How to Teach
Piano Successfully

Third Edition

How to Teach
Piano Successfully
Third Edition

by James W. Bastien

With contributions from

E. Gregory Nagode
Joseph Banowetz
Richard Chronister
Robert Roux
Sharon Lohse Kunitz
Maurice Hinson

George Lucktenberg
Nelita True
Rosina Lhevinne
Adele Marcus
James Dick
Irl Allison

kjos

Neil A. Kjos Music Company, 4380 Jutland Drive, San Diego, California 92117

International Standard Book Number 0-8497-6168-9
Library of Congress Catalog Card Number: 88-80602
Printed and bound in the United States of America.

For
Jane, Lisa, and Lori

About the Author

James Bastien has been a faculty member at Notre Dame, Tulane, and Loyola Universities, and a summer faculty member at Tanglewood and the National Music Camp at Interlochen, Michigan. While teaching piano and piano pedagogy at Loyola University in New Orleans, Mr. Bastien wrote this pedagogy text which was first published in 1973.

Mr. Bastien studied with Gyorgy Sandor at the Music Academy of the West in Santa Barbara, California, and also at Southern Methodist University in Dallas where he received bachelor and master degrees in piano performance.

He now resides in La Jolla, California, where he and his wife, Jane Smisor Bastien, write music and methods for piano students. Mrs. Bastien is shown teaching in her studio in many of the photographs in this book.

Preface to the Third Edition

Piano teaching is an art that requires special study, aptitude, application, and expertise. This book discusses those qualities and presents a program of study and a general survey of the teaching scene, providing guidelines for the successful practice of piano teaching. Because of the basic information included, this book may serve as a pedagogy text as well as a general reference book for professional teachers.

The four major areas of this Third Edition concentrate on the different areas of teaching. **Part One** discusses various organizational aspects of teaching and includes information on studio management, scheduling lessons, and business matters. A special feature is the survey of current piano methods, where special emphasis is given to the important beginning stages of instruction.

Part Two surveys the broad spectrum of teaching from the preschool student through the intermediate student, and offers specific recommendations in the areas of repertoire, technique, theory, and supplementary materials.

Part Three includes a variety of special subjects dealing with specialized teaching situations such as preparatory departments, college classes, computers in studios, considerations for fingerings, and how to prepare students for competitions. Many chapters were contributed by outstanding authors who are recognized authorities in their fields.

Part Four contains interviews with distinguished musicians and provides personal insights into their own views on teaching and learning.

Part Five contains Appendices of numerous subjects ranging from basic theory to a list of concert pianists.

The lists of recommended materials are intended to serve as representative guidelines, not *complete* lists. The music books suggested are intended for students of average ability. When surveying materials in a pedagogy class, it is helpful to have the recommended music available for a thorough examination.

Although the book was planned with a specific sequence, the reader should not feel bound to a chapter-by-chapter reading. Since each chapter is independent, the instructor or general reader can begin anywhere.

I am especially grateful to the many individuals who helped make this book possible. Special acknowledgements are given to Joseph Banowetz, Richard Chronister, Maurice Hinson, Sharon Kunitz, George Lucktenberg,

E. Gregory Nagode, and Robert Roux for contributing chapters; to Irl Allison, James Dick, Rosina Lhevinne, Adele Marcus, and Nelita True for their generosity in granting interviews. Finally, special thanks to my editor, Beverly McGahey, for her time and effort on this project!

For those using this text as a reference, or in a pedagogy class, I hope it will be of value in learning how to teach in a manner beneficial to all involved—teachers and students.

James W. Bastien
La Jolla, California

Contents

PART ONE
Pedagogical Considerations

An Overview of Teaching 1

The basic qualities of a successful teacher consist of knowledge, personality, enthusiasm, self-confidence, and many other personal attributes. These qualities distinguish a brilliant teacher from a mediocre one.

Stop to reflect for a moment on your own experiences. Who was the teacher who inspired you the most? Why was this person outstanding? What were the most memorable characteristics of this teacher?

Although there are many pedagogical procedures, there is no one magic blueprint that can be described as the method. Instruction varies widely and is largely dependent on the teacher's personality. One teacher might be quite formal and another informal; one might be a taskmaster, another easygoing; one might be impatient, another very patient. Since teachers work with people, they must be searching constantly for new and effective lines of communication. Methods, goals, and objectives must be periodically evaluated and reevaluated.

THE TEACHER'S CONCEPT OF TEACHING

If you are studying to become a teacher, why do you want to teach? If you are already teaching, what is your motivation?

The successful teacher usually is a positive person, concerned with others, and has chosen teaching as a career. Like other occupations, teaching has its share of rewards and frustrations. However, the teacher usually derives a great deal of satisfaction from working with people of varying ages, and this is often an important factor in choosing teaching as a career.

The glaring generality, "Teachers are born, not made," is an inaccurate assumption. Although teaching is a personal art, it must be studied and not left to "doing what comes naturally."

For those who elect teaching as a career, it can be a satisfying experience that becomes increasingly more interesting. Positive, meaningful, effective teaching comes from individuals who are genuinely interested in others. In short, they *care* about their students.

PRECOLLEGE TRAINING

A musician's career often depends on a chain of events that may date back to beginning instruction. If the training was solid in pianistic and

4

theoretical practices, then there probably is a firm foundation on which to build continued progress. However, if the training was sketchy, it would be necessary to spend a considerable amount of time and effort trying to gain missing skills.

Consider your own training as a young student, and evaluate your accomplishments. Answer the following questions by rating yourself on a ten-point basis. If your score is 70-100, you had excellent beginning instruction! However, if your rating is below 70, then you had some serious gaps in your precollege training.

1. Was your advancement carefully guided through thoughtful selection of materials that insured steady, gradual progress?
   1   2   3   4   5   6   7   8   9   10
2. Were you taught theory as a regular part of your basic instruction?
   1   2   3   4   5   6   7   8   9   10
3. Did your teacher stress ensemble playing, improvisation, ear training, sight-reading, harmonization, and transposition?
   1   2   3   4   5   6   7   8   9   10
4. Were you assigned music written in a variety of keys, and did you eventually play as well in one key as another?
   1   2   3   4   5   6   7   8   9   10
5. Were you taught all key signatures, all major, minor, diminished, and augmented chords?
   1   2   3   4   5   6   7   8   9   10
6. Were you taught to analyze form and harmony?
   1   2   3   4   5   6   7   8   9   10
7. Did you receive adequate technical instruction regarding posture at the piano; hand position; drills in scales, chords and inversions, arpeggios, and double notes?
   1   2   3   4   5   6   7   8   9   10
8. Was your teacher particular about correct fingering, phrasing, balance between melody and accompaniment, dynamics, tempo, and the mood of the composition?
   1   2   3   4   5   6   7   8   9   10
9. Did you learn terminology used in the compositions studied; did your teacher suggest that you use a music dictionary?
   1   2   3   4   5   6   7   8   9   10
10. Were you instructed to study the background of composers and the time in which they lived?
    1   2   3   4   5   6   7   8   9   10

Ideal Precollege Training

The training and development of a young pianist is entrusted almost exclusively to the independent teacher. Therefore, it is vitally important for a young student to have a competent and qualified teacher, because the beginning teacher can "make or break" a young pianist.

The instruction received during the precollege period may be difficult to assess. Competent instruction is not always assured by the number of years one has taken lessons.

Generally, young students begin formal piano lessons around the age of seven or eight. If lessons are continued without interruption throughout high school, the total length of precollege study would be about ten years. However, it is not safe to assume that because a student has had ten years of lessons prior to college that a high degree of proficiency will have been developed. Perhaps the student did not practice very much or was not motivated towards serious piano study. If this was the case, little would have been accomplished in relation to the time engaged in study.

Repertoire

Consider a model student who is about to enter a college music department. This student had ten years of piano instruction and was highly motivated by a gifted teacher.

The student's repertoire consists of literature from four periods, providing a broad style background. The performance level upon entering college should include representative works like the following.

Baroque Period
Bach: *Two-* or *Three-Part Inventions*, preludes and fugues from *The Well-Tempered Clavier*, *French Suites*
Scarlatti: any of the *Sonatas*
Handel: *Aylesford Pieces*, any of the *Suites* or *Sonatas*

Classical Period
Haydn: easier *Sonatas*
Mozart: *Sonatas*, *Variations*, or easier *Concertos*
Beethoven: easier *Sonatas*, *Variations*, or *Concertos*

Romantic Period
Representative works by Schubert, Schumann, Chopin, Liszt, Mendelssohn, Brahms, etc.

Contemporary Period
Bartók: *Rumanian Folk Dances*, *Three Rondos*, later books of the *Mikrokosmos*
Barber: *Excursions*
Bloch: *Poems of the Sea*
Copland: *The Cat and the Mouse*
Debussy: *Children's Corner Suite*, easier *Preludes*, or either of the *Arabesques*

Dello Joio: *Suite for Piano*
Hindemith: *Sonata No. 2*
Kabalevsky: *Twenty-four Preludes*
Muczynski: *Six Preludes, Op. 6*
Poulenc: *Mouvements perpetuels*
Tcherepnin: *Bagatelles, Op. 5*

Technique

The student should have sufficient technique to play with a clean sound, good phrasing, tonal balance, clear pedaling, and appropriate dynamics. In addition to musical considerations, technical studies should be selected from the following list.

Applied Technique
Clementi: *Gradus ad Parnassum*
Czerny: *The School of Velocity, Op. 299* or *The Art of Finger Dexterity, Op. 740*
Moszkowski: *15 Études de Virtuosité*

Pure Technique
Dohnányi: *Essential Finger Exercises*
Hanon: *The Virtuoso Pianist in Sixty Exercises*
Philipp: *Exercises for the Independence of the Fingers*
Pischna: *Sixty Progressive Exercises*
Major and minor scales, arpeggios, and broken chords in all keys.

Sight-Reading Ability

The ability to read new music easily is a necessary skill which should be developed from the beginning stages of lessons and continued through the more advanced levels. Teachers should help their students develop sight-reading skills by assigning music that is slightly less difficult than the pieces used for study and performance. The assignment of duets, two piano pieces, and chamber music works (piano trios, violin and cello sonatas, vocal music) is also helpful in developing reading skills. Accompanying the school chorus or church choir is another way to develop reading ability.

Theory

The teacher should provide systematic theory instruction to all students (either privately or in a group situation). An understanding of keys, intervals, chords, and harmonic structure is essential to the understanding of the music studied. In addition, students should receive ear training, improvisation, transposition, and harmonization as a basic part of the general theory program.

Pedagogical Considerations

Music History and Literature

Although there is little time for formal music history classes, an independent teacher can do much to develop concepts in this area. Attendance at musical events such as piano recitals, chamber music programs, symphonic and operatic performances, and other selected concerts are helpful in developing a rapport with music literature. Lectures, workshops, master classes, and other informative presentations should also be included. Students should be encouraged to listen to recordings of works studied. These experiences will develop an awareness of basic information about music history and literature.

COLLEGE TRAINING FOR THE PIANO PEDAGOGY MAJOR

In a general sense the term "college" may imply any formal schooling beyond high school. Titles of schools differ (Department of Music, School of Music, College of Fine Arts), and their curricula are often dissimilar. In addition, degrees offered in various music departments appear under such designations as Bachelor of Music, Bachelor of Arts, Bachelor of Fine Arts, and many more. Therefore, the student should choose a school which will best fit his or her personal interest.

Information and guidelines regarding college piano pedagogy may be found in *The Piano Pedagogy Major in the College Curriculum*. Part 1 deals with the undergraduate level, and Part 2 deals with the graduate level. These booklets are published by the National Conference on Piano Pedagogy and may be ordered, for a nominal fee, by writing to P.O. Box 24C54, Los Angeles, CA 90024.

Course Offerings for the Pedagogy Major

Classes in theory, composition, music history and literature, ensemble, conducting, orchestration, and a heavy emphasis on the student's primary instrument will generally comprise the basic courses. In addition, the piano pedagogy major will be required to elect specific courses in pedagogy, piano literature, accompanying, and practice teaching.

Since academic requirements vary greatly among colleges it is difficult to make a composite listing. However, English, psychology, foreign languages, history, and philosophy generally provide some of the basic arts and science courses. It is also beneficial for the pedagogy major to elect some of the general education courses such as introductory education, educational psychology, child and/or adolescent psychology, and a basic business course.

Accomplishments During the College Years

During the college years the student must continue to build on the precollege background. If the background is weak, the student will have to work harder than other classmates.

Because of variances in background and ability, each student must be evaluated on an individual basis. But regardless of background, talent, or other factors, some students achieve a great deal during college while others fall short of their potential. The determining factor in accomplishment is *motivation*.

A student may be motivated by influences such as peer group pressures, a desire to maintain a high grade point average, or a desire to please the piano teacher. These factors are necessary, but the most beneficial factor is self-motivation. After graduation, grades or a teacher's inspiration are no longer present, and it is entirely up to the individual to develop the highest potential possible.

OPPORTUNITIES FOR THE TEACHER

Independent Piano Teaching

Independent teaching may be done at home or at a separate studio. This is an ideal career for any person desiring to be self-employed. Possibilities for a beginning teacher's employment include teaching piano in a music store or a private school, or teaching as an assistant to an established teacher. However, a beginning teacher does not need to feel that it is necessary to teach for someone else. An ambitious, self-confident person may have far more success in a self-employed situation.

College Piano Teaching

College teaching is limited to those who have advanced training, advanced degrees, and some experience in the field. It is a position to which many young pianists aspire, but one which is becoming more and more crowded with talented, well-qualified applicants. Music schools are turning out well-trained piano performers, and the demand for employment is not as great as the supply.

Degrees. Administrators look for applicants who have attained a doctoral degree. This is not an absolute necessity for employment, but it adds to the attractiveness of an applicant's credentials. It often makes the difference between choosing one person over another.

The Doctor of Musical Arts degree (DMA) is specifically designed for the pianist interested in performance. Requirements may include recitals, chamber music performances, concerto performances, and lecture-recitals. For a student interested in teaching pedagogy, a Doctorate of Piano Pedagogy is offered at some universities.

Credentials. In applying for a college position, students need to prepare credentials carefully and accurately. Credentials usually include transcripts of course work, personal information, a picture, recital programs, and recommendations from college teachers. The Placement Bureau at the university normally helps the student with these matters. Graduate students should watch university bulletin boards for announcements of positions, read professional magazines, and join the College Music Society. In addition, candidates may write to colleges throughout the country to learn of job opportunities.

At the interview, the dean and the faculty search committee will meet with the job applicant and possibly observe a demonstration teaching session and listen to an audition.

Job offerings. Competition is keen for any new position. Music enrollments have decreased, and many college positions have been terminated. Therefore, the graduate desiring college employment must be prepared to compete against many others. A more desirable applicant is one who can perform; teach piano, pedagogy, and class piano; and be qualified to teach various other music classes.

THE TEACHER'S PERSONALITY

The teacher should generate as positive a personality as possible in working with students. One might be vivacious or dull, energetic or lethargic, optimistic or pessimistic, pleasant or unpleasant. Negative aspects detract and should be eliminated. It is helpful to portray the following qualities:

Be pleasant. A pleasant attitude is one of the most valuable attributes a teacher can possess. A genuine display of kindness can often defuse even the most hostile and disagreeable child. Although moods vary greatly from day to day, teachers need to conduct themselves with as much poise and self-control as possible when dealing with others.

Be enthusiastic. An enthusiastic person is one who evidences a positive, bright outlook in relationships with others.

Be encouraging. Realistic encouragement whenever possible is a sign of an outgoing personality. Rather than trying to get results by negative remarks, the positive teacher can bolster and uplift the student with encouraging remarks.

Be patient. Working with children either privately or in groups can be trying at times. However, the teacher should be able to cope with frustrations that may arise. An understanding teacher will "keep cool" and not resort to negative remarks.

SUMMARY

The total composite of one's training, background, personality, and motivation are combined to produce a skilled professional. The level and area in which the teacher will be working, whether independent or employed, will be determined largely by personal interest. Some teachers have a desire to work with children, others may prefer working with adults at the college level. Whatever the level, the teacher must be well qualified and an effective communicator capable of helping others to learn.

FOR DISCUSSION & ASSIGNMENT

1. What is your view on teaching as a career?
2. Do you think you would enjoy working with children or adults? Describe your reasons.
3. Compare your precollege training to the ideal training discussed in this chapter. How would you rate the teaching you received?
4. Describe the college program that you think would be the most advantageous as preparation for a teaching career.
5. Do you have aspirations of teaching in a college? If so, in what capacity?

FOR FURTHER READING

Adams, Sam, and John L. Garrett, Jr. *To Be a Teacher.* Englewood Cliffs: Prentice-Hall, Inc., 1969. PB. Designed as an introductory educational text, this book seeks to answer the vital question: Shall I be a teacher? Pertinent questions are asked which relate to such teaching decisions as what kind and what level, where would one want to teach, and many others. Specific suggested readings are Chapter 1 "What Is a Teacher?," Chapter 2 "Who Should Become a Teacher?," and Chapter 5 "What Are Some Decisions For the Teacher?"

Allen, Jeffrey G. *How to Turn an Interview Into a Job,* New York: A Fireside Book/Simon & Schuster, Inc., 1983. PB. Many helpful ideas are contained in this well-written book by this authority on the hiring process.

Donaho, Melvin W., and John L. Meyer. *How to Get the Job You Want.* Englewood Cliffs: Prentice-Hall, Inc., 1976. PB. This is a valuable reference book which clearly describes how to prepare resumés, conduct interviews, and develop job-hunting strategies.

Dyer, Wayne W., *The Sky's the Limit,* New York: Simon & Schuster, Inc., 1980. PB. This is a vital, dynamic book which offers helpful advice on developing a sense of purpose in life and goal achievement.

Highet, Gilbert. *The Art of Teaching.* New York: Vintage Books, 1950. PB. This well-written book outlines a general treatise on the philosophy of teaching. The book begins by considering the character and abilities that make a good professional teacher, and then goes on to examine specific methods to meet those goals. Readings of special interest are I. "Introduction," II. "The Teacher," and V. "Teaching in Everyday Life."

Maltz, Maxwell. *Psycho-Cybernetics*. Englewood Cliffs: Prentice-Hall, Inc., 1960. PB. Designed as a do-it-yourself psychology text for the layman, this book offers many important suggestions for creating a positive personality and a successful life.

Waitley, Denis. *The Winner's Edge*. New York: The Berkley Publishing Group, 1980. PB. This is an outstanding book on developing the human potential, and is a "must read" for those who would like to succeed.

Aspects of Independent Teaching 2

The piano teaching profession encompasses a vast panorama of areas. Therefore, teachers should decide which age groups they would be most interested in teaching. Some teachers like to work with very young children; others prefer working with traditional-age beginners, intermediate students, adult beginners, or advanced students. Serious consideration should be given to the type of student desired before embarking on a teaching career.

The teacher referred to in this chapter is one who teaches either at home or in a studio.

THE STUDENTS

Young Beginners

The prime consideration in this category is do you want to work with preschool children, or beginners from about age seven? Teaching youngsters can be a satisfying experience for teachers who like to work with young children. The early years are critical, and there is a decided advantage to starting beginners yourself. This is the time when students must learn basic skills such as hand position, phrasing, voicing, and a feeling for melodic contours. It is easier to instill these concepts yourself rather than work with transfer students who may not have been taught these fundamentals correctly.

Adult Beginners

Traditionally, adult beginners represented a small portion of the teacher's class. Today, with increased leisure time, more and more people are looking for a creative, stimulating activity. Music lessons offer an important outlet to adults who are searching for some form of aesthetic fulfillment.

Teaching adult beginners can be a rewarding experience. Presumably, adults study music because they are interested, whereas children often take lessons because of parental insistence.

Adult beginners generally do not reach astonishing heights in technical proficiency since finger facility has not been developed. Also, the ability to read music fluently, which demands a complicated coordination of intellect, eyes, ears, and hands, probably will progress slowly. Occasionally, though, an adult will cover an amazing amount of material in a short time.

Teachers who specialize in teaching adults enjoy the intellectual stimulation of working with adult terminology rather than the simple language used in teaching children. Another plus is that some adults can come for lessons when children cannot. Adult beginners can derive a great deal of satisfaction from piano playing and the study of music in general, and their accomplishments will be rewarding for teachers interested in working with this age group.

Intermediate Students

Students who continue into the intermediate level generally are motivated, interested, and have a genuine desire to learn. The intermediate student usually is in junior high school (grades 7, 8, 9).

Working with this age group can be either a joy or a source of frustration. This transitional period from childhood to adulthood often produces behavioral anxieties. Their need for acquiring status and independence is important as well as peer recognition and acceptance. These developments, both physical and mental, may keep them on edge for a number of years. Teenagers often are moody and seemingly apathetic for no apparent reason. Due to these conflicts it takes a great deal of imagination and determination on the part of the teacher (and parents) to keep the students practicing and making progress.

However, working with this age group can be rewarding because signs of pianistic accomplishment are beginning to emerge. The rewards of early practice are now coming to fruition, and as a result, technique and musicianship are evolving into a more structured and unified whole.

Advanced Students

A small percentage of the students will be continuing lessons in senior high school (grades 10, 11, 12). Their persistence is highly commendable. In spite of the demands of homework, dating, participation in sports and other extra-curricular activities, the possibility of holding part-time jobs, and other duties that make extraordinary demands on this age group's time, they have persevered in their musical endeavors.

Some students are still taking piano lessons because their love of music is so strong that they are seriously considering a career in music. Most of them are beginning to think about career choices, and if the choice is music, this will directly involve the piano teacher.

Pedagogical Considerations

The teacher working with this age group must be prepared to act in an informal advisory role. Many students who cannot establish a close relationship with their parents will seek out adults, frequently their teachers, for consultation. This kind of rapport with teachers and the ability to communicate with them is of vital importance to high school students.

PRIVATE OR GROUP LESSONS

Before a teacher begins to organize a studio and purchase equipment for it, decisions should be made to teach private lessons or group lessons, or a combination of the two. Therefore, one should consider the following:

1. Do I enjoy working with groups of children?
2. Am I confident that I can organize group activities and make classes interesting?
3. Am I convinced students will learn as much in group lessons as they would privately?

Some teachers give group lessons and are enthusiastic about the results. Most teachers, however, still teach only privately and give little or no class work. This is due to a number of reasons—lack of teaching space, a general uneasiness about group work, lack of training and experience with group situations, and a general conviction that private lessons accomplish more and produce better results than group lessons.

Richard Chronister states that it is the teacher who is the determining factor in successful teaching, not the situation. "The problems in music education run far deeper than is suggested by those who would have us believe that the choice of group teaching or private teaching is anything but a superficial aspect of successful teaching."[1]

A combination of both private *and* group teaching often produces effective results. The private lesson can be used for individual attention to items such as note learning (for beginners), counting aloud while playing, and repertoire. The group lesson (approximately forty-five minutes long) can emphasize skills such as theory, keyboard harmony, ear training, sight-reading, and ensemble playing.

A few teachers advocate teaching entirely in groups. Two possible combinations of group lessons are:

1. two lessons per week, one being a small group of two to six for the "private" lesson, and a larger group of six or more for the class lesson

[1]Richard Chronister "The Irrelevant Controversy: Group Teaching vs. Private Teaching," *Keyboard Arts* Spring 1972), p. 17.

2. one or two lessons per week comprised of a large group of six or more students

Because certain aspects of piano study can be presented easily to more than one student at a time, there are decided advantages to including some group teaching. Theory, keyboard harmony, ear training, sight-reading, and ensemble playing can be presented more effectively in a class situation. Also, competition from peer groups can provide stimulating sessions which do a great deal to spark enthusiasm among the individual members as well as to create class spirit.

While the many advantages of class lessons seem to be self-evident, there is little research available comparing the results of private piano lessons versus class instruction and, as far as we are aware, no statistical evidence available showing the advantages of one system of teaching over the other.

LEARNING HOW TO TEACH

How does a college piano major suddenly become a piano teacher? Are there teacher training programs available in colleges throughout the country for prospective piano teachers?

A number of colleges now offer programs designed to prepare students for private teaching. This area of the college music curriculum is called *piano pedagogy*. In such a program students are engaged in:

1. examining beginning, intermediate, and advanced teaching materials
2. preparing research papers based on topics relating to piano teaching
3. observing piano teachers and writing reports on the methodologies used
4. presenting reports based on analytical study of various periodicals
5. garnering experience in practice teaching supervised by the instructor

THE TEACHER'S STUDIO

Unless a teacher gives itinerant lessons (traveling from one home to another), a studio location is needed. A teaching location should be in close proximity to students and may be either at home, which is most frequently the case, or at a studio. A neat, attractive, well-equipped studio will provide a pleasant atmosphere in which to work, and students will look forward to their lessons in such surroundings.

Studio Location

Teaching at home can be frustrating if there is not sufficient privacy. If the phone rings or the teacher's children barge in on lessons, the teacher will be interrupted many times and full attention cannot be given to teaching. Therefore, if the teacher has small children at home, a baby sitter should be employed.

If privacy and appropriate facilities can be ensured, teaching at home does have some advantages—there is no need to travel outside the home to another studio, and there are numerous tax deductions for the portion of the home used as a studio.

Very few teachers use a teaching space apart from home. However, for a teacher who has a large class, there are some advantages in studio rental. If the teacher's home is not ideally located, an outside studio may be rented in a more convenient location such as a suburban shopping center.

Studio Size

The studio should be large enough to accommodate a piano (or pianos), chalkboard, table and chairs, and other equipment. It should also be sufficiently large enough to allow some class teaching (theory, preschool class, etc.). Two diagrams of piano studios are shown here. The first diagram (Example 1) shows a room with two pianos, chalkboard, table and chairs, and file cabinet. The second diagram (Example 2) contains more pianos and is intended for group teaching.

STUDIO EQUIPMENT

The following items range from essential to optional in furnishing a studio.

Pianos

A minimum of two. The choice includes grands, uprights, studio uprights, spinets, and/or electronic instruments (see next page).

Piano Chair or Bench

An adjustable piano chair or piano bench is a good solution to comfortable seating for all sizes of students. If the adjustable chair or bench cannot be found locally, it may be ordered from Hui's Imports (9608 Tallahassee Lane, Knoxville, TN 37923). An adjustable "concert chair" is available at Yamaha dealers.

Pedal Extension

For very young children who cannot reach the pedal, the foot-pedal stool may be ordered from Hui's Imports.

Aspects of Independent Teaching

Example 1 Studio for teaching private and group lessons.

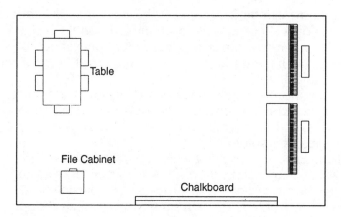

Digital Keyboards • Sound Modules/Sequencers
 Whether using the least or the most advanced keyboards, they will greatly enhance any teaching situation. While the more progressive instruments have a sound module/sequencer built in, it is also possible to obtain a separate sound module/sequencer which can be used with a keyboard without recording/playback capabilities, or even with an acoustic piano. Students love to play digital keyboards and are especially motivated by the interactive accompaniment disks, which can be played with a built-in sound module, or separate one.

Metronome
 There are many kinds available at most music stores.

Chalkboard
 Either a stationary or portable chalkboard, and/or small erasable slates.

Felt Board or Magnetic Board
 Both boards are useful and can be purchased from a school supply store.

Charts
 Good motivators for displaying progress, honor roll, etc. *Bastien Student Boosters* is a package of four different charts for studio use.

Flashcards
 Cards with notes, key signatures, intervals, chords, music terms, rhythm patterns, and melodic patterns may be made or purchased.

Writing Instruments
 Pencils, pens, crayons, and felt-tipped pens are needed for student classes and making the assignment or corrections. (Try using a different colored marker each time a mistake has to be noted.)

Pedagogical Considerations

Example 2 Studio for teaching group lessons.

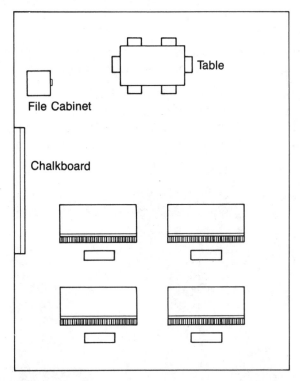

Bulletin Board
Especially useful for displaying items of special interest (contest or recital information, newspaper/magazine articles, etc.).

Telephone Answering Machine
A happy solution for those who do not wish to be disturbed while teaching.

Typewriter
Useful for writing policy statements, letters, invoices, recital programs, etc.

Computer
Useful for the same projects done on a typewriter (with more variety of type styles and sizes) plus student theory programs, etc.

Tape Recorder
Since many students own cassette recorders, lessons or ear training drills may be recorded and sent home for practice.

Record and/or Compact Disc Player
Various benefits can be gained from listening to recordings of different artists and styles periods.

Videotape Recorder (Camcorder)
The advantage of *seeing* the performance is remarkable.

A well-equipped studio should be an attractive place in which to teach. The studio shown in Example 3 includes decorations for Halloween, wall charts, and other imaginative features. Also included are seven pianos, chalkboard, file cabinet, desk, table and chairs, and other equipment.

Example 3 A well-equipped studio.

HOW TO OBTAIN STUDENTS

Unless a teacher is lucky enough to inherit a class of students from a teacher who is moving or retiring, it generally takes time to build one's own class of students.

Pedagogical Considerations

Example 4 Chalkboard work for learning key signatures.

Locate in an Area of Children

Before opening a studio, investigate the community into which you are planning to settle. Are there numerous children in the area? A suburban area is often ideal because the demands for lessons may be greater than the supply of teachers.

Join Music Teacher Organizations

Membership in one or more music organizations is essential for professional recognition. Music teacher organizations are largely responsible for the improvement in teaching standards that have taken place in this country. These organizations are interested in the best means of training students, establishing reasonable lesson fees, teacher certification, sponsoring workshops and recitals for the benefit of both student and teachers, sponsoring contests and auditions, and providing a membership list to the public as a reliable source for selecting music teachers.

The following music teacher organizations are of special interest to many piano teachers.

Music Teachers National Association (MTNA), The Carew Tower, 441 Vine Street, Suite 505, Cincinnati, OH 45202-2814.

This organization is closely associated with the needs of independent teachers, and it is responsible for independent teacher certification. MTNA publishes a magazine, *American Music Teacher.*

National Guild of Piano Teachers (The Guild), Box 1807, Austin, TX 78767.

The Guild sponsors national student auditions and awards scholarships. The Guild publishes a magazine, *Piano Guild Notes*.

National Federation of Music Clubs (the Federation), 1336 North Delaware, Indianapolis, IN 46202.

The Federation sponsors national student auditions and publishes the *Junior Keynotes* magazine.

Give Student Recitals

The recital may be either informal or formal. A recital is effective if the students are well-prepared and play their pieces with assurance.

The musical quality of the performers is the determining factor in a successful program. Therefore, work to the fullest capacity with the students to prepare them adequately for the recital. Generally, the recital pieces are memorized, and each student should know the piece securely to give an adequate performance—one devoid of memory slips!

Utilize Direct Mail

When soliciting students by sending letters or brochures, outline specifically what kind of a musical program you offer (see Example 5). If you prefer working with adult beginners, say so. List any special features about your program such as group piano, class theory, or private lessons/theory class combination. Letters may be sent to parents of children in nearby schools and churches if the lists can be acquired.

Consider Advertising in Print

Advertisements placed in the Yellow Pages or neighborhood newspapers, whether by an individual teacher, or an organization, could be considered. An ad could be a simple announcement of basic information seen in Example 6.

Pedagogical Considerations

EXAMPLE 5 Direct mail letter.

LORI WILLIAMS PIANO STUDIO
**6943 JUTLAND STREET
BEDFORD, WA 12345
555-1212**

Dear Parents:

Do you realize that children who study a musical instrument learn responsibility and discipline, they gain pride in their accomplishments which in turn makes them confident, they learn to think in a logical manner, and they will perform better in school. These are just a few of the benefits that your child can gain.

Piano lessons have changed quite a bit since you might have experienced them in your childhood. In my studio students receive a thirty-minute lesson AND a forty-five-minute class lesson, with other students at the same level. Besides just learning to actually *play* the piano, students will engage in flashcard drills, chalkboard work, and other activities to strengthen their overall knowledge of music. This will prepare them well for continued study in piano, for playing other instruments or singing, and for enjoying music in general.

Lessons and classes are also offered for adults!

You and your children are invited to come to my **Open House, August 10, Sunday afternoon from 2–5** to discover more about piano study "today's" way. Refreshments will be served. If you are not able to come, but would like further information, please call me between 9 a.m. and 9 p.m. any day.

I look forward to meeting you!

Sincerely,

Lori Williams

Example 6   A small advertisement.

Learn to Play the Piano!
Any age student is welcome.
Special classes for adults
who want to play the piano again.

For more information call

LORI WILLIAMS
555-1212
6943 Jutland Street
Bedford, WA 12345

Certified by
the Music Teachers
National Association
and the
National Guild
of Piano Teachers.

HOW TO INTERVIEW PROSPECTIVE STUDENTS

The purpose of an interview is to assess the aptitude of the potential student and to discuss various aspects of study: lesson time, fees, best times for practice, amount of practice, etc. Since cooperation is essential for optimum results, a good rapport must be established at the initial meeting and maintained through lessons.

To gain the confidence of the child and parents, the teacher should explain goals and what will be expected. The teacher should define objectives and outline the teaching program regarding the type of methods that will be used, participation in theory classes (obligatory or optional), length of lessons, lesson attendance, and others. Both the child and parents should know exactly what they are getting into *before* enrolling for lessons.

It is helpful to interview the child alone, without the parents, to determine if the child really wants lessons, or if the parents want lessons for their child.

When interviewing a new student the teacher should learn as many facts about the child as possible. Since different situations require different questions, the following questions are divided into three sets. The first series of questions is designed for beginners, the second for the parents, and the third for transfer students.

Questions for Beginners, Ages 7–10

To put the child at ease, ask questions to elicit the following information:

Pedagogical Considerations

1. Name (for correct spelling)
2. Address
3. Telephone
4. Age and grade in school

Generally, it is easier to teach beginners if they can read. Parents will need to understand that their supervision of practice sessions will be needed if the student cannot yet read well.

Even though the parents say the child is "quite talented," the teacher needs to do a little testing at the interview. If you have more than one piano in the room, have the child match tones that you play. Show the groups of two and three black keys with your second, third, and fourth fingers, and ask the child to cover the three black keys with the same fingers. Play some simple patterns on your piano using only the three black keys. Ask the child to match the tones you played.

Clap simple rhythms for the child, such as ♩ ♫ ♩. Ask the child to clap each rhythm after you have done one.

Have the child sing a simple melody ("Mary Had a Little Lamb") while you play and sing the tune with the child. About halfway through, drop out and let the child finish the song alone. A child who cannot sing on pitch probably has not done much singing.

Tell the child that the music alphabet consists of seven letters, A through G. Then ask him to say the alphabet backwards from G. This will give you a feeling for how the child thinks, and it will provide an insight into whether he or she can reason well.

Finally, ask the child if he or she wants to take piano lessons. Most children are forthright and honest, and if they really do not want to take lessons, they will tell you so. Sometimes it is the parents who want lessons for the child, rather than the child who wants lessons.

After interviewing the child alone, invite the parents back into the room to ask them a few more questions.

Questions for Parents

1. Do either of you play the piano or another musical instrument? It is helpful to know what expertise will be available from the parents during the early stages of lessons.
2. Does your child have many outside activities? A child who has ballet lessons on Monday, swimming on Tuesday, soccer practice on Wednesday, and Scouts on Thursday, will certainly not have time to do justice to them all!
3. Discuss the amount of daily practice that will be required with both the child and parents. Beginners should practice at least thirty minutes a day, six days of the week. Make sure this is clear to the

child and parents, and ask them if there is time in their schedule for this daily routine. Piano lessons can be fun if a sustained effort is given by the child and by parental encouragement.

4. Explain the scheduling of lessons, and give parents a printed brochure which lists the calendar (regular lesson days plus holiday interruptions), tuition, payment of fees, policy on missed lessons, how to cancel lessons if allowed, and the lesson times. This policy statement helps to prevent any misunderstandings that might arise later. It may be printed in letter or brochure form. A sample policy statement is shown in Example 7.

5. Clearly explain your policy concerning payment of fees. Some teachers require payment in advance for the month, quarter, or semester. Also explain about how music should be paid for. If the teacher buys the music and sells it to students, the price will be added to the monthly statement; if parents are required to purchase the music, suggest the best sheet music store(s) in town.

6. If parents do not know much about music, it is helpful to have them buy the booklet, *A Parent's Guide to Piano Lessons*, by James Bastien (Neil A. Kjos Music Company, 1976).

Parents should be advised to let the teacher know if they want to have their child take lessons.

Questions for Transfer Students

To put the student at ease, ask questions to elicit the following information:

1. Name (correct spelling)
2. Address
3. Telephone
4. Name for billing
5. How long the student has studied piano
6. What grade the student is in

After asking these questions, try to assess the transfer student's musical ability. Have the student play one or more pieces for you. From the performance you can detect any lack of training in technique, phrasing, hand position, steady tempo, balance of hands, etc.

Next, have the student read some music below the grade level performed. Some students are unable to sight-read music even after several years of study. Students who have been taught by rote cannot name notes. Finally, have the student name the music terms that are used in the piece just read. Also ask questions about the key signature, harmony, and tempo marks.

Pedagogical Considerations

Example 7 A Studio Policy Statement.

LORI WILLIAMS PIANO STUDIO
6943 JUTLAND STREET
BEDFORD, WA 12345
555-1212

CALENDAR
FALL SEMESTER
  Sept. 13 Monday. Classes begin
  Nov. 25–28 Thursday through Sunday. Thanksgiving recess
  Dec. 19 Sunday. Christmas holidays begin
  Jan. 3 Monday. Classes resume
  Jan. 15 Saturday. Last day of the Fall Semester

SPRING SEMESTER
  Jan. 17 Monday. Classes resume
  Mar. 30–Apr. 15 Thursday through Wednesday. Spring recess
  May 20 Saturday. Last day of the Spring Semester

SUMMER TERM
  Dates and tuition to be announced.

TUITION
Based on 32 weeks of lessons, tuition is $450 for the school year. This includes one 30-minute private and one 45-minute group lesson each week.

For those students taking the 30-minute private lesson only, tuition is the same.

PAYMENT OF FEES
Fees, payable in advance of lessons, are to be made on the basis of $225 per semester; or, if you prefer are payable in nine equal payments of $50 each. Make checks payable to Lori Williams.

MISSED LESSONS
Missed lessons will be made up at the teacher's discretion depending on the student's need and the time available. Lessons missed by the teacher will definitely be made up.

CANCELLED LESSONS
If you wish to cancel a lesson, please call 555-1212 before noon the day of the lesson.

LESSON TIMES
Private _____
                              Day   Time

Group _____
                              Day   Time

Have the student play some scales, chords and inversions, and arpeggios. The teacher can also test the student's aural ability by playing various intervals to identify and by playing major and minor chords for identification. When playing the aural test, have the student stand where the keyboard cannot be seen.

After the interview, invite the parents back into the room and discuss the

Aspects of Independent Teaching

same general things that were mentioned previously for parents of beginners.

When the interview has been completed for either beginners or transfer students, the next step is to decide whether or not to accept the student into your class. Carefully consider the pros and cons *before* enrolling a new student.

If the child seems willing and cooperative and if the parents are enthusiastic, you can add this new student to your class. However, if the child is either apathetic about beginning piano lessons, or seems too immature to handle the complexities of lessons at this time, it would probably be better not to get into a losing situation. Discuss the problems with the parents with the child out of the room, and explain why you would not advise piano lessons now.

HOW TO SCHEDULE LESSONS

Once a new student has been accepted, the next consideration is how to arrange a suitable lesson time. The hours available for teaching include early morning (before school) and after school. Sometimes school hours are available for teaching, if released time is allowed.

Since the teacher's class is probably comprised of students of all ages, careful consideration should be given to the most advantageous times of the day and week for scheduling lessons. The following outline and discussion of various age groups is offered as a general guide for scheduling all types of lessons.

Preschool Beginners
Preschoolers are available during the day. However, with many parents working and children in day-care centers, the scheduling may not be as flexible as it used to be.

Beginners, Average Age
Average age beginners are in the second, third, or fourth grades. They may be given an early afternoon (or Saturday) time.

2nd, 3rd, 4th year Students
This age group may be given afternoon (or Saturday) time.

Intermediate Students
Intermediate students are usually about junior high age, and generally more involved with extracurricular activities than younger children. It may help to find out if there are certain nights of the week when school sports activities are held and try to avoid those times. Early morning times before school starts can be considered as well as afternoon and evening times.

Pedagogical Considerations

Advanced Students

Advanced students are senior high age, and there are numerous considerations for this age group. Homework, sports, dating, jobs, and many other activities pose possible conflicts in scheduling. Lesson times for this group may be scheduled before or after school, and into the evening.

Adult Students

Adults may be scheduled for lessons at varying times, depending on the time they have available. If they work, early morning hours should not be overlooked.

For the uninitiated, scheduling lesson times can be problematic. To help alleviate a number of the typical pitfalls that may be confronted in scheduling, suggestions are given for three different types of schedules: private lessons, a combination of private and group lessons, and small and large groups.

Private Lessons

Teachers giving only private lessons generally offer three types: thirty-minute lessons, forty-five-minute lessons, and hour lessons. An hour lesson can become tedious if the student is young or in the beginning stages. Therefore, most teachers give one thirty-minute lesson per week instead of one extended lesson. The following schedule is based on private lessons only.

Example 8 All private lessons.

Thirty students are scheduled during the week.
  The class distribution is:
  4 Kindergarten students (indicated on the chart with K–1, K–2, K–3, K–4)
  4 Beginning students (indicated with B–1, etc.)
  6 Second-year students (2nd–1)
  5 Third-year students (3rd–1)
  3 Fourth-year students (4th–1)
  3 Intermediate students (I–1)
  3 Advanced students (A–1)
  2 Transfer students (T–1)

Note that this schedule utilizes four 7:30 a.m. times.

	Monday	Tuesday	Wednesday	Thursday	Friday
7:30		2nd–2	3rd–1	3rd–2	2nd–6
2:30	K–1	K–2	K–3	K–4	3rd–4
3:00	B–1	B–3	B–4	3rd–3	3rd–5
3:30	B–2	2nd–3	2nd–4	2nd–5	
4:00	2nd–1	I–2	T–1	I–3	
4:30	I–1	A–2	A–3	T–2	
5:00	A–1	4th–1	4th–2	4th–3	

Aspects of Independent Teaching

Combination Private & Group Lessons

The private-group combination is very effective. The private lesson (thirty minutes) deals almost exclusively with repertoire, sight-reading, some technique, and individual problems. The group lesson (forty-five minutes) emphasizes theory, ensemble playing, sight-reading, technique, and general musicianship. There is sufficient time between these two weekly lessons to cover a great deal of material, and students are exposed to a complete musical program. The result is usually superior musicianship.

There are a number of advantages in the combination of private and group lessons:

1. Teaching time is used efficiently.
2. Effective presentation of materials can be provided more efficiently.
3. Motivation can be generated among class members.
4. Contact with peers stimulates competition.

Example 9 is based on a combination of one thirty-minute private lesson and one forty-five-minute group lesson per week for each of thirty pupils.

Example 9 Combination of private and group lessons.

	Monday	Tuesday	Wednesday	Thursday	Friday
7:30		Private	Private	Private	Private
2:30	Private	Private	Private	Private	Private
3:00	Private	Private	Private	Private	Private
3:30	Private	Private	Private	Private	Private
4:00	Group–K	Group–B	Group–3rd	Group–Int.	Private
4:30					Private
5:00	Private	Group–2nd	Group–4th	Group–Adv.	Private
5:30	Private				Private
6:00	Private	Private	Private	Private	Private

Small & Large Group Lessons

Some teachers offer group instruction only. There are several possibilities for scheduling group lessons:

1. one large group (6–8) lesson per week
2. two large group lessons per week
3. one small group (4–6) lesson plus one large group (8–12) lesson per week

If teachers do not have enough students to form large groups, an alternative of "overlapping" groups may be considered. For instance, have two students come at 3:30 for their lesson. At 4:00 two more students come and the four students work together for thirty minutes. At 4:30 the first two students leave and the second two continue for their small class lesson. Punctuality is a must for this schedule!

SUMMARY

A teaching career is generally built by a steady chain of events that are carefully planned. Self-preparation is the first step in obtaining the desired goal. Although college study culminating in one or more degrees is a basic necessity, learning does not end there. On the contrary, experience is one of the most important factors in successful teaching. A great deal of learning will come by doing.

It often takes time to build a beginning class and to develop a reputation in the community. Financial rewards can eventually be gained for the well-trained, aggressive, conscientious teacher.

Matters of organizing a studio, obtaining students, interviewing students, and scheduling lessons should be given serious consideration before embarking on an independent teaching career.

FOR DISCUSSION & ASSIGNMENT

As a class project, interview three independent piano teachers in your community and report on various aspects of their teaching situations. Make an oral or written report to the class on the following questions:

1. How did these three teachers learn to teach? Do you think their training was adequate? If not, what should be done to upgrade their competency?
2. What is the total number of students in each teacher's class? How many are beginners, second year students, transfer students, advanced students, and adult students? Do you think you would enjoy teaching a class of this mixture? If not, why?
3. Describe their studios. Are the studios in their homes? How many pianos are in each studio? What additional equipment is used? Do you think the studios and equipment in them are adequate? If not, what would you do to improve the situation?
4. How did these teachers obtain students when they first began to teach? What additional advertising might have been employed? Do they presently have all the students they would like to have?
5. Describe the type of interview these teachers use. Describe the type of studio brochures these teachers give to parents.
6. Describe the schedules these teachers follow. Do any of the teachers give group lessons? If so, how are these scheduled? Could you offer any suggestions for economizing teaching time?

Aspects of Independent Teaching

FOR FURTHER READING

Dyer, Dr. Wayne W. *What Do You Really Want For Your Children?* New York: Avon Books, 1985. PB. This is an excellent book for dealing with childrens' problems in a positive manner. Teachers can gain useful insights on how to develop a pleasant rapport with children from this well-written book.

Eyre, Linda and Richard. *Teaching Children Responsibility.* New York: Ballantine Books, 1984. PB. This book discusses parental responsibility for teaching obedience, building character, and for developing innate talents and work ethics. An excellent summary story is given at the end of each section.

Ginott, Hiam G. *Between Parent and Child.* New York: Avon Books, 1965. PB. Although written primarily for parents, this best-selling book offers practical suggestions for solutions to a variety of problems that will be of interest to teachers. Topics such as communication, praise and criticism, jealousy, and others are treated with skill. Readings of special interest are Chapter 1 "Conversing with Children," Chapter 2 "New Ways of Praise and Criticism," Chapter 3 "Avoiding Self-Defeating Patterns," and from Chapter 4, the portion on "Music Lessons."

Sandstrom, Carl Ivor. *The Psychology of Childhood and Adolescence,* Translated by Albert Read. Baltimore: Penguin Books, 1968. PB. From Sweden comes this intelligent, well-written book designed as an introductory textbook for teachers. The author speaks with authority on a broad spectrum of subjects ranging from growth and development to the development of language and thought. Chapters of special interest are Chapter 4, "Survey of Development," Chapter 7 "Motivation and the Development of Learning," and Chapter 12 "Development of Personality."

Business Procedures 3

Piano lessons should be conducted in a businesslike manner. It is advisable to charge by the month, semester, or term rather than by the lesson. If payment is made by the lesson, pupils will feel free to cancel lessons. Some months have fewer weeks due to holidays such as Thanksgiving, Christmas, and Easter. Since tuition is based on a fixed number of weeks in the school year, monthly payments should be the *same* regardless of the number of weeks in the month.

Statements should be sent to parents. If music is purchased by the teacher, it should be added to the statement. If audition or competition fees are paid by the teacher, these should also be added.

LESSON FEES

The amount charged per lesson, month, semester, or school year varies throughout the country. An artist teacher may command a high fee, while an independent teacher may ask a fee commensurate to the community. Lesson fees are dependent on the:

1. background and capability of the teacher
2. income bracket of the community
3. length of lessons
4. type of lesson—private and/or group

Background & Capability of the Teacher

The teacher's background includes precollege training, college training, pedagogy background, advanced study with artist teachers, and other professional experiences. All are relevant factors in determining lesson fees. One would expect to pay more for lessons from a teacher with a Master's degree than from a teacher with a Bachelor's degree or no degree at all. An experienced, successful teacher may charge a proportionately higher fee than a less experienced teacher.

Income of the Community

The socioeconomic status of the community is determined by various factors. The cost of living is usually determined by the area in which one lives. Generally, the price of land, home or apartment, taxes, and other items are usually higher in a large city than a small one. Monthly lesson tuition in New York may be several times the tuition in a small town. Therefore, fees should be scaled to the community in which one teaches.

Lesson Fee Structures

Some teachers have varying rates for half-hour lessons, forty-five minute lessons, and hour lessons, while other teachers charge a fixed tuition.

Private instruction is generally more expensive than class instruction, but not proportionately. Fees for private lessons may run $18 to $20 an hour; however, a fee of $5 per pupil for a class of ten would net the teacher $50 for an hour of group instruction.

The following gives some typical ways to structure fees.

Private Lessons Only

General prices for one half-hour private lesson per week range from $40 to $60 per month, or a comparable amount paid by the semester. This rate is based on a lesson fee of $10 to $15.

Combination Private & Group Lessons

Prices for one half-hour private lesson and one forty-five minute group lesson per week range from $40 to $50 per month, or a comparable amount paid by the semester.

Combination Small & Large Groups

Fees are about the same as for private and group, from $40 to $60 per month, or a comparable amount paid by the semester.

Large Classes

Fees for this type of instruction may be less. One hour per week ranges from $30 to $50 per month, or a comparable amount paid by the semester.

Most full-time professional teachers teach between forty and fifty pupils per week. Private lessons based on fifty pupils at $40 per month each would produce a nine-month income of $18,000. Additional income could be gained by teaching lessons in the summer.

Combination private and group lessons would produce a nine-month income of $22,500, based on forty pupils at $50 per month each. The best return for the teacher would be gained from some type of group lesson in addition to the private lesson. It is also the best investment for students because they receive more time for their money.

Pedagogical Considerations

INCREASING THE INCOME

Raising Tuition

It is best to raise rates at the beginning of a new school term rather than in the middle of the year. The change to the higher fee will not be so abrupt, and parents will have time to adjust their budgets. A brief letter similar to that shown in Example 1 should be sent to the parents sometime in May. Reasons for the tuition increase do not have to be spelled out. A simple statement will suffice.

EXAMPLE 1 Raising Tuition Letter.

LORI WILLIAMS
6943 JUTLAND STREET
BEDFORD, WA 12345
555-1212

May 1

Dear Parents:

The tuition for the coming school year will be $70 per month.

I will be contacting you soon about scheduling classes for the summer. You can look forward to information about some new "special focus" classes that will be offered!

Sincerely,

Lori Williams

Teaching in the Summer

Summer income may be obtained by continuing regular lessons, or offering special programs for regular students, or by offering classes for new beginners for six to eight weeks.

Some of the "regular" students will continue lessons during part of the summer. If you are teaching the private/group combination during the regular school year, it might be difficult to continue this same program during the summer due to a reduced number of students.

There are several possible summer programs that may be offered: high school theory, music appreciation classes, piano pedagogy for older high school students, and classes in accompanying and ensemble literature.

BOOKKEEPING PROCEDURES

Since the independent teacher is self-employed, careful records must be kept of income and expenses for tax purposes. Monthly fees are easy to keep track of by marking each time a payment is received, on a chart similar to that shown in Example 2.

EXAMPLE 2 Recording student payments.

Student Names	Sept.	Oct.	Nov.	Dec.	Jan.	Feb.	Mar.	Apr.	May
Kim Park									
Dee Parsons									
Ginny Price									

etc.

Accounting is not difficult if the amount of each bill and payment is entered onto an expense form similar to that shown in Example 3. If book-keeping is not kept up to date, a number of deductible items may be overlooked. Be sure to keep *all* receipts and cancelled checks for several years for tax purposes.

For bookkeeping procedures see the *Music Teacher's Record Book* by Jane Smisor Bastien (Neil A. Kjos Music Company, 1976) and *A Business Guide for the Music Teacher* by Beth Gigante (Neil A. Kjos Music Company, 1987).

TAX DEDUCTIONS

Tax laws are subject to change, and the teacher should consult an accountant about itemized deductions. However, the checklist of deductible expenses in Example 4 is a general guide.

Annual Expenditures

Records of income and expenses must be accurately noted as they occur. Otherwise it is extremely difficult to gather this information when income tax time approaches. To compile information for tax records, all items must be itemized as shown in Example 3 for the entire year.

Pedagogical Considerations

EXAMPLE 3 Monthly accounting form.

EXPENSES FOR THE MONTH OF_____

1. Music purchased   _____
   Music sold   _____
   Balance   _____

2. Rewards, favors, incentives purchased   _____

3. Studio rent if applicable   _____

4. Portion of utilities   _____

5. Reference materials
      books   _____
      music   _____
      records   _____
      tapes   _____
            TOTAL   _____

6. Office supplies
      envelopes, paper   _____
      postage   _____
      printing   _____
      statements or receipts _____
      other   _____
            TOTAL   _____

7. Telephone   _____

8. Additional expenses
      dues, workshops, tunings, etc.   _____

      GRAND TOTAL   _____

EXAMPLE 4 Checklist of deductible expenses.

Instruments, Equipment, Supplies
   Instruments: depreciation, rental, maintenance, repairs
   Depreciation for record player, tape recorder, typewriter, computer, video recorder,
      other equipment
   Records, tapes, books
   Metronome, stop watch, etc.
   Sheet music, music paper, etc.
   Office supplies: stationery, business cards, postage, etc.

Studio
   Depreciation and portion of mortgage, real estate tax
   Rent if applicable
   Overhead: portion of heat, light, cleaning, etc.

Business Procedures

Recital Expenses
Hall rental, flowers, programs, refreshments, etc.

Fees & Dues
Profesional organizations
Bookkeeping or accounting (consult an accountant for application on Schedule C form)

Maintenance of Professional Skills
Professional magazines and books
Conventions and workshops: travel and hotel, 80% of meals

Miscellaneous
Advertising: any expense to promote business
Business telephone
Local transportation (mileage to and from music store)
Possibly: entertainment and gifts; childcare

FOR DISCUSSION & ASSIGNMENT

Under this heading in Chapter 2, questions were to be asked of three independent teachers in the community. Further information about studio management can be learned by asking the following questions from the same teachers.

1. What method of payment does each teacher use: by the lesson, month, or semester? Discuss briefly the merits or demerits of each teacher's method.
2. What policy is used for a missed lesson? Are students charged for missed lessons? Are missed lessons made up?
3. How is payment handled for months of varying teaching weeks?
4. What fees are charged for lessons?
5. Are summer lessons given? If so, are any additional summer programs offered? How are fees handled for summer lessons?
6. Did any of the teachers raise their rates during the past few years? If so, how was it handled?

Survey of Methods for Beginners 4

Piano instruction is an excellent added dimension to a child's education. It is usually not the intent or purpose of those studying to become professional musicians. Rather, for the majority who study, music becomes a satisfying experience that gives direction to the basic needs of self-expression.

Due to the great popularity of piano instruction, this country has produced a large body of teaching materials over the past sixty years. The sheer bulk of this output is sufficient to overwhelm anyone who endeavors to become knowledgeable on the subject.

TEACHING GOALS OF METHOD BOOKS

The word "method" is defined by Merriam-Webster as "a systematic plan followed in presenting material for instruction." The word further connotes a procedure that develops an integrated system of learning. Since method books have planned objectives for systematic progression, one should consider the specific goals outlined by each book or series.

Without thought or reference to any particular method of instruction, list your own teaching objectives. Consider basic skills that beginning students should have attained after a few years of instruction. The following list of objectives is offered as a guide. These ten points represent general goals that would be endorsed by most piano teachers—no doubt you will think of many more.

After a few years of instruction, students should be able to:

1. understand the entire keyboard, not just part of it
2. recognize notes fluently, including ledger line notes
3. recognize chords and be able to play them (major, minor, augmented, and diminished)
4. understand tempo markings, meter signatures, key signatures, and music terms
5. improvise

6. respond to ear training activities
   a. repeat a melodic pattern played by the teacher
   b. play an answer to a question phrase
   c. recognize intervals and chords
7. harmonize melodies
8. sight-read
9. participate in ensemble music (one piano-four hands, two pianos)
10. memorize a number of pieces each year

Educational Philosophies

Philosophical concepts in education have changed greatly during the past six decades. Years ago, it was thought that elementary education had to be strict. Fortunately, much of this stern autocratic approach to teaching is gone. However, it is difficult for some teachers to adjust to today's methods because of the way they were taught, even though teaching methods have progressed markedly over the years.

Teaching methods employed today reflect the general evolution that has occurred in all phases of education. Teaching should be relevant, and should focus on the needs and objectives of students today.

The Middle C Method

The middle C method was made popular by John Thompson's *Teaching Little Fingers to Play*, published by the Willis Music Company in 1936. The instructional procedure requires the student to place both thumbs on middle C and begin playing, as shown in Example 1.

Example 1 Typical middle C beginning melody.

Without previous keyboard experience the student begins to play little melodies while simultaneously learning notation and rhythm. Later, melodies are written mostly in two parts as shown in Example 2. Finger numbers are given for every note in most courses. The keys of the pieces are limited almost exclusively to C, G, and F. Theoretical concepts such as intervals, chord structure and use, transposition, harmonization, the order of sharps and flats, key signatures, etc., may or may not be included; generally, these presentations, if given, come later in the course.

Example 2 Typical middle C two-part melody.

Landmark Reading

An alternative to middle C methods was first introduced in 1955 by Frances Clark's *Library for Piano Students*, published by Summy-Birchard (now Birch Tree Group Ltd.). Directional reading is developed from given landmarks (Example 3): bass clef F, middle C, and treble clef G. The student reads intervals up and down from these landmarks.

Example 3 Landmark reading: F C G.

The series *Music Pathways* by Lynn Olson, Louise Bianchi, and Marvin Blickenstaff, published in 1974 by Carl Fischer, uses landmark reading from five C's on the staff.

Example 4 Landmark reading: five C's.

Multiple Key Method

The multiple key method is a completely different approach to beginning instruction from either middle C methods or landmark reading. Robert Pace was one of the originators of this style of learning to play the piano, in his series *Music for Piano* published in 1961 by Lee Roberts Music

Survey of Methods for Beginners

Publications, Inc. The procedure of the multiple key method is to learn all twelve five-finger positions within the first few months of instruction.

The twelve major positions are most easily learned by dividing the keys into groups according to those that are related by both sight and touch. Example: Group 1 keys (C G F) have all white keys in the tonic chords; Group 2 keys (D A E) have a white, black, white composition in their tonic chords; Group 3 keys (D♭ A♭ E♭) have a black, white, black composition in their tonic chords; Group 4 keys (G♭ B♭ B) are not related by sight or touch because each is different.

Directional reading is developed by establishing the concept of intervallic relationships, mainly steps (seconds), skips (thirds), and repeated notes as shown in Example 5.

Example 5   Basic patterns for directional reading.

Almost from the beginning, I and V⁷ chords are used and melodies are harmonized with these two chords, as in Example 6. Elements of theory are covered thoroughly in multiple key methods to include intervals, basic chords (tonic, subdominant, dominant, major, minor, diminished, augmented), the order of sharps and flats, key signatures, transposition, and harmonization.

Example 6   Melody harmonized with I and V⁷ chords.

Gradual Multiple Key Method

The gradual multiple key method allows the beginner sufficient time to learn each group of keys over several years of study. The four key groups are still presented, but at a slower pace than the initial multiple key approach. This concept of learning was introduced by James and Jane Smisor Bastien in the *Bastien Piano Library* (1976), published by the Neil A. Kjos Music Company. Many teachers are now using this concept of teaching to allow beginners sufficient time to grasp and learn beginning fundamentals. Reading, theory, harmonization, and other basics can be developed more gradually.

Pedagogical Considerations

The following comparisons of middle C and the gradual multiple key method (Example 7) reflect basic changes in old and new methods. Although it might be concluded that the student would experience a greater variety of material using the gradual multiple key method, one should not forget that the correct presentation of any material is essential. Success cannot be guaranteed automatically by the method chosen. The teacher, not a set of books, is the determining factor in quality results.

CRITERIA FOR THE EVALUATION OF PIANO METHODS

Upon close scrutiny it can be discovered that *all* method books have strong and weak features. No one series has a corner on the market for a magic blueprint that will automatically produce first-rate pianists. However, there are some guidelines which may be used to determine quality features in method books and to help determine approaches that will assist the skilled teacher in developing knowledgeable musicians. The following criteria are offered as general guidelines in evaluating beginning method books. This material, used with permission, is based on a set of guidelines used by David Piersel at South Dakota State University.

Design & Format
1. Basic approach
   a. Middle C?
   b. Gradual multiple key?
   c. Other?
2. Format
   a. Is color used?
   b. Are pictures and/or drawings used?
   c. Is the music legible?
   d. Is the size of the type and music realistic for younger students?
   e. Is the marginal material helpful without being cluttered, and is it written in children's language?
   f. Is the book long enough to be practical, but short enough to give the student a feeling of accomplishment?
3. Sequence and progression of materials
   a. Does the series as a whole keep the student advancing in a *steady* manner, not by spurts?
4. Purpose of the method
   a. For individual study?
   b. For group study?
   c. For a combination of individual and group study?
5. Note range
   a. Does the series guide the student to gradually explore more and more of the keyboard?
   b. Is the range confined to a central portion of the keyboard?

Survey of Methods for Beginners

Example 7 Comparison of middle C and gradual multiple key methods.

	Middle C Method	Gradual Multiple Key Method
Melodies	Centers around middle C, especially in the early lessons.	Begins on black keys, then the C five-finger position, middle C position, and additional key groups.
Notation	Confined to a two-octave range and limited mainly to the white keys, with the exception of F$\sharp$, B$\flat$, and C$\sharp$.	Develops a four-octave range to include all sharps and flats, and ledger lines above, below, and between the staffs.
Rhythm	Somewhat restricted to $\frac{4}{4}$, $\frac{3}{4}$, $\frac{2}{4}$, especially in the early lessons; $\frac{6}{8}$ is introduced later.	Presented similarly, although $\frac{6}{8}$ is usually introduced much earlier.
Theory	Basically nonexistent. "Theory" is often nothing more than exercises in drawing the treble and bass clefs, note spelling, writing note values, writing counts, etc.	Considerable. Intervals, chords, key signatures, and keyboard harmony are interwoven as basic ingredients in the general musical program.
Chord usage	Quite limited. Block chords are almost never used or explained; however, various types of broken chord accompaniments are used.	Frequently used. All major, minor, diminished, and augmented chords are used in both block and broken form; they are clearly explained and systematically used.
Order of sharps and flats	Excluded. The order of sharps (F C G D A E B) and flats (B E A D G C F) is *not* used or explained in this approach.	Included. Students learn the order of sharps and flats in the second year and review them in subsequent years.
Key signatures	Quite limited. The student is told that if there is an F$\sharp$ in the key signature, the piece is in G, but there is no attempt to systematically teach all the key signatures.	Emphasized continually. All major (and later, minor) key signatures are explained and used; by frequent reference to "key," the student becomes aware of the tonal center.

Pedagogical Considerations

	Middle C Method	Gradual Multiple Key Method
Transposition	Some. Suggestions for transposition are sometimes given, but keys suggested usually are those of C, G, or F.	Considerable. Students are directed to transpose the pieces into other keys.
Harmonization	Quite limited. The harmonization of given melodies is virtually nonexistent in this approach.	Frequently used. Single line melodies are presented for students to harmonize in various keys.
Improvisation	Excluded.	Included. Students are given question phrases and are told to improvise or create their own answer phrases.
Creative work	Very limited, almost nonexistent.	Limited to writing harmonies for melodies, and question and answer phrases.
Technique	Included. Finger drills are used mostly in the key of C, and scales are presented early in this approach.	Included. Finger drills are used in all keys in various ways: legato and staccato touch, balancing of tone, phrase studies (down-up wrist motion), forearm rotation; scales are presented later in this approach.
Sight-reading	Limited to C, G, and F keys.	Reading facility is developed in many ways.
Comprehensive music program	Somewhat limited. Confined mostly to the learning of pieces, technical studies, and scales.	Repertoire, sight-reading, theory, technique, and creative work constitute the general music program.

Survey of Methods for Beginners

6. Methods of counting
   a. Numerically?
   b. Syllabically?
   c. Other?
7. Presentation of rhythm
   a. What types of rhythms are encountered as the series progresses?
8. Chords and scales
   a. How and when are these presented?
   b. Are both block and broken chords used?
   c. How many different types of chords are used?
   d. Are both major and minor scales presented?
9. Theory
   a. Are intervals used?
   b. Are chords presented?
   c. Is keyboard harmony included?
   d. Is functional harmonization included?
   e. Is transposition emphasized?
   f. Is creative work included?
   g. If separate books are used, how well does it integrate with the basic method books?
10. Supplementary materials
    a. What variety is available within the course?
11. Form and structure
    a. What opportunities are offered throughout the course to teach form?
12. Musicianship
    a. Is the student given an opportunity to develop musicianship or creativeness?
    b. Is undue emphasis given merely to the mechanics of playing the piano?

Fundamental Features
1. Is it a comprehensive course of study?
   a. Does it include a logical, practical *sight-reading* program?
   b. Does it include a sensible *theoretical* program based primarily on keyboard harmony?
   c. Does it include a practical *technical* program geared to basic keyboard fundamentals?
   d. Does the method offer a variety of *supplementary* books for reinforced learning at different levels of advancement?
2. Does the music make sense to the student?
   a. Is the music tasteful and appealing to children?
   b. Is the rate of progression gradual?
3. What will the student have learned upon completion of the method?
   a. Will he be able to sight-read fluently?

Pedagogical Considerations

b. Will he be musically literate in basic theory?

c. Will technique be developed sufficiently to perform various levels of repertoire accurately?

4. What length of study time will it take for the student to become musically literate?

a. Two years?

b. Three years?

c. Never?

THE TEACHER'S ATTITUDE TOWARD NEW APPROACHES

It is immediately apparent that there are numerous ways of starting beginners. No one music educator or one set of books has all the answers. It is up to the teacher to produce students who become musically literate in fundamentals within a two- or three-year span. To accomplish this, the teacher has an immense amount of beginning materials from which to select an effective program for each student.

An open mind should be kept toward new or innovative methods. However, this does not mean that one should blindly accept a new method simply because it is the latest publication available. The pros and cons should be weighed carefully before embarking on a new system merely for the sake of trying something new.

Teachers should realize that a method alone will not do the job for them. Some teachers become so attached to one author's course that they will not consider using another method even for supplementary purposes. This is a very narrow view and unnecessarily limiting. Quality teaching is determined by the *results* achieved, not necessarily by the methods used.

Times change, pupils' needs change, and basic goals need periodic reevaluation. Therefore, a functional approach to teaching is helpful in the beginning stages of lessons. Elements of keyboard harmony, theory, improvisation, and creative work lay a better fundamental foundation than merely learning to play a few pieces each year. Many of the older methods simply do not include these elements of practical musicianship.

METHOD BOOKS

The United States has produced more method books than any other country. Some methods are old, some are recent publications. Seen on display at a major music store, the number of methods is overwhelming. Not all stores are able to carry a complete stock due to the expenses involved. Best-sellers are usually stocked; other methods may be ordered.

The following alphabetical list includes the better-known authors of method books. An asterisk indicates that their methods for children (age five or older) and/or adults are surveyed in this chapter. Methods for pre-school children are reviewed in Chapter 5.

*Bastien, James and
 Jane Smisor Bastien
 Brimhall, John
*Clark, Frances
 Diller-Quaille
 Fletcher, Leila
*Glover, David Carr
*Lyke, James and Denise Edwards
*Noona, Walter and Carol
*Olson, Lynn Freeman,
 Louise Bianchi and
 Marvin Blickenstaff
 Oxford Piano Course
*Pace, Robert
*Palmer, Willard,
 Morton Manus and
 Amanda Vick Lethco
 Schaum, John W.
*Suzuki, Shinichi
*Thompson, John

The teacher should make an effort to be aware of new methods published. Information on new methods can be found in magazines such as *American Music Teacher, Clavier,* and *The Piano Quarterly.* One of the best reference sources on new publications is the *Maxwell Music Evaluation Notebook* edited by Carolyn Maxwell (1245 Kalmia Avenue, Boulder, CO 80302).

To acquaint teachers with methods that are used with some frequency, ten authors' methods for both children (age five and older) and adults are surveyed. It is helpful to have these methods available for pedagogy students to evaluate themselves.

Bastien, James and Jane Smisor Bastien

BEGINNING METHODS FOR CHILDREN

BASTIEN PIANO BASICS Neil A. Kjos Music Company (1985-87)

Method
Piano for the Young Beginner, Primer A, Primer B (ages 5-6), leads into Level 1.
Piano, Primer-Level 4 (ages 7-10)

Pedagogical Considerations

Theory
Theory & Technic for the Young Beginner, Primer A, Primer B (ages 5-6), leads into Level 1.
Theory, Primer-Level 4 (ages 7-10)

Technique
Technic, Primer-Level 4

Repertoire
Performance, Primer-Level 4

Supplementary
Boogie, Rock, & Country, Levels 1-3 (1988)
Dinosaur Kingdom, Level 2/3 (1988)
1st Parade of Solos, Primer/Level 1 (1988)
2nd Parade of Solos, Level 1/2 (1988)
3rd Parade of Solos, Level 2/3 (1988)
4th Parade of Solos, Level 3/4 (1988)
Nursery Songs at the Piano, Primer/Level 1 (1988)
Popular Christmas Songs, Primer-Level 4 (1986)
Popular Hymns, Primer-Level 3 (1987)
Indian Life, Levels 1-3 (1987)
Space Adventures, Level 3/4 (1987)
Two Sonatinas, Level 4 (1987)
Other books are available.

Bastien Piano Basics is a comprehensive, gradual multi-key series featuring a step-by-step approach for beginning students. Each level contains original pieces, selected folk songs, and popular-style pieces. The concise explanations of concepts, the clean layout, and the attractive full-color illustrations that reinforce concepts and provide extra interest, continue throughout the series.

One of the special features of this method is that there are two sets of primers—one for the young beginner 5-6 years of age, and the other for the more common beginning age of 7-10. After completing either set, the student would continue with Level 1.

Although the *Bastien Piano Basics* series presents the same concepts at the same levels as does the *Bastien Piano Library* (see page 52), there are many differences. Of primary importance is the difference in writing style: the left hand is less chordal, thus creating a stronger independence of hands and more interesting music. Also, concepts are presented in a more concise manner, giving less for the students to read, and providing a cleaner layout. It is easy to plan lessons because on each Contents page all books at that level are coordinated page-by-page. The illustrations are contemporary and colorful.

Method
Piano for the Young Beginner, Primer A is designed especially for the

five- or six-year-old student. Pre-staff notation is used until page 28, when the grand staff is introduced. The counting systems suggested include both note name (say "quarter" for each quarter note, "half note" for each half note, etc.), and number counting beginning on page 22. The music is a combination of original pieces, selected folk songs, and seasonal pieces. Duet accompaniments are included for many of the pieces.

Piano for the Young Beginner, Primer B introduces these new materials: eighth note pairs, dynamic signs, intervals through the fifth, rests, sharp and flat signs, slurs and ties, and staccato touch. Duet accompaniments are provided for many of the pieces. After completing this primer along with the corresponding theory book, the young student is to continue with Level 1.

Piano, Primer Level is for the average-age beginner from seven to ten. Piano contains pre-staff notation until the grand staff is introduced on page 26. First pieces begin on the black keys using a variety of finger patterns. The student is introduced to basic rhythms ($\quarternote$, $\halfnote$, $\wholenote$, $\dottedhalfnote$, $\eighthpair$), intervals through the fifth, rests, sharp and flat signs, legato-staccato touches, tonic chord, and music signs and terms. The counting systems suggested include both note name counting (count "quarter" for each quarter note, "half note" for each half note, etc.), and number counting beginning on page 18. Staff reading is taught by recognition of step, skip, and repeat. Duet accompaniments are provided for many of the pieces.

Piano, Level 1 introduces the two-note V^7 chord (using root and seventh), tempo marks, key signatures, music form, dynamic shading, the damper pedal, upbeat, single eighth note and rest sign, dotted quarter note, and the Group 1 keys (C G F). Many pieces include changing hand positions.

Piano, Level 2 includes half and whole steps, one-octave major scales with tetrachords identified (C G F D A E), binary and ternary forms, intervals of sixths and sevenths, moving the thumb or little finger (to extend out of five-finger positions), primary chords, triads and inversions, chord progressions (I IV$^6_4$ V$^6_5$), $^6_8$ time signature, order of sharps, and the Group 2 keys (D A E).

Piano, Level 3 introduces various bass style accompaniments, relative minor scales of a and d, minor key signatures, major-minor triads, primary chords in minor, triplets, chromatic scale, order of flats, and the Group 3 keys (D♭ A♭ E♭).

Piano, Level 4 includes overlapping pedal, e minor scale, identifying first and second inversion chords, sixteenth notes, dotted eighth notes, augmented and diminished triads, syncopations, parallel major and minor scales, and the Group 4 keys (G♭ B♭ B).

Theory
Theory & Technic for the Young Beginner, Primers A and **B** contain a

combination of written work, technique studies, and short pieces to reinforce concepts presented in the *Piano* books. Upon completion of these two books, along with the corresponding *Piano* books, the young student is to continue with Level 1 of *Bastien Piano Basics*.

Theory, Primer Level contains drills, games, and short pieces to provide a variety of written and playing activities. Materials include notes, bar lines, alphabet letters, rhythms, melodic and harmonic intervals through the fifth, dynamics, slur and tie, rests, tonic chord, and the sharp and flat signs.

Theory, Level 1 includes chord accompaniments, tempo marks, key signatures (C G F), accent sign, crescendo and diminuendo signs, the damper pedal, upbeat, the Group 1 keys (C G F), how to transpose, single eighth note and rest signs, dotted quarter note, octave sign, and natural sign.

Theory, Level 2 includes half and whole steps, major scale formation with tetrachords, intervals of sixths and sevenths, primary chords, chord progressions, question and answer phrases, $\frac{6}{8}$ time signature, the order of sharps, major sharp key signatures, ledger lines, and the Group 2 keys (D A E).

Theory, Level 3 includes various bass styles, minor scales, minor key signatures, triads and inversions, recognizing inverted triads, triplets, chromatic scale, the order of flats, major flat key signatures, and the Group 3 keys (D♭ A♭ E♭).

Theory, Level 4 includes writing key signatures, identifying inverted chords, intervals of the scale, sixteenth notes, dotted eighth note, altered intervals, augmented and diminished triads, syncopation, parallel major and minor scales, and the Group 4 keys (G♭ B♭ B).

Technique

Technic, Primer Level contains both pre-staff and staff finger drills. A variety of exercises are provided for legato-staccato touch, tonic chord practice, phrase groups (down-up wrist motion), slur, and tie. The exercises are limited to five-finger patterns in the C, middle C, and G positions.

Technic, Level 1 contains a variety of five-finger studies for legato and staccato touch, slurred notes (down-up wrist motion), pedal, solid and broken chords, dotted quarter note, octave sign, double notes, and reading in the keys of C G F.

Technic, Level 2 includes major scales (C G F D A E), intervals of sixths and sevenths, primary chords (I IV$^6_4$ V$^6_5$), triads and inversions, $\frac{6}{8}$ time signature, and double note exercises.

Technic, Level 3 includes various bass style accompaniments, relative minor scales of a and d, major-minor triads, primary chords in minor, triads and inversions, triplets, the interval of an octave, chromatic scale, and studies by Hanon, Schmitt, and Czerny.

Technic, Level 4 has wrist staccato, overlapping pedal, first and second inversion chord studies, triads and inversions, sixteenth notes, dotted eighth note, augmented and diminished triads, syncopation, and studies by Gurlitt, Schmitt, Lemoine, and Czerny.

Repertoire
The **Performance** books (**Primer** through **Level** 4) contain a variety of original works, folk songs, and popular styles. The sequence is carefully correlated with the *Piano* books. These pieces may be assigned for extra reading, and for performance in recitals, auditions, and contests.

THE BASTIEN PIANO LIBRARY Neil A. Kjos Music Company (1976)

Method
Piano Lessons, Primer-Level 4
Traditional Primer—Piano Lessons (1981)

Theory
Theory Lessons, Primer-Level 4
Traditional Primer—Theory & Technic Lessons (1981)
Note-Speller, Level 1

Technique
Technic Lessons, Primer-Level 4
First Hanon Studies, Level 3

Sight-Reading
Sight Reading, Levels 1-4

Repertoire
Piano Solos, Primer-Level 4
Traditional Primer—Piano Solos (1981)

Supplementary Books
Christmas Favorites, Primer-Level 4 (1979-80)
Duet Favorites, Levels 1-4 (1980)
Favorite Classic Melodies, Primer-Level 4 (1981)
Folk Tune Favorites, Primer-Level 4 (1979)
Happy Halloween, Primer/Level 2 (1983)
Happy Valentine's, Primer/Level 2 (1983)
Hymn Favorites, Primer-Level 2 (1978)
Nutcracker Suite, The, Level 4 (1980)
Piano Recital Solos, Primer-Level 4 (1980-81)
Pop Piano Styles, Levels 1-4 (1980)
Scott Joplin Favorites, Level 4 (1975)
Other books are available.

Pedagogical Considerations

The Bastien Piano Library is presented in a gradual multi-key sequence. Each level contains original and selected folk song materials. These books are to be used with the companion books *Theory, Technic, Piano Solos,* and *Sight Reading.* The result of this correlation of materials is a step-by-step method presented in an enjoyable manner.

Method

Piano Lessons, Primer Level is designed for beginners about seven to ten. This book contains six units divided into three units of pre-staff notation and three units of staff notation. The C, G, and middle C five-finger positions are emphasized. The main materials introduced are rhythm ($\quarternote$, $\halfnote$, $\wholenote$, $\dottedhalfnote$, $\eighthnotes$), music alphabet, intervals through the fifth, transposition, notation, tonic chord, legato-staccato touches, and music signs and terms. A written review page is included for each unit. Duet accompaniments are provided for many of the pieces.

Traditional Primer—Piano Lessons introduces reading in middle C and in the C major five-finger position. Included are fundamentals such as notation, rhythm, legato and staccato touches, sharp and flat signs, and dynamics (forte and piano). Teacher duets are provided for many of the pieces.

Piano Lessons, Level 1 introduces the two-note V^7 chord (using root and seventh), key signatures, upbeat, the Group 1 keys (C G F), dotted quarter note, and the pedal. Duet accompaniments are provided for some of the pieces.

Piano Lessons, Level 2 includes half and whole steps, one-octave scales (C G F D A E), interval of the sixth, I IV$^6_4$ V$^6_5$ chords, $^6_8$ meter, the order of sharps, the Group 2 keys (D A E), and minor chords. Transposition is suggested for many of the pieces.

Piano Lessons, Level 3 has various bass style accompaniments, triads of the scale, triplets, relative minor scales, minor key signatures, chromatic scale, inversions of triads, the order of flats, and the Group 3 keys (D$\flat$ A$\flat$ E$\flat$).

Piano Lessons, Level 4 includes overlapping pedal, intervals of sevenths and octaves, sixteenth notes, parallel major and minor scales, augmented and diminished triads, syncopation, and the Group 4 keys (G$\flat$ B$\flat$ B).

Theory

Theory Lessons is designed to be used simultaneously with each level of *Piano Lessons.* The theory books contain a combination of written and playing work to reinforce concepts presented in the basic course.

Theory Lessons, Primer Level includes staff work, note spelling, rhythm drills, harmonizing melodies, key signature drills, drawing notes, intervals, transposition, the Group 1 keys, and music signs and terms.

Traditional Primer—Theory & Technic Lessons provides parallel materials

Survey of Methods for Beginners

correlated with the *Traditional Primer—Piano Lessons*. Included are writing and playing drills, technique exercises for legato and staccato touches, chords, phrasing patterns, and exercises for finger dexterity.

Theory Lessons, Level 1 materials include recognizing half and whole steps, writing and playing major scales (C G F D A E), question and answer phrases, harmonizing lead lines, rhythm drills, note drills, intervals, the order of sharps, the Group 2 keys (D A E), and music signs and terms.

Theory Lessons, Levels 3, 4 provide expanded theoretical work to parallel the materials presented in Levels 3 and 4 of *Piano Lessons*.

Note Speller, Level 1 is designed to introduce basic information about the staff, notes and rests, accidentals, and ledger line notes. Materials are divided into twenty-seven written lessons plus one review lesson.

Technique

Technic Lessons provide additional materials to reinforce concepts presented in the *Piano Lessons*. A combination of pure and applied technique studies is presented in this series. The general goal is to develop hand and finger coordination and facility, and to develop ease and control at the keyboard.

Technic Lessons, Primer Level contains six units divided into three units of pre-staff notation and three units of staff notation. Teacher's notes are included for the first three units which give student practice suggestions. Materials introduced in this volume include playing clusters, playing intervals (seconds, thirds, fourths, fifths), playing the C and G five-finger positions, playing chords (tonic chords), phrasing, legato and staccato touch, and hand-over-hand arpeggio.

Technic Lessons, Level 1 contains a variety of keyboard studies for five-finger drills, chords (solid and broken), touch (legato and staccato), phrasing, thumb crossings (scale preparation), moving hand positions, chromatics, pedal, and double notes.

Technic Lessons, Levels 2, 3, 4 continue to expand the student's facility at the keyboard. Included in these three books are studies for scales, chords, finger extension, chromatic scale, double notes, phrasing, pedal, finger independence, triads and inversions, trill, and the Alberti bass. A variety of rhythms, touches, and keys are utilized in the exercises and etudes in these books.

Sight-Reading

Sight Reading, Levels 1, 2, 3, 4 contain graded reading material ranging from elementary to early intermediate levels using legato and staccato, chords, and different styles and moods. Some excerpts are not identified and are to be "discovered" by the student. The teacher should assign two pages per week and require the student to sight-read one exercise each day. At the next lesson the teacher can hear one or more exercises.

Pedagogical Considerations

Repertoire
Piano Solos provides additional repertoire and reading to supplement each level of *Piano Lessons*. The music consists of original pieces and familiar folk songs. These pieces may be assigned for extra reading, and for performance in recitals.

Traditional Primer—Piano Solos contains additional pieces to reinforce concepts learned in the *Traditional Primer—Piano Lessons* book. Included are original pieces, familiar songs, and folk song arrangements.

INTERMEDIATE METHOD

INTERMEDIATE PIANO COURSE (Bastien) Neil A. Kjos Music Company (1982)

Method
Intermediate Repertoire 1, 2, 3

Theory
Intermediate Theory 1, 2, 3

Technique
Intermediate Technic 1, 2, 3

Repertoire
Intermediate Multi-Key Solos 1, 2, 3

The **Intermediate Piano Course** is intended to be used after the completion of any beginning method.

Method
Intermediate Repertoire books contain an excellent selection of Baroque, Classic, Romantic, and Contemporary literature by master composers as well as some original compositions in each of those styles by James and Jane Bastien. Also included are descriptions of each period, complete with photos of paintings, architecture, and historic keyboard instruments; a list of famous composers from each period; and examples of compositional styles and forms.

Theory
Intermediate Theory books provide written and playing material and contain numerous examples from standard literature for harmonic analysis. Each book has a final review of all the theory information presented.

Technique
Intermediate Technic books contain an organized program of preparation studies followed by etudes from the standard technical composers, as well as new imaginative studies by the Bastiens.

Survey of Methods for Beginners

Repertoire
Multi-Key Solo books give the intermediate student an opportunity to play music in many keys that are not found in the standard early intermediate literature. These pieces may be used for sight-reading and recital use.

BEGINNING METHOD FOR ADULTS (age 12 and up)

OLDER BEGINNER PIANO COURSE (Bastien) Neil A. Kjos Music Company (1977)

Method
Older Beginner Piano Course, Levels 1, 2

Theory/Technique
Musicianship for the Older Beginner, Levels 1, 2

Supplementary
Classic Themes By the Masters (1978)
Easy Piano Classics (1978)
Favorite Melodies the World Over, Levels 1, 2 (1977)
Religious Favorites (1978)
Solo Repertoire (1982)

The *Older Beginner Piano Course* (two books, 96 pages each) is designed for students from about age twelve and up. The course is designed functionally, allowing the student to play and harmonize melodies from the beginning using a chord approach. Each book has ten units with a review page at the end of the unit. A combination of original and familiar music is used. Multi-key reading is introduced gradually through the course. Each course book is to be supplemented with the companion book *Musicianship for the Older Beginner*.

Method
Older Beginner Piano Course, Level 1 includes reading in the keys of C G F and D A E, I IV V^7 chords, transposition, major scales, $\frac{4}{4}$ and $\frac{6}{8}$ meters, minor chords, and the pedal.

Older Beginner Piano Course, Level 2 has bass styles, syncopated rhythm, minor scales and minor key signatures, triads of the scale, inversions of triads, the chromatic scale, augmented and diminished triads, sixteenth notes, and the keys of D♭ A♭ E♭ and G♭ B♭ B.

Theory/Technique
Musicianship for the Older Beginner, Levels 1, 2 (48 pages each) is designed to be used as a companion to the *Older Beginner Piano Course*. Each book is divided into ten units containing theory, technical drills, and sight-reading materials correlated to the method books.

Pedagogical Considerations

REVIEW COURSE FOR ADULTS

Piano: 2nd Time Around (Bastien) Neil A. Kjos Music Company (1981)

This is a basic review course for adults who have played the piano previously and are wanting to play again. It is appropriate for adults studying with an independent teacher and/or at the college level when a beginning class would be too elementary.

There are five main sections in the book:

Section 1 *Where Are You?* is intended to be used as an initial evaluation of the student's skills.

Section 2 *Once Over Lightly* is specifically for those students who are not familiar with multi-key experiences, as well as for those who need the review.

Section 3 *Shape Up!* contains exercises and etudes for building and improving technical skills.

Section 4 *Attention Getters* includes pieces from master composers representing the four periods of music literature.

Section 5 *Handy References* presents a "one stop shop" approach to basic music theory, books about music, chronological list of composers and other helpful information.

Clark, Frances

BEGINNING METHOD FOR CHILDREN

FRANCES CLARK LIBRARY FOR PIANO STUDENTS Birch Tree Group Ltd. (1973)

Method
The Music Tree:
   Time to Begin Frances Clark and Louise Goss
   Parts A, B, C Clark and Goss

Supplementary
Playtime A, B, C Clark and Goss
Supplementary Solos edited by Clark and Goss
Other books are available.

Repertoire
Themes from Masterworks, Books 1, 2, 3 (1963) arranged by Jon George and David Kraehenbuehl
Piano Literature, Book 1 (1964)
Piano Literature, Books 2, 3 (1954)
Piano Literature, Books 4A, 4B (1957)
Piano Literature, Books 5A, 5B (1956-57)
Piano Literature, Books 6A, 6B (1956-58)
Contemporary Piano Literature, Books 1, 2, 3, 4, 5, 6 (1955-57)

Survey of Methods for Beginners

The *Frances Clark Library for Piano Students* is a well-written series designed in a logical manner. Emphasis is given to reading up and down from given landmarks. Additional materials include intervals, key signatures, sharps and flats, and technical drills.

Method
Time to Begin, in *The Music Tree* series, develops a feel for the topography of the keyboard and teaches direction (high and low), rhythm, key names, dynamics, intervals through the fifth, and other basics. The book is divided into nine units; each unit has two parts: "Discoveries" (new concepts) and "Using What You Have Learned" (reinforcement material). In addition, some rhythm drills, technical warm-ups, written and creative work are provided at the end of most of the units. Directional reading is introduced within pages 4-27 in pre-staff notation style, almost entirely on the black keys. From page 28 to the end of the book the staff is developed gradually from two lines; reading is limited to white keys only. Bass staff reading is introduced on page 58, stressing the F line (F clef). Treble staff reading is introduced on page 59, stressing the G line (G clef). The grand staff is introduced on page 61, and the reading on pages 61-62 emphasizes the *landmarks* bass clef F, middle C, and treble clef G. Interesting duet accompaniments are provided for many of the pieces. This approach, reading from given landmarks, offers teachers an alternative from either middle C courses or multiple key courses.

Part A consists of ten units organized similarly to *Time to Begin*. Reading is developed from landmarks by intervals up or down. Hand spans are limited to the interval of a fifth. New information includes staccato touch, tied notes, upbeats, rests, sharps and flats, and letters A and B to show the parts of a piece. The music is limited to single-line melodies using quarter, half, and whole notes. Useful technical warm-ups for all units are provided on pages 62-64.

Part B presents eighth notes, major and minor five-finger positions, perfect fifths as accompaniments, note against note reading, new landmarks, and shifting hand positions.

Part C includes key signatures; intervals of sixths, sevenths, and octaves; triplets; $\frac{3}{8}, \frac{6}{8}, \frac{9}{8}, \frac{12}{8}$ meter signatures; crossing fingers over the thumb (scale preparation); and sliding the thumb under.

Supplementary
Playtime, Parts A-C contain supplementary solos, many with optional accompaniment. The original music is by various composers such as Dittenhaver, Kraehenbuehl, and McArtor. Some folk song arrangements are also included.

Supplementary Solos is a sixty-four page collection of previously published materials from Jon George's *Student's Choice*, David Kraehenbuehl's

Jazz and Blues (Books 3 and 4), and five other solos. The pieces are about levels 3 and 4 in difficulty.

Repertoire Books
The **Piano Literature** nine-book series offers an excellent selection of tastefully chosen pieces from the seventeenth, eighteenth, and nineteenth centuries.

Piano Literature, Book 1 consists primarily of folk song arrangements and serves as an introduction to the literature series; it is designed for first and second year students who are not yet ready for the complexities of music by master composers.

Piano Literature, Books 2-6B survey three centuries of keyboard music at successive levels. Representative composers are Couperin, Rameau, J.S. Bach, Handel, Scarlatti, C.P.E. Bach, Haydn, Clementi, Mozart, Beethoven, Schubert, Mendelssohn, Chopin, Schumann, Tchaikovsky, Grieg, and MacDowell. Short biographical sketches are also included.

Contemporary Piano Literature is a six-book series that includes standard composers of children's music such as Bartók, Kabalevsky, Shostakovich, and others. In addition, these books also contain first-rate music by Finney, Kraehenbuehl, Moore, Siegmeister, Tansman, and Tcherepnin. Short biographical sketches are also included.

BEGINNING ADULT METHOD

KEYBOARD MUSICIAN (Clark, Goss, Roger Grove) Birch Tree Group Ltd. (1980)

This is designed to teach the older beginner similar concepts to those in *The Music Tree* series. Included are twenty-two units, each containing five parts: 1. subjects (concepts), 2. repertoire (mostly original or folk song arrangements), 3. rote pieces (slightly more complicated than the student's supposed reading ability), 4. technique-rhythm-improvisation, and 5. sight-reading material. The reading in the beginning uses the landmark system. Many of the beginning pieces have duet accompaniments; some duets are provided later in the book.

Glover, David Carr

BEGINNING METHOD FOR CHILDREN

PIANO LIBRARY Belwin/Columbia Pictures Publications (1967)

Method
The Piano Student, Primer-Level 4 David Carr Glover and Louise Garrow
The Piano Student, Levels 5, 6 (1971) Glover

Theory
Piano Theory, Primer-Level 4 Mary Elizabeth Clark and Glover
Piano Theory, Levels 5, 6 (1971) Clark and Glover
30 Notespelling Lessons, Books 1, 2 (1977) Glover

Technique
Piano Technic, Levels 1-4 Glover and Garrow
Piano Technic, Levels 5, 6 (1971) Glover
Write and Play Major Scales Clark and Glover
Write and Play Minor Scales Clark and Glover
Piano Arpeggios (1970) Glover and Clark

Supplementary
Christmas Music, Primer-Level 3 (1968-75) Glover and Garrow
Chords and Keys, Levels 1, 2 Clark and Glover
Piano Duets, Levels 1, 2 (1970) Glover and Garrow
Piano Duets, Levels 3, 4 (1971) Glover
Piano Repertoire Primer-Level 3 Glover and Garrow
Other books are available.

Repertoire
Piano Repertoire, Level 4 edited by Glover and Garrow
Piano Repertoire, Level 5 (1971) edited by Glover
Piano Repertoire, Level 6 (1971) edited by George Lucktenberg and Glover
Contemporary Piano Repertoire, Levels 5, 6 (1971) edited by Maurice Hinson and Glover

The *Piano Library* course by Glover and Garrow is essentially middle C oriented, but not in the traditional sense. Emphasis on chords (major, minor, augmented, diminished), key signatures, scales, and arpeggios provide adequate material for a basic foundation. The course books plus theory, technique, and repertoire books are well coordinated.

Method
Piano Student, Primer Level is designed for beginners about six to eight years old. Almost all the pieces are in the middle C position. Duet accompaniments are provided for many of the pieces.

Piano Student, Level 1 includes tonic chords having only a root and fifth (rather than the three-note triad), and dominant seventh chords having only a root and seventh. Key selections are limited to C, G, and F, but some other keys are suggested for transposition (D E A B).

Piano Student, Level 2 has full chords (I V_5^6 IV$_4^6$), some one-octave scales (C G F D), $_8^6$ meter, and the use of the damper pedal.

Piano Student, Level 3 includes triads and inversions, relative minor scales, major and minor cadence chords, and key signatures.

Piano Student, Level 4 includes sixteenth notes, trills, augmented and

Pedagogical Considerations

diminished triads, the chromatic scale, syncopation, and major and minor arpeggios.

Piano Student, Levels 5, **6** contain a combination of original compositions by Glover, and a great deal of literature by composers from various periods.

Theory
Piano Theory, Levels 1-4 contain mostly written exercises correlated to the materials in the basic method books. Programmed instruction format is used; answers are given in the back of each book. Materials presented include note and note value recognition, accidentals, music terms, key signatures, transposition, chords, scales, intervals, cadences, and information about form and style. The materials are well-organized and easy to comprehend.

Technique
Piano Technic Books by Glover and Garrow provide additional studies to reinforce concepts learned in the method books. The types of exercises presented in **Levels 1-4** consist of slurred notes for down-up hand motion, legato and staccato five-finger patterns, scale etudes, rhythmic patterns (♩. ♪ ♫), and some arpeggio drills. **Levels 5** and **6** consist mainly of etudes by well-known composers (Czerny, Hanon, Streabbog, etc.) and some original etudes by Glover.

Supplementary
Piano Repertoire, Primer, Levels 1, 2 provide additional supplementary material to accompany the basic method series. These books contain a combination of folk song arrangements and original solos. **Level 3** contains arranged works by master composers such as "Elegie" by Massenet, "Dance Macabre" by Saint-Saëns, etc.

Repertoire
Piano Repertoire, Levels 4, 5, 6 contain standard literature from the Baroque, Classic, and Romantic periods.

Contemporary Piano Repertoire has music by Bartók, Kabalevsky, Rebikov, Gretchaninoff, Prokofiev, Stravinsky, Shostakovich, and Khachaturian ranging in difficulty from about third year through intermediate levels.

BEGINNING METHOD FOR ADULTS

ADULT PIANO STUDENT Books 1, 2, 3 (Glover) Belwin Mills/Columbia (1970)

This basic adult method is designed for an older beginner and provides a logical stepwise progression of materials for easy comprehension and steady progress. Based on five-finger patterns, the books progress through most of the compositions, and incorporate the I IV V^7 chords in various accompanying figures. Ensemble drills, some aspects of theory, scales,

Survey of Methods for Beginners

chords, arpeggios, technique drills, and a combination of original compositions and arrangements of famous melodies are comprised in this series.

Lyke, James and Denise Edwards

BEGINNING METHODS FOR ADULTS

KEYBOARD FUNDAMENTALS Stipes Publishing Company (1986)

This book is designed for non-music majors in a college piano class, as well as for independent teachers to use with beginning adult students. The book is divided into five chapters. *Chapter 1* presents finger numbers, hand position, note values, and reading and improvising on the sets of two and three black keys. Also included is "landmark" reading from bass F, treble C and G. *Chapter 2* includes major pentachords, sharps, flats, naturals, eighth notes, rests, harmonizing with fifths, repertoire, technique, and theory review. *Chapter 3* introduces new pentachords, major triads, major scales, key signatures, new intervals, repertoire, technique, and theory review. *Chapter 4* introduces minor pentachords, major and minor triads, dotted notes, $\frac{6}{8}$ meter, lead sheet harmonization, repertoire, technique, and theory review. *Chapter 5* introduces primary triads, pedaling, syncopation, sixteenth notes, harmonization, repertoire, technique, and theory review.

Noona, Walter and Carol

BEGINNING METHODS FOR CHILDREN

THE YOUNG PIANIST SERIES The Heritage Music Press (1981)

Method
Piano Book, Primer-Level 4

Theory
Theory Pages, Primer-Level 4

Solos
Solo Book, Primer-Level 4

Supplementary
Christmas Carols, Primer-Level 4 (1983)
Hymns, Primer-Level 4 (1985)
Other books are available.

The Young Pianist Series is written in a gradual multi-key approach. The materials are well coordinated between the method books and the other books in the series.

Pedagogical Considerations

Method

Piano Book, Primer Level uses pre-staff notation until page 30; staff notation begins on page 31. Steps, skips, and repeats are clearly explained and used. Basic fundamentals contained include intervals (seconds-fifths), time signatures, phrasing (drop-lift wrist motion), ledger line notes, ties, rests, sharps, flats, and natural signs. Duet accompaniments are provided for many of the pieces.

Piano Book, Level 1 includes first and second endings, upbeat, accidentals, I and V^7 chords, and the five-finger positions of C, G, F.

Piano Book, Level 2 introduces tetrachords, major scale explanation, intervals of the sixth, transposition, pedal, primary chords (I IV V^7), $\frac{6}{8}$ time signature, the order of sharps, and the Group 2 keys (D A E).

Piano Book, Level 3 includes various bass patterns, major scales, ledger lines, triplets, inverted triads, interval of the seventh, explanation of form, harmonic minor scales, the order of flats, and the Group 3 keys (D♭ A♭ E♭).

Piano Book, Level 4 presents the relative minor scales (natural, harmonic, melodic), parallel minor scales, sixteenth notes, interval of the octave, chromatic scale, whole-tone scale, syncopation, augmented and diminished triads, and the Group 4 keys (G♭ B♭ B).

Theory

The **Theory Pages** series is designed to be used in conjunction with the *Piano Book* series. Each level provides a well coordinated sequence of both written and playing drills, improvisation activities, harmonization studies, and melodies to transpose. A final review is included at the end of each book.

Solos

Each **Solo Book** contains original and arranged folk song material to supplement the basic method books. Theory concepts are included at the top of many of the pages in the same sequence as they are used in the *Piano Book* series.

MAINSTREAMS IN MUSIC (Noona) The Heritage Music Press (1973)

Method
The Pianist, Phases 1-4

Theory
Pencil and Paper, Phases 1-4

Technique
Projects, Phases 1-4

Repertoire
The Performer, Phases 1-4

Survey of Methods for Beginners

Supplementary
The Contemporary Performer, Phases 1-4 (1975-76)
The Improviser, A, B, C (1975)
Improviser Projects, A, B, C (1975)
Other books are available.

The *Mainstreams in Music* course is basically multi-key oriented, although Phase 1 begins in the middle C hand position. Additional books in each phase provide materials for reinforcement of concepts in a well-related manner. Because the materials covered in the four "phases" are extensive, this method could be handled better by a slightly older beginner of nine to eleven.

Method
The Pianist, Phase 1 introduces the beginner to basic middle C reading using middle C as the first "guidepost." Explanations of directional reading (step, skip, repeated notes) assist in first reading experiences. The F and G guideposts are added (similar to the Clark "landmark" concept). Hands together playing (note against note) is introduced about halfway through the book. Reading is limited to the five-finger span with occasional hand position shifts. Duet accompaniments and experimental suggestions are provided for many of the pieces.

The Pianist, Phase 2 introduces intervals, I and V^7 chords, multi-key presentation in groups of keys somewhat related to the circle of fifths, eighth notes, parallel major-minor chords, the order of sharps and flats, and pedaling.

The Pianist, Phase 3 includes syncopated rhythm, major scales, one-octave harmonic minor scale, dotted notes, inversions of triads, primary chords (use of the IV chord for the first time), $\frac{6}{8}$ meter, and triplet rhythm.

The Pianist, Phase 4 includes minor scales (three forms), relative minor key signatures, parallel minor scale, primary chords in minor, chromatic scale, whole-tone scale, sixteenth notes, trill, augmented and diminished triads, arpeggios, and seventh chords.

Theory
The **Pencil and Paper** books are designed to be used in conjunction with *The Pianist* books. Answers are given in the back of each theory book.

Pencil and Paper, Phase 1 contains written drills for naming keys on the keyboard, drawing music signs, and naming notes.

Pencil and Paper, Phase 2 contains drills in writing minor scales, major-minor key signatures, cadences, altered intervals, sixteenth-note rhythms, augmented and diminished chords, scale degree names, seventh chords, and arpeggios.

Pedagogical Considerations

Pencil and Paper, Phase 3 contains drills in naming ledger notes, building major scales, inversions of chords, $\frac{6}{8}$ rhythm, primary chords, and triplet rhythm. Some materials from the previous level are reviewed.

Pencil and Paper, Phase 4 contains drills in writing minor scales, major and minor key signatures, cadences, altered intervals, sixteenth note rhythms, augmented and diminished chords, scale degree names, seventh chords, and arpeggios.

Technique
The **Projects** books are an imaginative multi-purpose series containing three sections in each book: Exploring, Creating, and Technical Studies.

Projects, Phase 1 "Exploring" deals with experimentation in rhythms and sampling keys at the keyboard. "Creating" consists of improvising and composing activities at the elementary level. "Technical Studies" contains exercises in dropping and lifting, contrary motion, two-note slurs, and legato and staccato touches.

Projects, Phase 2 "Exploring" provides sight-reading material in all twelve keys with suggestions for tranposition and pattern analysis. The "Creating" section stresses melodic variation, question and answer phrases, and harmonizing and improvising using I and V^7 chords. "Technical Studies" contains five-finger patterns in legato and staccato touches, hand-over-hand arpeggios, phrasing, and interval studies.

Projects, Phase 3 "Exploring" provides sight-reading material with suggestions for transposition and analysis. Included in the "Creating" section are improvising studies with scales and chords, twelve-measure blues, as well as composing a piece in binary and ternary form. "Technical Studies" contains exercises using triplets, thirds and sixths, scales, and inversions of chords.

Projects, Phase 4 "Exploring" contains sight-reading studies using the materials presented in *The Pianist, Phase 4*. In the "Creating" section the student is directed to compose musical answers to question phrases, play cadences, and compose several pieces. The "Technical Studies" consist mainly of major and minor scales and arpeggios.

Repertoire
The **Performer** books consist of supplementary original pieces, folk songs, and some well-known composer pieces to provide additional materials at each phase. **The Contemporary Performer** books are designed to introduce the student to idioms of twentieth-century style such as polyrhythms, clusters, polytonalities, twelve-tone rows, and ostinato patterns. The materials are well-organized and provide an excellent introduction to contemporary sounds.

Survey of Methods for Beginners

THE GIFTED PIANIST (Noona) Roger Dean Publishing Company/Heritage (1986)

Method
Gifted Pianist, Books 1-4

Theory
Scrivia, Books 1-4

Solo
Divertimenti, Books 1-4

Repertoire
Styles, Books 1-4

This method offers the talented student an opportunity to play challenging, sophisticated classical music. One problem the teacher might encounter is how to determine if the beginner is gifted or average before piano lessons commence. However, if the child started piano lessons at a young age (4-6), the teacher would be better able to make an accurate assessment of the youngster's ability to continue lessons in this method. For special students, this piano method could be an excellent choice.

Method
Gifted Pianist, Book 1 provides an excellent description of the history of the piano with sketches of early keyboard instruments. The counting system suggested is ♩ = ta, ♩ = ta-ah, ♩. = ta-ah-ah, o = ta-ah-ah-ah. Some pieces incorporate modal sounds divided between the hands (aeolian, dorian). Landmark reading is presented about midway in the book. Materials used include intervals (seconds-fifths); anacrusis (upbeat); sharp, flat, natural signs; octave sign; legato-staccato touch; and dynamics. Form is well defined for some of the pieces (AB, ABA). Some excellent rhythm drills are given, as well as useful etudes for technical drills. A thorough music glossary and dictionary is included at the end of the book.

Gifted Pianist, Book 2 includes half and whole steps, ledger lines, intervals of sixths and sevenths, pedal, scales in tetrachords, $\frac{6}{8}$ meter, the order of sharps and flats, and the Group 1 and 2 keys. Master composer pieces include those by Kabalevsky, Türk, Haydn, and Shostakovich. Etudes are also included by Gurlitt, Köhler, Czerny, and Hanon.

Gifted Pianist, Book 3 has major and minor scales, inversions of triads, triplets, sixteenth notes, cadence practice, pentatonic scales, and whole-tone scales. Master composers include J.S. Bach, Lully, Beethoven, Burgmüller, Kabalevsky, Haydn, Schumann, and Prokofiev.

Gifted Pianist, Book 4 includes $\frac{3}{8}$ meter, relative minor scales, parallel major and minor scales, ornamentation, chromatic scale, major-minor triads, and arpeggios. Master composers include Scarlatti, J.S. Bach, Kabalevsky, Chopin, Beethoven, and Burgmüller.

Pedagogical Considerations

Theory
The four books of **Scrivia** provide an outstanding presentation of written, playing, improvisation, and ear training activities. These theory books progress rapidly and reach early intermediate level in **Book 3**. These books offer the student complete information about period styles, composers from each period, and an opportunity for analysis of the form used in representative pieces from each period. Modes are clearly explained and used, and students may write their own modal scales. **Book 4** contains useful explanations of each Baroque ornament with appropriate written work to be done by the student. These four books offer the student a thorough presentation of theory from easy to late intermediate.

Solos
The **Divertimenti** books provide students with imaginative original pieces in a variety of styles. Many of the pieces have unusual titles such as "Tiger Cat," "Milanese Bells," "Firewheel," "The Ill-tempered Cuckoo," etc. In addition to original pieces there are many arranged folk songs from different countries.

Repertoire
The **Styles** books provide additional repertoire for study and performance. Beginning with **Book 2** there are pieces by Kabalevsky, Haydn, Mozart, Beethoven, Shostakovich, and others. This series contains useful supplementary pieces in various styles.

Olson, Lynn Freeman, Louise Bianchi, and **Marvin Blickenstaff**

BEGINNING METHOD FOR CHILDREN

MUSIC PATHWAYS Carl Fischer (1974)

Method
Discovery, 1A, 1B, 1C; 2A, 2B

Theory
Activity, 1B, 1C; 2A, 2B
Muscianship, 3A, 3B; 4A, 4B; 5A, 5B

Technique
Technique, 3A, 3B; 4A, 4B; 5A, 5B

Supplementary
Performance, 1C, 2A, 2B
Ensemble, 3, 4, 5 (1975)
Something Light, 3, 4, 5 (1975)

Repertoire
Repertoire, 3A, 3B; 4A, 4B; 5A, 5B

Music Pathways is a well-designed course integrating method, theory, technique, and supplementary books. The materials are well coordinated to give students a thorough background in beginning fundamentals.

Method

The five books of *Discovery* contain a synthesis of learning paths combining the landmark reading approach (five C's) and the multiple key approach. The music is originally composed. The first three books contain a vinyl record of some of the pieces. "Discovery" learning is the featured element in the learning process, and in many instances the student is asked to experiment and discover things independently rather than being given facts for memorization.

Discovery, Book 1A is designed for average-age beginners (7-10) and contains fourteen chapters. The first eight chapters are written in pre-staff notation, the remaining six chapters use staff notation. Directional reading from multiple C's is the main feature of the book. The materials introduced include rhythm (♩ ♩ ♩.), skips and steps, intervals through the sixth, notation (all over the staff, including ledger lines), legato-staccato touches, and music signs and terms. The counting system used is

♩ ♩ ♩

tah tah tah-ah. Mostly single-line melodies are used. A few duet accompaniments are provided.

Discovery, Book 1B has melodies accompanied by fifths, whole and half steps, sharps and flats, eighth notes, five-finger positions in the Group 1 and 2 keys.

Discovery, Book 1C includes five-finger positions in the Group 3 keys, intervals of the seventh, question and answer phrases, dotted quarter rhythm, and pedal.

Discovery, Book 2A includes major key signatures, $\frac{6}{8}$ meter, tonic-dominant relationships, major triads, and triplet rhythm.

Discovery, Book 2B contains sixteenth notes, minor five-finger patterns, I and V^7 chords, some major scale practice, major-minor five-finger patterns.

Theory

Activity books in this series contain materials paralleling those used in the *Discovery* books. The activities are to be written and played.

The **Musicianship** books contain some of the best materials in the *Pathways* program. Discussions of style, rhythm, melody, harmony, form, and expressive elements in each book are related to the repertoire pieces in a meaningful, intelligent, imaginative manner. These books are well-organized, comprehensive, and of considerable merit.

Pedagogical Considerations

Technique
Technique books in the *Pathways* program begin when the student has completed the "method" part of the course. At this point the student is playing repertoire and technique studies, and is beginning a comprehensive theory program. Each book is divided into three sections: "Finger drills" (for finger independence and strength), "technical skills" (to develop scale, chord, arpeggio facility; hand independence; and pedaling), and "etudes" (studies from the repertoire). Each book has only sixteen pages.

Supplementary
Performance books contain supplementary pieces in the first and second levels of the *Pathways* program. Some of the pieces have duet accompaniments. Each book has only sixteen pages.

Ensemble 3, 4, 5 each have standard duet literature from famous and not-so-famous composers.

Something Light 3, 4, 5 each has a potpourri of styles such as blues, boogie, western, rock, and arrangements of familiar tunes and pieces by other composers.

Repertoire
Repertoire books contain useful material from four-period literature by J.S. Bach, Bartók, Beethoven, Kabalevsky, Lynes, Tansman, Telemann, Türk, and other composers. The music is well-graded to allow students sufficient time to progress gradually through this six-book series. An excellent glossary of terms is included in each book.

Pace, Robert

BEGINNING METHOD FOR CHILDREN

MUSIC FOR PIANO Lee Roberts Music Publications, Inc. (1979-85)

Method
Music for Piano, Books 1-4 (1979-84)

Theory
Theory Papers, Books 1-4 (1979-85)

Technique
Finger Builders, Books 1-4 (1979-84)

Supplementary
Creative Music, Books 1-4 (1979-84)

Originally published in 1961, this was a landmark in the field of piano education at that time. The later series is a revised one. Repertoire, technical drills, improvisation, ear training, transposition, and harmonization are interwoven in an intelligent manner. Creative thinking is encouraged on the part of both the student and teacher through numerous improvisational studies. Basic musicianship is the primary concern throughout the entire series.

Method

Music for Piano, Book 1 is a multi-key approach and contains original pieces and folk song arrangements. The first six pages are written in pre-staff fashion. Staff notation is presented next using pieces comprised of steps and skips in different keys. Some two-part music is provided beginning on page 21, and the pieces become quite difficult for a beginner at this stage of learning. Chords are introduced on page 30 with minimal explanation. The student is confronted with $\frac{6}{8}$ meter on page 34; minor chords are introduced on page 40. Although this sequence appears logical, there are a great many facts confronting the beginner at the outset: a variety of keys, the entire staff, notation and rhythm, and all major key signatures. A young beginner (6-7) often finds concepts in rapid sequence (without development) somewhat confusing. However, a beginner of at least age 8 to 11 will be better able to comprehend this *gestalt* multi-concept approach.

Music for Piano, Book 2 presents use of the pedal, modal scales, the subdominant chord, triads of the scale, diminished triads, sixteenth notes, and pieces by Türk, Mozart, and Schumann.

Music for Piano, Book 3 includes augmented triads, twelve-tone music, blues progressions, canon form, and all the modal scales. Also included are original compositions, folk song arrangements, duets, and pieces by master composers.

Music for Piano, Book 4 contains mainly master composer pieces at the intermediate grade level by the following composers: J.S. Bach, Clementi, Dello Joio, Schumann, Persichetti, Telemann, Schubert, Mozart, Frescobaldi, Buxtehude, Chopin, Kabalevsky, Türk, Prokofiev, Haydn, Rameau, Grieg, Beethoven, and Bartók.

Theory

The **Theory Papers** series contains a variety of written drills, keyboard harmony assignments, and creative work.

Theory Papers, Book 1 consists of alphabet letter drills, exercises for steps and skips, treble and bass clef signs, time signatures, all major key signatures, question and answer phrases, all major triads, some minor triads, and a variety of broken chord bass patterns.

Theory Papers, Book 2 includes major and minor key signatures, intervals, diminished triads, triads of the scale, and altered intervals.

Theory Papers, Book 3 includes inversions of triads, augmented triads, twelve-bar blues progressions, and twelve-tone music to be written by the student.

Pedagogical Considerations

Theory Papers, Book 4 has cadence patterns, four-part harmony, first and second inversions, chord structure, and major and minor seventh chords.

Technique
Finger Builders consists of a variety of five-finger patterns, phrase groups (down-up wrist motion), scale and chord studies, some Hanon studies and some double note exercises.

Supplementary
Creative Music contains a variety of playing and written exercises similar to those in *Theory Papers*. For students who like to write their own music, these books have a useful purpose.

Palmer, Willard, Morton Manus, and **Amanda Vick Lethco**

BEGINNING METHOD FOR CHILDREN

ALFRED'S BASIC PIANO LIBRARY Alfred Publishing Company (1981-88)

Method
Lesson Book, Levels 1A-6 (1981-84)

Theory
Theory Book, Levels 1A-6 (1981-85)

Technique
Technic Book, Levels 1A-4 (1984-85)

Repertoire
Recital Book, Levels 1A-6 (1981-85)

Late Beginner
Lesson Book, Level 1 (1983)
Theory Book, Level 1
Technic Book, Level 1
Recital Book, Level 1

Supplementary
Duet Book, Levels 1B, 2, 3 (1986)
Fun Book, Levels 1B, 2, 3 (1985)
Hymn Book, Levels 1B, 2, 3 (1985)
Merry Christmas, Levels 1A, 1B, 2, 3, 4 (1982)
Other books are available.

This attractive series contains a nice variety of materials and clearly explained concepts. The main emphasis in the lower levels is given to interval reading.

Method
Lesson Book, Level 1A contains pre-staff notated pieces to page 26 and

notated pieces on the staff in the remainder of the book. The first pieces begin on the black keys using quarter, half, and whole notes. Two counting systems are suggested: for a quarter note count "1" or "quarter," for a half note count "1 2" or "half note," and for a whole note count "1 2 3 4" or "whole note hold down." Note reading is first initiated by relating notes to the F clef and the G clef in an approach similar to Frances Clark's "landmarks." The C position is used next, followed by the G position. Rests are introduced one at a time beginning on page 41. Near the end of the book the sharp and flat signs and staccato touch are introduced. Duet accompaniments are provided for many of the pieces.

Lesson Book, Level 1B introduces the student to the accent sign, tempo marks, two eighth notes, $\frac{2}{4}$ meter, the damper pedal, octave sign, single eighth note and rest sign, half and whole steps, tetrachords, and the major scales C and G.

Lesson Book, Level 2 includes the dotted quarter note, intervals (sixths, sevenths, octaves), crossing fingers, triads, primary triads, chord progressions, dominant seventh chord, and the D major scale and primary chords.

Lesson Book, Level 3 has extended position, major scales in contrary motion, the chromatic scale, relative minor scales of a and d, primary chords in minor, overlapping pedal, and the $\frac{3}{8}$ and $\frac{6}{8}$ meter signatures.

Lesson Book, Level 4 includes triplets, inversions of triads, major scales in parallel motion, syncopated rhythm, seventh chords, relative minor scales of e and g, the B♭ major scale, sixteenth notes, and the dotted eighth note.

Lesson Book, Level 5 presents ornaments, arpeggios, major scales of A and E♭, and relative minor scales of b and c. Much of the music is by well-known master composers at the intermediate level.

Lesson Book, Level 6 includes diminished and augmented triads, thirty-second notes, dotted sixteenth notes, and arpeggios. Master composers include Kabalevsky, Beethoven, and C.P.E. Bach.

Theory
The **Theory Books** contain materials coordinated to the Lesson Books. Included are written and playing exercises, puzzles, and games.

Theory, Level 1A includes notes to draw, dynamics, keys to name, music signs, slur and tie, melodic and harmonic intervals (second to fifth), and the sharp and flat signs.

Theory, Level 1B begins with a review of materials presented in *Level 1A* and includes these new concepts: eighth note pairs, single eighth note and rest sign, half and whole steps, tetrachords, and the C and G major scales written and played in tetrachords.

Pedagogical Considerations

Theory, Level 2 includes the dotted quarter note, intervals through the octave, triads, chord progressions, and the dominant seventh chord.

Theory, Level 3 contains broken chords, the chromatic scale, major and minor triads, relative minor scales, and primary chords in minor.

Theory, Level 4 includes triplets, triads and inversions, syncopated rhythm, seventh chords, sixteenth notes, dotted eighth note, and major and minor scales.

Theory, Level 5 has scale degree names, trill, ornaments, arpeggios, major and minor scales.

Theory, Level 6 presents perfect and diminished fifths, diminished and augmented triads, double sharp, circle of keys, authentic cadence (major and minor), and plagal cadence (major and minor).

Technique

Technic, Level 1A contains both pre-staff and staff notated finger exercises. The materials are organized into groups in all four *Technic* books. The student can practice one group each week until the book is completed. Exercises include phrasing (down-up wrist motion), legato-staccato touch, slur and tie, and melodic and harmonic intervals.

Technic, Level 1B includes parallel and contrary motion exercises, single and double note studies, and pedal.

Technic, Level 2 has intervals of sixths, sevenths, and octaves; finger crossings; scale practice; triads; and two studies by Hanon.

Technic, Level 3 includes finger extensions, chromatic scale, broken chord bass patterns, minor scales, major-minor triads, and syncopated pedal.

Technic, Level 4 includes triplets, first and second inversion triads, inverted triads, syncopated rhythm, seventh chords, sixteenth notes, $\frac{6}{8}$ meter, and double notes.

Repertoire

The **Recital Books** contain a wide variety of pieces to supplement the *Lesson Books*. The music consists mainly of original works in the lower levels. Some arranged folk songs are included beginning at **Level 2** and some arranged famous themes are included beginning at **Level 3**. These pieces may be used for additional reading practice, and for performance in recitals.

Late Beginner

This series of four books (*Late Beginner* Level 1 of **Lesson, Theory, Technic, Recital**) is designed for a student who starts piano lessons later than most beginners, about age eleven. The materials presented combine the principles introduced in books **1A** and **1B** of the basic library. Most of the music is the same as used in those books; however, staff reading is introduced sooner. These books are a good solution for a later beginner who might be turned off by books written for young children.

BEGINNING METHOD FOR ADULTS

ALFRED'S BASIC ADULT PIANO COURSE (Palmer, Manus, and Lethco) Alfred Publishing Company (1983-85)

Method
Lesson Book, Levels 1, 2 (1983-84)

Theory
Theory Book, Levels 1, 2 (1984-85)

Supplementary
Christmas Book, Levels 1, 2 (1984)
Pop Song Book, Levels 1, 2 (1984-85)
Sacred Book, Level 1 (1985)
Other books are available.

Alfred's Basic Adult Piano Course is a well-written method that teaches reading, intervals, key signatures, and has melody-chord style of writing. It is well-designed for beginning adult students.

Method
The two **Lesson Books**, ninety-six pages each, are written in a melody-chord fashion. A combination of original and familiar music is used. Each method book may be supplemented with companion books.

Lesson Book 1 includes reading in various keys (C G F, a and d minor), intervals, chords (I IV V⁷), sharp and flat signs, scales, major-minor triads, and the pedal.

Lesson Book 2 has extended positions, $\frac{6}{8}$ meter, new keys (e minor, D, B♭, g minor, E♭), chromatic scale, first and second inversion triads, seventh chords and their inversions, sixteenth notes, diminished and augmented triads, and the trill.

Theory
Theory Book, Levels 1, 2 are designed to be used in conjunction with the method books. Materials include clef signs, staff, time signatures, intervals, chords, dynamics, sharps, flats, natural signs, pedal, half and whole steps, scales, primary chords, chromatic scale, triads and inversions, two-part writing, sixteenth notes, and the circle of fifths.

Suzuki, Shinichi

BEGINNING METHOD FOR CHILDREN

SUZUKI PIANO SCHOOL Birch Tree Group Ltd. (1970-78)

Method
Suzuki Piano School, Volumes 1-6

With the exception of **Volume 1**, this series contains classical music by various master composers, and some technique drills. Theory books are not included, so the teacher must select a companion theory book by another author to use with each volume. Additional books may also be needed to teach reading.

The pieces in *Volume 1* begin with sixteenth and eighth notes for "Twinkle, Twinkle, Little Star." Most of the pieces are in two-part style. The Alberti bass is used for some pieces. The level would be about second or third year in another method.

Each piece in the Suzuki books is generally expected to be taught by rote for an extended period of time. A recording of each book is available separately. Students are required to listen to the recordings at home as an aid in learning the repertoire.

For a better understanding of the Suzuki method, the following books are recommended:

An Introduction to the Suzuki Method. Birch Tree Group Ltd., 1984. Paper.

Kataoka, Hanuko. *Thoughts on the Suzuki Piano School*. Birch Tree Group Ltd., 1985. Paper.

Suzuki, Shinichi, translated by Waltrund Suzuki. *Nurtured by Love*, 2nd edition. A Senzay Publications, 1983. Paper.

Thompson, John

BEGINNING METHOD FOR CHILDREN

MODERN PIANO COURSE Willis Music Company (1936-42)

Method
Teaching Little Fingers to Play (1936)
The First Grade Book (1936)
The Second Grade Book (1937)
The Third Grade Book (1938)
The Fourth Grade Book (1938)
The Fifth Grade Book (1942)

From a historical perspective, Thompson's **Modern Piano Course** is an important series, being one of the first middle C piano methods. The materials are well-organized and provide beginning students a useful approach to playing the piano in the middle C position.

Method
Teaching Little Fingers to Play is a middle C course containing introductory rote playing, steps and skips, single line melodies divided

Survey of Methods for Beginners

between the hands for half of the book, some note against note playing in the last half of the book. Finger numbers are used for every note.

The First Grade Book primarily has note against note pieces in five-finger positions. Useful explanations of phrasing, two-note slurred groups, and an actual photo of the down-up wrist motion are included. In addition, scales in tetrachords, explanations of intervals, chords, and inversions are included. Harmonizations are confined essentially to broken chord accompaniments. Tonalities are mainly C, G, F (later also D, A, B♭, E♭, E, A♭).

The Second Grade Book has arrangements of some pieces by master composers, explanations of the pedals, major and minor scales, cadence chords, arpeggios, and numerous technical drills.

The Third Grade Book consists of much more difficult pieces than the previous books—mostly arranged pieces by the following master composers: J.S. Bach, Bizet, Burgmüller, Clementi, Ellmenreich, Grieg, Handel, Liszt, and others.

The Fourth Grade Book and **The Fifth Grade Book** are similar to *The Third Grade Book*, primarily consisting of piano literature.

FOR DISCUSSION & ASSIGNMENT

1. List the goals you consider to be of prime importance in a method series.
2. What basic function should a method serve?
3. Describe the approaches used in the following methods: middle C, landmark, multiple key, and gradual multiple key.
4. A complete program consists of reading, theory, technical studies, and supplementary repertoire. Which of the methods surveyed provides these materials? Are these methods "complete," or should additional supplementary books be used?
5. Would you use one series exclusively, or would you use a variety of books by different authors or composers?
6. Make a detailed survey of a piano method for a class report. Discuss presentations of notation, rhythm, intervals, chords, etc. Discuss the basic concepts presented. Make a critical judgement as to the progression of materials. What will the student have learned upon completion of this method?
7. Using your knowledge gained from examination of beginning methods, write a first lesson presentation as it would appear in a printed course. Design it the way you would like to begin teaching. Demonstrate it for the class.

Pedagogical Considerations

FOR FURTHER READING

American Music Teacher, Suite 2113, 441 Vine Street, Cincinnati, OH 45202-2982.

In order to receive this magazine you must be a member of the Music Teachers National Association. It contains articles, reviews, and information about activities (certification, conventions) related to the organization. The magazine is published six times a year.

Clavier, 200 Northfield Road, Northfield, IL 60093.

This magazine has a useful review section of new publications as well as articles, interviews, an annual listing of summer workshops, question and answer page, and classified ads. It is published ten times a year.

Maxwell Music Evaluation Notebook, 1245 Kalmia Ave., Boulder, CO 80302.

This notebook is published once a year and is probably the most thorough reference source for teachers. The notebook contains excellent evaluations of methods, theory books, technique books, editions, duets, sheet music solos, two-piano music, jazz and popular books, and supplementary books. An index lists all composers in alphabetical order. This is one of the best teacher reference sources available.

The Piano Quarterly, Box 815, Wilmington, VT 05363.

This magazine contains articles, interviews, and reviews of new publications. It is published four times a year.

PART TWO

Pedagogical Techniques

The Advantages of Early Instruction 5

Elementary instruction of all kinds is of inestimable value. Television programs such as "Sesame Street" and various Head Start programs have taught us the advantages of early learning. Introductory structured learning may help the preschool child understand basic concepts and simple reasoning processes. In addition to introducing the youngster to music through piano study, the knowledge learned will transcend purely musical facts and will carry over into other learning experiences. Developmental sensory-motor skills assimilated through piano study will generally aid the child in coordination of his or her small and large muscles.

A really talented child will have a head start and will be playing interesting music by the second or third grade. One of the prime advantages of preschool music instruction is that it will give the youngster a definite interest and activity aside from play and nursery school or kindergarten.

Some teachers are skeptical about preschool instruction: they question if a preschool child has sufficient concentration to accomplish anything constructive at the piano, and if a child of seven or eight would accomplish more faster. Other questions are sure to arise. However, if home conditions are conducive to learning, and if the youngster is ready to begin piano lessons, a great deal will be gained from early instruction.

When Is a Child Ready for Lessons?

Not every preschool child will be ready to begin piano instruction. The maturity level of four- and five-year-olds varies greatly. Girls generally are better coordinated and exhibit better dexterity than boys at an early age. Before rushing headlong into piano lessons, parents should ask themselves a number of questions concerning their child's readiness level:

1. Does the child show an interest in learning to play the piano by trying to pick out melodies on the piano, or by singing, or by just listening to music?
2. Is the attention span long enough to practice ten minutes at a time?
3. Is there fairly good coordination of the small muscles? Can the child handle a pencil fairly well? Parents who have taught their child how

to draw letters, numbers, and how to write his or her name will probably be willing to assist with practicing.

If a significant number of these prerequisites are missing, it is recommended that piano lessons be started later when conditions are more conducive for learning. The readiness age will vary with each individual.

Practice Assistance Required

Parents who are interested in starting a young child in piano instruction often are not aware that the youngster will need supervised practice sessions. If the preschool child cannot read, the directions will have to be read by someone else. Even simple tasks will have to be organized, for this may be the child's first experience in a structured learning situation, and guidance will be needed, especially in the beginning. Efficient practice can be achieved with the following guidelines.

1. The preschool child will need a supervised practice period every day for about ten or fifteen minutes. For a child whose attention span is shorter than average, two brief practice sessions are advised.
2. The person helping should sit near the youngster to assist in reading directions and to point out any mistakes that might occur, as well as to give praise.
3. It is ideal to set aside a specific time each day for practice when there will be no outside interference from family members, television, etc. This will help to establish the *habit* of practicing which is vital to the learning of any skill.
4. It is a good idea to keep a record of the practice time (in a music notebook), and explain that regular practice will help the child become proficient at playing the piano.

Piano lessons can, and definitely should, be an enjoyable experience for a young child. However, parents and teachers should be cautioned to begin formal instruction only when a child is able to absorb instruction and practice on a regular basis. Lessons will be enjoyable *only* with a certain amount of work on the part of both the child and parent(s).

PRIVATE OR GROUP INSTRUCTION?

Instruction on any level may be given individually or in a group, and valid reasons may be made for either case. However, young children function especially well in group activities, and they gain a great deal of satisfaction from friendly competition with their peers. The group provides impetus for numerous musical experiences such as rhythm drills, note flashcard drills, creative work, listening games, and ensemble experience. Any or all of the experiences may be taught privately, but usually they are more effectively presented in a group situation.

Class Size

Group lessons for young children should be limited to about four to six students. In working with smaller groups the teacher will have more flexibility in moving from one concept to another, and each child will have a better opportunity for individual participation and demonstration.

General Activities

Young children will benefit from a combination of singing, playing, and writing activities. Singing games, singing finger numbers, and singing words to pieces will help train the ear and develop a sense of pitch. Playing the piano will be the main focal point of the lessons, but additional activities such as creative work, ensemble playing, and eurhythmics will be beneficial for the preschool child.

EQUIPMENT

Class interest and enthusiasm is heightened by using various teaching aids such as flashcards, keyboards, musical games, and rhythm instruments. In addition, other class aids can be made by a creative teacher.

One of the most valuable reference sources for homemade materials is *The Carabo-Cone Method Series, Book 2* by Madeleine Carabo-Cone (MCA Music/Hal Leonard, 1971). Miss Carabo-Cone lists a quantity of imaginative, original class materials in this excellent book.

In addition to homemade equipment, materials may be purchased from a music store, school supply store, or by direct mail from a catalog such as Music in Motion (109 Spanish Village, Suite 645, Dallas, TX 75248). This catalog contains numerous items that are ideal for use in working with young children.

Homemade Equipment

Letter flashcards (A B C D E F G) and number flashcards (1 2 3 4 5) are useful for playing games teaching recognition. The flashcards can be made out of construction paper with stenciled letters or numbers pasted on as shown in Example 1.

The Advantages of Early Instruction

84

Example 1 Use of flashcards in a group situation.[1]

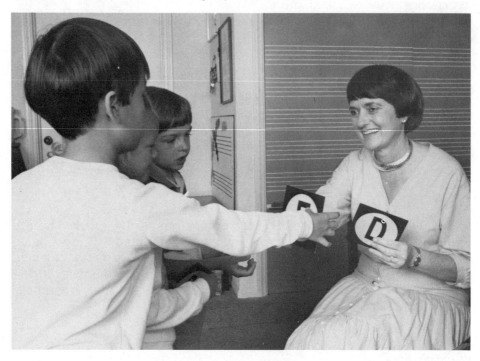

As shown in Example 2, felt-backed cards (letters, numbers, notes, rhythm patterns, etc.) may be made and placed on a large felt board to teach a variety of concepts.

A grand staff may be drawn on cardboard or on the studio floor, and round bean-bags may be made for students to toss or place on the staff and identify as shown in Example 3.

Outside help may have to be enlisted to make a large keyboard for young children to climb around on.

Purchased Equipment

A magnetic board may be purchased at a toy or school supply store. The order of numbers and letters can be reinforced by having the students place them in order on the magnetic board.

A chalkboard of any size, portable or stationary, may be obtained from a toy or school supply store.

A plastic keyboard is extremely useful for demonstration as well as reinforcement.

Crayons, pencils, markers, etc. are necessary for student use in the studio.

[1]Jane Smisor Bastien and some of her students in Mrs. Bastien's home studio.

Pedagogical Techniques

Example 2 Learning rhythm recognition with felt-backed cards.

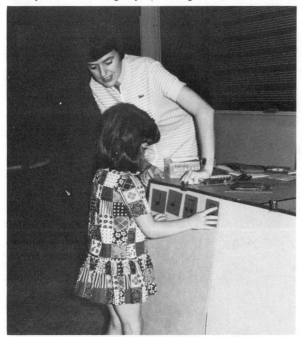

Example 3 Placing a bean-bag to be a specified note.

The Advantages of Early Instruction

Example 4 Learning topography and letters with "feet on" approach.[2]

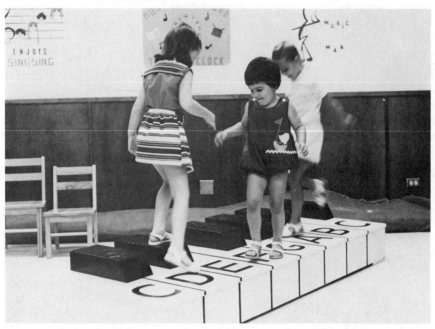

Example 5 Arranging numbers in order.

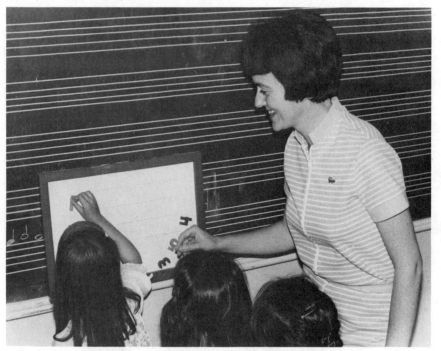

[2]Photo courtesy of the Southern Methodist University Preschool Department.

Pedagogical Techniques

Example 6 Learning note values by writing them.

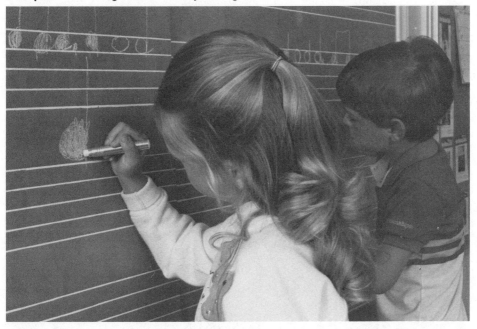

Example 7 Note-finding drill with a plastic keyboard.

The Advantages of Early Instruction

Example 8   Coloring in conjunction with ear training.

MUSIC READINESS PROGRAM

Lessons for young beginners (and average age beginners as well) should be a type of readiness program that will prepare children for the complete staff and its complexities.

Numerous parallels may be drawn between the teaching of word reading and music reading. An infant learns words by imitating parents or older brothers and sisters. The vocabulary expands as the child matures. Usually, a child is quite conversant before beginning to read. Kindergarten prepares children for reading by teaching the alphabet, phonetic sounds, etc. Thus, language is used before actually reading the printed page. Similarly, children should be taught to play and make music before actually being confronted with the complexities of the printed page.

A number of exploratory conceptual experiences should be initiated in preschool music classes. The following list represents specific items providing a beneficial background towards the music reading goal.

Pedagogical Techniques

Awareness of hands (right and left) and coordination between the two. When first beginning to teach children right and left hands, do not face them. Turn your back to them and show them what you want them to do, such as "Right hand up, right hand down; left hand up, left hand down."

Demonstrate high and low sounds on the piano. Then have the children go to the piano and play the following: a high key, low key, key in the middle of the piano, three high keys which go up, etc.

Have children trace their hands and then number the fingers traced. Utilize different colors for perception growth—i.e., color the third finger blue, the second finger red, etc.

Finger-number games may be played with the teacher holding up specific fingers and the children imitating. Also, a cut-out paper hand, or a stuffed glove, is useful for demonstration.

The music alphabet, both forward and backward. Tell the children that the music alphabet names the white keys. At first let them trace the alphabet from examples given to them. Most youngsters have a good working knowledge of the alphabet, but often are slow at drawing it. The teacher will need to move from student to student to give assistance.

Example 9   Teaching right/left hand requires the teacher to turn so each hand can be seen correctly by the students.

The Advantages of Early Instruction

Example 10 Learning finger numbers.

Rhythmic concepts. Rhythmic perception can be developed by clapping and counting, and by "stepping" and counting note values using the following terminology:

    Whole note (looks like a football) count: "hold that whole note"

    Half note (with a "clean face") count: "half note"

    Quarter note (with a "dirty face") count: "quar-ter"

    Eighth notes ("two quarters holding hands") count: "two eighths"

The children's concept of long and short pulses will also be heightened by having them chant and step the rhythms as in Example 13.

Example 11 Practicing the alphabet in class.

Example 12 Chanting and clapping note values.

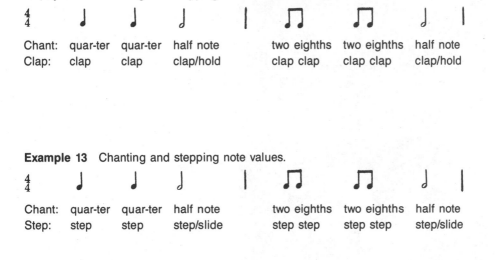

Chant:	quar-ter	quar-ter	half note		two eighths	two eighths	half note
Clap:	clap	clap	clap/hold		clap clap	clap clap	clap/hold

Example 13 Chanting and stepping note values.

Chant:	quar-ter	quar-ter	half note		two eighths	two eighths	half note
Step:	step	step	step/slide		step step	step step	step/slide

The Advantages of Early Instruction

While one student plays a certain rhythm on one note, assist the others in chanting and clapping the counts. If there is more than one piano in the room, allow one child to "present" a rhythm and ask the other students to imitate it on their piano.

Antiphonal response also is effective for teaching rhythm skills. Allow each child to be the leader. The leader "discovers" a rhythm, and the class responds as an echo:

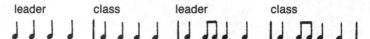

Clapping and responding in rhythm can help teach the concept of continuity. Also, because the group activity is enjoyable, it can help lengthen attention spans.

Pre-staff notation. After the children know their finger numbers, a few rhythms, and have been shown the groups of two and three black keys, they may play simple melodies in pre-staff notation as in Example 15.

From the beginning it is essential to develop an "eyes on the page" approach to reading. This will help to establish the correct habit of not looking down at the hands while playing.

Example 14 Playing and chanting rhythms.

Example 15 Pre-staff melody on the black keys.

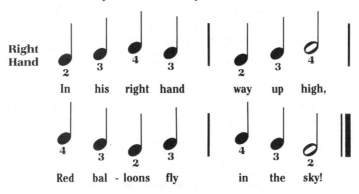

From *Piano for the Young Beginner, Primer A* by James Bastien (Neil A. Kjos Music Company, 1987).

Example 16 Playing while keeping the eyes focused on the book.

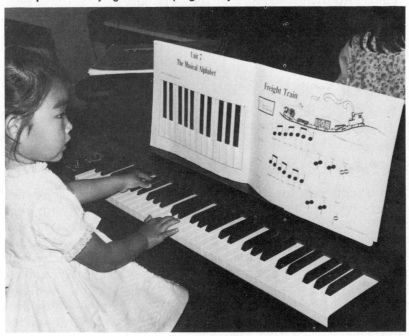

The Advantages of Early Instruction

Creating simple melodies and rhythmic patterns. Most children are imaginative and inventive; generally, they gain a great deal of satisfaction from experimentation. Learning by doing, or "discovery learning," is an excellent methodology for beginning instruction. Children can experiment with five-finger positions, simple familiar melodies, and making up their own melodies.

In the beginning the child may create a melody for a nursery rhyme as shown in Example 17. Improvisation such as this benefits the child both in the development of finger coordination and aural perception.

Example 17 A student-composed melody for a nursery rhyme.

Listening to music and discovering the difference between fast and slow, or loud and soft. Constructive listening is essential in promoting aural perception. The teacher should improvise a variety of pieces in various moods and tempos, and have children describe sounds such as thunder, raindrops, etc. In addition, have children play their own heavy and light sounds and then discuss what they played.

BASIC TECHNIQUE FOR THE PRESCHOOL CHILD

Sitting At the Piano

One of the first concerns for the preschool child is how to acquire the proper alignment with the keys, so that the hands and forearms are in a straight line with the keys. An adjustable piano chair, cushions, or even several telephone books can raise the child to the correct level. If an adjustable piano chair or bench cannot be found in a local store, either may be ordered from Hui's Imports (9608 Tallahassee Lane, Knoxville, TN 37923). Once the child is raised to the correct height, a new problem arises: the child's feet are now swinging freely back and forth in the air, unsupported! To balance the child, use a footstool as shown in Example 18.

Example 18 An adjustable chair and feet support for a young student.

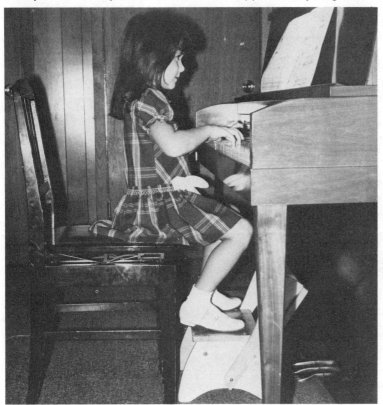

Posture & Hand Position

Posture and hand position are prime concerns for students of all ages. The preschool child must be shown how far to sit from the piano, to sit up "straight like a tree," and to hold the forearms in a straight line with the keys. Once these basics have been acquired, the next consideration is hand position and finger placement. The hands, wrists, and forearms should be held in a straight line, and the fingers should be curved as shown in Example 19. Tell the child to imagine holding a ball. This will give the image of curved fingers. Flat fingers, wrists hanging below the keys, and other unsatisfactory approaches should be discouraged from the beginning.

INCENTIVES & REWARDS

Rewards for work well done will produce a positive response from children (and all other ages). Praise is a necessary ingredient in the entire motivation factor. Young children respond to stickers, candy, bubble gum, and other prizes.

The Advantages of Early Instruction

Example 19 Preschool child with the correct hand position.

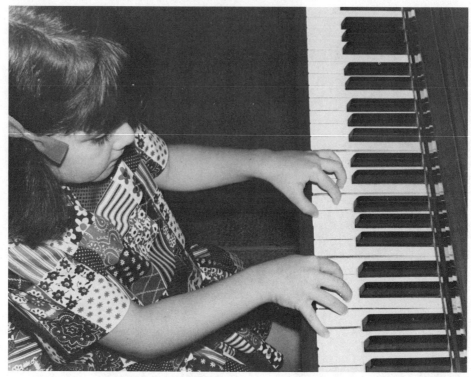

Many of the class activities can be conducted as games. Recognition and rewards for the winners will aid in promoting group spirit and enthusiasm. However, the teacher should be careful to measure the child on individual merits. If a sticker is given for work well done, the award should be made on the basis of progress, not because the playing was better than another student.

A music notebook is a valuable record of the child's progress. Achievement can be recorded in different colored markers for memorized pieces, recital participation, performances at the child's school, etc.

The preschool program should be geared to reasonable goals. Class activities should be organized so that achievement of even the simplest tasks is possible. Incentives, rewards, praise, and encouragement will constitute a happy beginning.

SUMMARY

According to Jean Piaget, the noted Swiss psychologist, a child's early years are the optimum period of intellectual growth. He ascertained that children progress through specific learning stages in an ordered sequence.

He labeled the "sensory-motor" period from birth to about two years, and the "pre-operational" period from two to seven years. During the "pre-operational" period, the child begins to think and respond through symbols such as language, drawings, dramatic play, and dreams. It is during this period that music instruction may be meaningful to the child who is ready for lessons. With proper assistance at home, the preschool child can learn a number of important facts and basic skills that will form a foundation for further study.

PRESCHOOL METHOD BOOKS

Bastien, James Piano for the Young Beginner, Primers A, B. 48 pp. each. **Theory & Technic for the Young Beginner, Primers A, B.** 40 pp. each. Neil A. Kjos Music Company (1987).

Piano for the Young Beginner, Primer A is designed especially for the five- or six-year-old student. Pre-staff notation is used until page 28, when the grand staff is introduced. The counting systems suggested include both note name (say "quarter" for each quarter note, "half note" for each half note, etc.), and number counting beginning on page 22. The music is a combination of original pieces, selected folk songs and seasonal pieces. Duet accompaniments are included for many of the pieces.

Piano for the Young Beginner, Primer B introduces eighth note pairs, dynamic signs, intervals through the fifth, rests, sharp and flat signs, slurs and ties, and staccato touch. Duet accompaniments are provided for many of the pieces. After completing this primer along with the corresponding theory book, the young student is to continue with Level 1 of *Bastien Piano Basics*.

Theory & Technic for the Young Beginner, Primers A and B contain a combination of written work, technique studies, and short pieces to reinforce concepts presented in the *Piano* books.

Bastien, Jane Smisor, Lisa, Lori Bastiens' Invitation to Music: Books A, B, C, D for Piano Party, Theory & Ear Training Party, Performance Party. Neil A. Kjos Music Company (1993-94), 48-24 pp. each.

For children age four and up. *Book A* introduces A-G, finger numbers, counting, and high and low. Black key clusters establish good hand position. All the pieces are in pre-staff notation. *Theory and Ear Training Party* reinforces concepts and *Performance Party* provides more reading and playing experiences. *Book B* introduces more rhythms, the staff (by use of steps and skips), I and two-note V7 chords in C, G, and F. *Book C* includes reading the grand staff by steps and skips then fourths and fifths. Slurs, ties, and $\frac{2}{4}$, $\frac{3}{4}$, $\frac{4}{4}$ concepts are mastered. *Book D* expands to D, A, E, D♭, A♭, E♭, G♭, B, B♭, and includes flats, sharps and key signatures. The Teacher's Notes at the back of all but *Performance Party* offer helpful suggestions for working with this age.

The Advantages of Early Instruction

Collins, Ann, and **Linda Clary** **Sing and Play, Books 1, 2, 3.** Stipes Publishing Co. (1981), Book 1, 40 pp; Book 2, 56 pp; Book 3, 64 pp.

These preschool piano books are designed for children ages three to five. Materials are organized into concept blocks with notes to teachers and parents on practice procedures. The concepts presented include directional reading, notes, landmark reading, steps and skips, and dynamics. The counting system suggested is to count 1 for all quarter notes, 1 2 for all half notes, 1 2 3 for all dotted half notes, and 1 2 3 4 for all whole notes. Book 1 has alphabet letter cards and note cards which may be cut out for home and studio drill. Books 2 and 3 have note cards and note pattern cards which may be cut out for extra drill. A separate teacher manual is provided, containing many helpful suggestions on how to organize reading, ear training, rhythm, technique, and improvisation. Additional supplementary books are available.

Cory, Cappy Kennedy **The Primer Pianist, Books A, B.** The Heritage Music Press (1977), 64 pp. each.

These two books are written specifically for beginners ages four to six. The concepts presented include black key groups, low and high sounds, finger numbers, alphabet letters, notes and rests, dynamics, rhythm patterns for clapping, steps and skips, and easy pieces. A checklist is provided at the end of each unit to review the materials presented in that unit. Additional supplementary books are available.

FOR DISCUSSION & ASSIGNMENT

1. Observe a preschool class taught by someone in your area. Report on the following items: the type of instruction offered (readiness program or piano lessons); the size of the class; the equipment used; the type of class activities presented; the effectiveness of the program.
2. What advantages do preschool beginners have over those who begin lessons later? Are there any disadvantages?
3. Should all preschool children be exposed to music instruction?
4. Do you think you would like working with preschool children? Give reasons, pro and con.

FOR FURTHER READING

Andress, Barbara. *Experiencing Music in Early Childhood.* New York: Holt, Rinehart, and Winston, Inc., 1980. Numerous helpful suggestions are offered to aid the teacher in working with young children in this informative book.

Arnoff, Frances Webber. *Music and Young Children.* New York: Holt, Rinehart, and Winston, Inc., 1969. Although directed to classroom teachers, there is an abundance of general information that would be helpful for piano teachers interested in this age group. Contains a useful bibliography.

Carabo-Cone, Madeleine. *A Sensory-Motor Approach to Music Learning, Book 1—Primary Concepts*. New York: MCA Music/Hal Leonard, 1969. PB. Numerous helpful suggestions are offered in this book to assist the teacher interested in learning new preschool class activities.

_____. *A Sensory-Motor Approach to Music Learning, Book 2—Materials*. New York: MCA Music/Hal Leonard, 1971. PB. Various class materials are discussed and specific directions for their use are given in this valuable book on preschool music activities.

_____. *A Sensory-Motor Approach to Music Learning, Book 3—Identification Activities*. New York: MCA Music/Hal Leonard, 1973. PB. Specific class activities are described for identifying such music fundamentals as landmarks (primarily F-line bass clef, middle C, and G line treble clef; staff; and time values). Photos of class activities and equipment enhance this useful book on preschool activities.

Dodson, Dr. Fitzhugh. *How to Parent*. New York: Signet/The New American Library, Inc., 1970. PB. Although this book is directed to parents, it has direct application for teachers interested in preschool children. The book deals only with children from infancy through preschool age. Of special interest to the teacher are the extensive appendices dealing with selecting good books, educational toys, play equipment, and records for children. The book is direct and well-written and is a valuable general reference.

Hefferman, Charles. *Teaching Children to Read Music*. New York: Appleton-Century-Crofts, 1968. PB. Teachers will find much useful information contained in this brief volume. For one interested in preschool activities, Chapter 2 "The Readiness Program" is of special interest.

Ibuka, Masura. *Kindergarten Is Too Late!* New York: Simon and Schuster, Inc., 1977. The advantages of early learning are clearly presented in this useful book on education for young children.

Melton, David. *How to Help Your Preschooler Learn More, Faster, and Better*. New York: McKay Co., Inc., 1976. Teachers and parents will gain many insights on how to help youngsters learn more, faster, and better in this informative book.

Average Age Beginners 6

The beginning piano student generally is between seven to ten years old. Teachers have diverse opinions regarding an optimum beginning age. Some children may be ready to begin lessons as early as five, while others would do better to wait until they are seven or eight. Gifted children especially benefit from starting lessons early. Teachers and parents will have to make the decision when it is best to begin lessons.

PARENTAL SUPERVISION

If the student is not capable of reading the instructions in the books being used, regular parental help will be needed for scheduling practice periods, checking on work in progress, creating an enthusiastic atmosphere for practice, and assisting when problems arise.

Parental cooperation and periodic supervision is extremely important in maintaining a healthy rapport between all parties concerned—the student, parents, and teacher. For an insight into specific solutions to many problems that often arise, parents will profit by reading *A Parent's Guide to Piano Lessons* by James Bastien, published by Neil A. Kjos Music Company, 1976.

PRIVATE OR GROUP INSTRUCTION?

Traditionally, average age beginners have been taught on a one-to-one basis. Students taught in this fashion, without any class participation, often lose interest after a year or two mainly because there is no external motivating force other than the teacher. True, the annual recital, plus auditions and competitions do offer some goals throughout the year, but these sparsely spaced activities cannot take the place of weekly exposure to group participation.

Group lessons can be an effective means of generating enthusiasm for piano study. Students so motivated continue to take lessons, enjoy studying, and are willing to play for others. Even infrequent get-togethers once a month, bi-monthly, etc. will provide incentives for students. Whatever the combination of private and group lessons the teacher offers, overall student achievement will be upgraded.

A SAMPLE FIRST LESSON

It is impossible to prepare an exact blueprint to fit the needs of each student for the all-important first lesson. However, some general guidelines may be considered.

First, a congenial rapport should be established between the teacher and student. Begin by putting the child at ease by maintaining a pleasant disposition. Don't forget to smile! After the preliminaries, present the beginner with an assignment book and the piano book (or books) to be used.

Concepts to be stressed in the first lesson include:

1. hand position and posture at the piano
2. right hand, left hand, and how the fingers are numbered
3. direction on the keyboard: up is to the right; down is to the left
4. the pattern of keys on the keyboard (black keys in groups of two's and three's)

Also, explain that the fingernails must be kept short for playing the piano! (Some teachers keep a fingernail clipper by the piano.)

Each lesson, even the first, should contain a balanced program of varied activities. The student should be exposed to four basic categories: repertoire, theory, technique, and supplementary books.

The repertoire in the beginning will probably be in the form of pre-staff pieces such as shown in Example 1. Pre-staff notated melodies allow the student to play and make music without the hindrance of learning staff notation simultaneously with other new concepts.

Example 1 Pre-staff notation of melody.

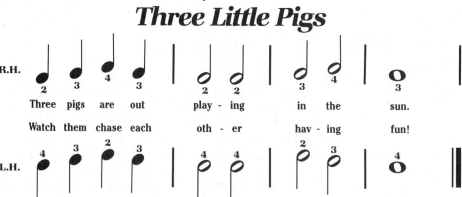

From *Piano, Primer Level* by James Bastien (Neil A. Kjos Music Company, 1985).

Pedagogical Techniques

Teach the beginner the correct reading procedure of keeping the eyes on the music, not looking up and down between hands and the book. The following steps will help a child learn a piece well:

1. understand and clap the rhythm before beginning to play
2. "play" the song in the air (or on a closed keyboard cover) singing the finger numbers aloud while moving the fingers
3. find the position for both hands before beginning to play
4. keep the eyes on the book
5. play straight through singing the finger numbers or words while playing

Theory, for the first lesson, may be no more than learning note values and discovering that some notes are short and some are long.

Technique work similar to that shown in the example should be given to help develop finger coordination. Most of the newer piano methods provide companion technique books for extra practice.

Example 2 Technique suitable for the first lesson.

Teeter-Totter Fun!

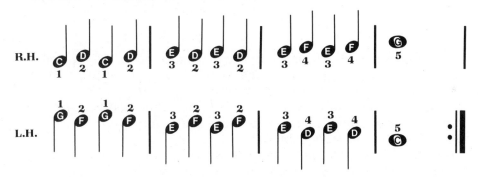

From *Technic, Primer Level* by James Bastien (Neil A. Kjos Music Company, 1986).

The materials presented at the first lesson probably will be based on whatever method series is being used. Since the concepts will be new to the student, make sure the beginner understands each item presented. Be specific. Write down the assignment in a music notebook. Tell the student what will be expected regarding practice time—about thirty minutes a day is sufficient in the beginning. Most importantly, describe *how* to practice.

Be pleasant and encouraging. The beginner who senses that this is going to be great fun will be eager to return. The student, above all, needs reassurance that the teacher believes that he or she will succeed. While this piano playing "game" requires serious application and responsibility, it can also be creative and pleasant.

Average Age Beginners

FIRST YEAR MUSIC PROGRAM

The beginning piano student is faced with learning numerous concepts during the first year of lessons! Fundamentals of reading, rhythm, technique, and theory must be assimilated. Comprehension of these new skills will depend largely on an intelligent presentation that encourages the student to think and reason. Good habits from the beginning will form a solid foundation on which to build.

Pre-staff Reading

The student who has been exposed to a period of pre-staff reading, as discussed previously in the first lesson, will be more likely to comprehend the complexities of the staff when it is presented. The student will have already played and read by direction and will have established an "eyes on the page" approach to reading. Most of the "newer" method books begin in this fashion. Some books require a pre-reading period as short as a week or two, others require up to two months or more. Whatever the duration, the time spent in the beginning to establish finger coordination and a feeling for the topography of the keyboard is well worth the effort.

Reading by Direction

Reading by shapes and contours is important for beginners. Spatial relationships such as *up*, *down*, or *same* are difficult for a young student to perceive on the staff. The student must judge how far the fingers should move on the keyboard to match what is seen on the book. This process must become automatic, and the student should develop a quick reflex response to the printed symbol.

There are three basic movements possible on the staff: *step*, *skip*, or *repeat*. When beginning to teach direction on the staff, it is advisable to start with just seconds (steps), thirds (skips), and repeated notes.

Example 3   The "direction" of step, skip, repeat.

Reading by Intervals

It is essential for the beginner to recognize intervals in the first year. This information is clearly explained and thoroughly used in most of the newer piano methods. Generally, the first book in a series contains intervals through the fifth; other intervals are introduced later in succeeding levels. The student should be able to name intervals either up or down.

Example 4 Intervals through the fifth.

Individual Note Recognition

Fluency with note names requires patience and perseverance on the teacher's part. A great deal of drill must be done in the first year of lessons on learning the notes thoroughly. Review in the second (and sometimes the third) year is often necessary.

In interviewing transfer students it is often discovered that they do not know the names of the notes in one or both clefs, ledger line and space notes, or the correct octave in which notes should be played!

There are several aids to learning note names:

1. use flashcards
2. sing note names
3. write note names
4. number the lines and spaces

1. Note flashcards may be made by the teacher or pupil, or they may be purchased from a music store. Examples of flashcards that may be purchased are *Music Flashcards* by Jane Smisor Bastien (Neil A. Kjos Music Company), *Flash Cards* Levels 1A, 1B, 2, and 3 (Alfred Music Company), and *Note Flashcards* from Music in Motion (109 Spanish Village, Suite 645, Dallas, TX 75428). *Bea's Keys* can also be used for drills on naming notes. The teacher can have students place each note card on a corresponding key on the piano for correct identification. These cards have to be ordered from Bea N. Carney, 1522 Driftwood Drive, Dallas, TX 75224.

Each student should have a set of note flashcards for home drill. The cards should be sorted out according to the sequence presented in the student's method book. When working at home, the student should name the note on the card and play it in the correct location on the keyboard. It is of little value to name the notes correctly, and be unable to play them in the correct octave on the piano.

Time students with a stopwatch to see how quickly notes on the staff can be named. Later in the first year, a beginner should be able to name all the notes on the staff, from bottom line bass staff to top line treble staff in one minute.

A few minutes of each lesson should be devoted to flashcard drill. For group lessons a game can be made using the cards. Have the students form

Average Age Beginners

two lines (Example 5): each line, or team, may be given a name such as the Cubs and Jets. Each team competes to get the correct answer first. Each student keeps the correctly identified card until all the cards have been used. The group with the most cards wins the game. Games such as this are stimulating and motivating. Other musical elements may be presented similarly such as intervals, key signatures, chords, etc.

Example 5   Group flashcard drill.

2. Singing or saying note names will aid the beginner in establishing good reading habits. While playing, the student should sing each note aloud while thinking about which direction the next note moves.

Methods written before the middle part of this century have a finger number over each note. Most students using these methods read the numbers and do not learn note names. Fortunately, newer methods use finger numbers sparingly, and it is easier to teach note names in this manner.

When both hands play at the same time, the student can sing the notes of first one hand, then the other. The teacher should persist in having the student name the notes aloud until note reading is secure.

Pedagogical Techniques

3. Writing note names as shown in Example 6 will help give a thorough comprehension of the staff. Any written work reinforces keyboard activity. Most methods have companion theory books containing note drills. In addition, the teacher might assign a note spelling book for extra work on individual note recognition.

Directions: Write the names of the notes, then play them on the piano.

Example 6   Writing note names.

4. Numbering the lines and spaces aids in creating a mental image of the staff.

Example 7   Identifying lines and spaces.

The invention of the staff is ascribed to Guido of Arezzo (c. 1000), who used the human hand as an aid in identifying line and space notes. The five fingers correspond to the five lines; the spaces in between each finger correspond to the four spaces.

Hold up your hand and tell your students that the staff is related to the hand. Pointing to corresponding fingers, ask "What note is on the first line, treble clef? What note is on the fifth line bass clef? What note is in the first space treble clef?" This physical representation of the staff makes a lasting impression on students, and it helps them remember pitch locations easily.

Beginning Technique

Technique is defined by the *Merriam-Webster Dictionary* as "the method or the details of procedure essential to expertness of execution in any art." For the young pianist this would mean the ability to play with clarity, evenness, and balance of tone.

The teacher should strive to establish the correct fundamentals from the beginning. It is important to present a technique program that will become a solid foundation.

Technique is just one component in the music program. Each item presented in this chapter can be incorporated into lessons to assist the

Average Age Beginners

Example 8a Incorrect finger position.

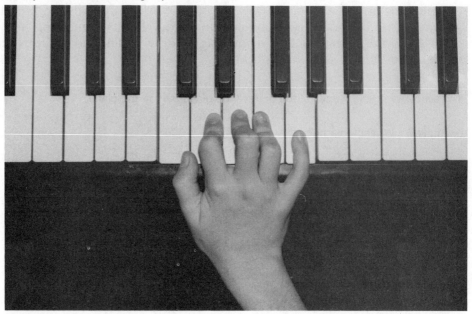

Example 8b Correct finger position.

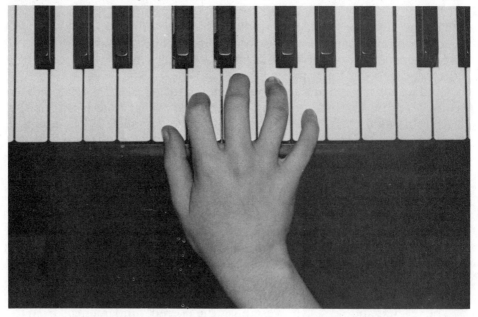

Pedagogical Techniques

beginner in establishing a secure approach to basic skills needed to play the piano correctly.

Although many books on technique have been written, most deal only with advanced levels. Terms like arm weight, forearm rotation, relaxation, etc., apply to students of all levels, but the beginner is confronted with more basic matters. Beginning technique should be pared down to simple concepts that relate to control and coordination at the keyboard. The terminology used should be easily understood by young students.

Within the first year of lessons the beginner must learn many concepts such as legato and staccato, phrasing, and basic finger coordination. Although teachers may disagree on the order in which technical items should be given, most agree that the following items are essential concepts for first-year students.

1. posture and hand position
2. arm drops, large muscle motions
3. legato touch
4. staccato touch
5. balance of melody and accompaniment
6. down-up wrist motion for phrasing
7. legato thirds

Posture and Hand Position

Matters of posture, hand position, height, distance from the keyboard, etc., were discussed in the previous chapter and the suggestions there apply as well to average age beginners.

When the correct sitting level is attained, instruct the student to lean slightly forward toward the keys. The hands, wrists, and forearms should be held in a straight line, and the fingers should be curved.

Example 9   Correct hand position for playing triads.

110

Example 10a Supported finger raised *over* the key.

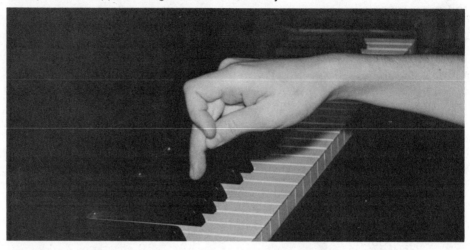

Example 10b Supported finger *on* the key.

Some young children have weak fingers, and the tendency to cave in at the first joint on the second, third, fourth, and fifth fingers.

It is beneficial for the beginner to play triads to help develop well-curved fingers as shown in Example 9.

Over a period of time, posture, hand position, curved fingers, etc., can be emphasized and repeatedly corrected by the teacher until they become natural to the student. The most important aspect of beginning lessons is to form *correct* habits.

Arm Drops

Some teachers like to have the student use the large muscles first, then concentrate on the smaller motions used in coordinating finger action. Arm drops may be taught in the beginning when key names are being learned. Have the student support the third finger with the thumb, raise the forearm in the air over a particular key, and drop the finger onto the key with arm weight. This gives the student the correct concept for holding the fingers in a curved position.

Legato Touch

The execution of the legato principle requires the student to play a key, hold it, and release it when the next key is played. This concept comes easily to some students and is difficult for others. The process requires intricate finger coordination that may take some time to develop. However, it is vitally important for the beginner to understand this process and be able to do it easily.

Legato may be explained to children by describing it in the following manner: when walking, one foot goes down while the other foot goes up. This is analogous to "walking on the keys"—one key is played and held until the next key is played.

Two common errors in first attempts at legato playing are blurring the tones by not releasing the first key after the second key has been depressed, or by bouncing the hand and arm up and down producing uneven, disconnected tones.

Studies for legato touch may be begun with just two notes (see Example 11) by simply alternating fingers: 1 2 1 2 1; 2 3 2 3 2, etc., in either hand.

Example 11 Beginning studies for legato touch.

Next, play five-finger positions up and down the keyboard on the white keys in a slow tempo as shown in Example 12.

Staccato Touch

For children, the technical means for producing staccato will be slightly different than for older students. Each finger should stay near the key and push up, rather than dropping from high and rebounding. The best way to teach staccato is by demonstration.

Average Age Beginners

Example 12 Legato five-finger positions on white keys.

Example 13 Beginning studies for staccato touch.

Once the idea of staccato has been established, simple studies can be devised for staccato practice. Example 13 presents a few ideas.

Balance of Melody and Accompaniment

A well-trained student is easily recognized by the ability to play with sufficient control to balance voices. Voicing, or balancing tones, at this level simply means playing one hand louder than the other. Demonstrate this so the student can *hear* the difference between the hands.

Example 14 Study for balance of melody and accompaniment.

Keep Your Balance!

From *Technic, Level 1* by James Bastien (Neil A. Kjos Music Company, 1986).

Down-up Wrist Motion for Phrasing

Phrasing on the piano is dependent on the correct motions of the hand, wrist, and arm. The mechanics of producing slurred groups can be taught to first year students when they have sufficient control to produce the proper motions, generally by the end of the first semester of lessons.

Demonstrate the motions used in playing a two-note slur to the student. Show what it looks like to drop on the key with a slightly lower wrist motion and release the key with a higher wrist motion (Example 15). Several terms may be used to describe this process: down-up, drop-release, or drop-roll (rolling in toward the piano and lifting at the same time). Arrows written in the score help depict the down-up motion.

Example 15a   Low wrist position.

Example 15b   High wrist position.

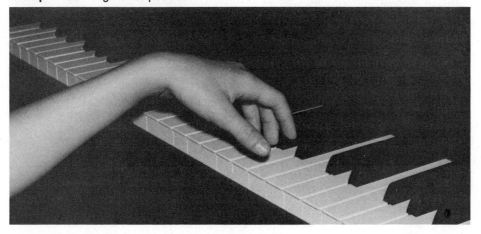

Example 15c   Arrows indicate wrist motion.

Average Age Beginners

The lifting of the wrist is the same at the end of a two-note slur or any phrase. When a longer phrase mark is used, relate the group of notes under the phrase sign to a vocal line—a breath would be taken after the last note of the phrase. At the piano the hand lifts, the legato line is broken, and the "breath" is accomplished.

Numerous exercises for slurring, as those suggested in Example 16, can be devised by the teacher. The first note of the slur should be slightly louder, and the last note should be slightly softer. Have the student "float" off the last note of a slurred group. Teach the student to make a break in the sound from the end of the slur to the beginning of the next slur.

Example 16 Beginning slur exercises.

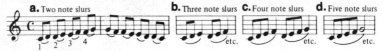

Many first year pieces have staccato and legato touches. For thorough comprehension, direct the student to *say aloud* the hand motions used in the composition. Say "up" for staccato, "down" for long notes or phrases, and "off" for phrase endings (Example 17). Verbalizing music symbols and transferring them into hand motions is the most effective means of getting the student to interpret the signs on the printed page. This technique is so important that it should be continued until the student automatically plays what is seen on the score.

Example 17 Verbalizing hand motions.

Legato Thirds

Although first year students will not need a great deal of drill on legato thirds, a few passages will be found in some of the music studied. The teacher should try to devise legato third exercises prior to use in first year pieces.

When practicing legato thirds, the student should play the first third clearly, with the other fingers raised as pictured in Example 19. If the other fingers are not raised sufficiently, they might accidentally play. It is important to release the first keys as soon as the next keys are played so there will not be a blur in the legato line.

Example 18   Beginning legato third exercises.

Example 19a   Hand position for legato thirds, first third.

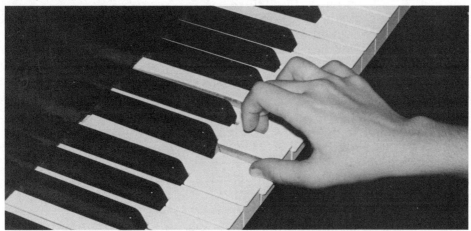

Example 19b   Hand position for legato thirds, second third.

Average Age Beginners

Beginning Theory

Theory should be presented as a combination of both playing and written work during the first year of lessons. This functional approach will lay the foundation for more complicated elements yet to come. Students will have the ability to understand and analyze the music studied, which will aid in the general learning process. If the student can analyze the music in terms of tonality, intervals, and chords, a comprehensive view of the music will have been acquired. It is for this goal that teachers should strive!

To make sure a student understands melodic and harmonic progressions in the score, the teacher must teach theory from the beginning as an integral part of the music program.

It is possible to integrate theory into a weekly thirty-minute private lesson. However, it might be easier and more thorough to cover the material in a theory lesson or class. A theory class can be scheduled each week (or month) in addition to the private lesson.

Suggested concepts to cover in a first year theory program include:

1. major five-finger positions
2. intervals using scale tones
3. sharp, flat, and natural signs (accidentals)
4. key signatures
5. tonic and dominant seventh chords

Major Five-finger Positions

Most methods include reading in the major five-finger positions of C, G, and F. Beginners must learn these, and be able to shift hand positions quickly from one to another.

Example 20 Major five-finger positions of C, G, and F.

Intervals

Since intervals form the basis for most theoretical study, it is important that students understand them clearly. In the beginning the terminology may be steps and skips rather than seconds and thirds. However, within the first year, students can be taught interval names.

Explain clearly that there are *two* types of intervals: *melodic* and *harmonic*. Melodic intervals are played separately; harmonic intervals are played together.

Pedagogical Techniques

Example 21 Melodic and harmonic intervals.

Most method books have companion theory books providing interval drills like Example 22. These drills help students form a mental picture of each interval. Interval flashcards are also helpful for students.

Example 22 Melodic and harmonic interval drills.

3. Write the names of these melodic intervals. Play and name these notes.

5. Write the names of these harmonic intervals, then play them.

From *Theory, Level 1* of *Bastien Piano Basics* by James Bastien (Neil A. Kjos Music Company, 1985).

It is important to incorporate ear training drills when teaching intervals. First, have the student play and sing intervals at the keyboard by singing the scale degree of the interval: "1 3, 1 5." Next, play intervals to be identified by the student.

Sharp, Flat, and Natural Signs

The first year student should experience reading, writing, and identifying sharp, flat, and natural signs (accidentals). Written work like Example 23 is useful to make sure students are able to position accidentals correctly on the staff.

Major Key Signatures

In teaching major key signatures, point out that the key signature at the beginning of each staff tells the notes to be played sharp or flat throughout the piece, and the key (or tonality) of that piece.

To find the key of a piece using sharps, have the student name the sharp farthest to the right. The next letter in the music alphabet is the name of the major key.

Average Age Beginners

Example 23 Drills for accidentals.

a. Draw a sharp sign before each note. Play and name these notes.

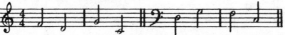

b. Draw a flat sign before each note. Play and name these notes.

c. Draw a natural sign before the second note in each measure. Play and name these notes.

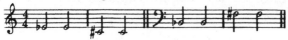

Example 24 Sharp key names.

Key of D   Key of A

To find the key of a piece using flats, have the student look at the next to the last flat. The name of that note is the name of the major key. Exceptions are the keys of C (no sharps or flats) and F (one flat only).

Example 25 Flat key names.

Key of Bb   Key of Eb

Only multiple key methods present the complete sequence of sharps and flats to first year students. The teacher not using a multiple key method may incorporate these if he or she feels it is necessary. The order of sharps and flats would have to be explained separately, apart from the student's theory book.

Example 26 The order of sharps and flats.

FIRST YEAR MATERIALS

The teacher should make a definite plan, with realistic goals, as to what will be covered in a year's time. The first year program contains many new concepts. Since drill and review are essential for assimilation of new concepts, the teacher must plan ahead so that new items are spaced evenly apart to allow time for absorption. The beginner should not be hit with a whirlwind series of new concepts at each lesson. The teacher should review old material and present only one or two new items each week.

The following chart lists objectives for first year students and is intended only as a general guide based on a nine-month year. Some students will need more time to assimilate the items presented. The purpose of this outline is to present basic information in the approximate sequence of a thorough music program.

FOR DISCUSSION & ASSIGNMENT

1. When first teaching beginners do you favor beginning with pre-staff notated pieces? Discuss pros and cons of this approach.
2. List some aids the teacher can give to help students read music notation.
3. Use a beginning student(s) to demonstrate hand position, arm drops, legato and staccato touch, balance of melody and accompaniment (voicing), down-up wrist motion, and legato thirds. Which items do you consider most important? Why? List other first year technical considerations you feel are important.
4. Should theory be incorporated as part of piano lessons? Why is it important?
5. At a music store or pedagogy library make a survey of first year supplementary books and solos. Present some of these for the class and tell why they would benefit first year students.
6. From your experience examining first year literature, compose a first year solo and point out the teaching features.
7. Outline a first year program for repertoire, technique, and theory.

FOR FURTHER READING

Bolton, Hetty. *On Teaching the Piano*. London: Novello and Co., Ltd., 1954. This brief 93-page book is worth reading. Chapter 4, "Teaching the Beginner," is of special interest.

Gat, Jozsef. *The Technique of Piano Playing*. London: Collet's Holdings Ltd., 1965. Although written for advanced students, the section called "Notes on Teaching the Technical Problems of Beginners" contains valuable information.

Last, Joan. *The Young Pianist*. 2nd ed. London: Oxford University Press,

Average Age Beginners

Example 27 Approximate sequence of first year concepts.

	REPERTOIRE	RHYTHM	TECHNIQUE	KEYBOARD HARMONY
Sept.-Oct.	5-finger melodies in pre-staff notation. Combination of folk songs, original melodies.	♩ ♩ ♩. 𝅝	Correct hand position. Curved fingers. Legato touch. Major chords.	Play some major chords. Dynamics.
Nov.-Dec.	Single line melodies (on staff) divided between hands. Some note-against-note playing. Some melody/chord playing. Supplementary reading: Christmas.	♫	5-finger exercises for: Legato/staccato touch. Voicing (balance of hands).	Melodic/harmonic intervals. Sharp, flat signs.
Jan.-Feb.	More complicated melodies/chord playing.	♩ ♩ ♩	Down-up wrist for phrasing.	Harmonize melodies with I, V7 chords. Key signatures. Crescendo, diminuendo signs.
Mar., April, May	Hand position shifts.	♪ 𝅘𝅥𝅮 ♩. ♪	Legato thirds. Some scales.	Octave sign. Natural sign.

Pedagogical Techniques

THEORY	EAR TRAINING	OTHER ELEMENTS
Identify steps, skips, repeats.	Match tones of 3 black keys. Match tones of 5-finger positions.	Say alphabet letters forward and backward. Learn names of keys. Begin to learn note names. Count aloud while playing.
Write and recognize 2nds-5ths.	Recognize 2nds-5ths. Sing intervals.	Sing note names while playing. Read melodies with 2nds-5ths.
Identify key signatures.	Match tones using melody and harmony (teacher plays & student responds).	Tone control (dynamics). Touch control. Pedal. Upbeat.
Group 1 keys.	Play answers to teacher's question phrases.	Identify chord symbols.

Average Age Beginners

1972. This book contains useful information on teaching young students. It should be read in its entirety.

Sandor, Gyorgy. *On Piano Playing*. New York: Schirmer Books/Macmillan, 1981. This book deals with the motions used to play the piano on an advanced level. However, many useful photos and music examples clearly explain basic approaches that may be applied to any level. This is an outstanding book on technique, and should be in the library of all piano teachers!

Second Year Students 7

Second year students usually are beyond beginning basics and are ready for new repertoire and expanded technical and theoretical concepts. Although they are still developing beginning skills at the elementary level, they can move into more interesting areas of musicianship.

The teacher, however, must constantly strive to keep each student interested in piano lessons through a positive approach and a wise selection of music. Parents should be counseled that their encouragement is still needed by their child.

Each higher grade in school produces increased homework and additional demands from outside activities such as sports. Parents should be forewarned that this may cause some conflict with piano lessons. However, if the child's interest is maintained, enthusiasm for lessons will continue.

SECOND YEAR REPERTOIRE

At the beginning of the second year, notes, key signatures, chords, etc., should be reviewed and checked for a few weeks before introducing new concepts.

The continuation of an effective music program should include and correlate the four major areas of concentration begun during the first year of lessons: repertoire, technique, theory, and sight-reading.

It is quite difficult to state the exact repertoire for each student, because factors such as age, ability, amount of practice, interest, encouragement from parents, competition from peers, etc., play an important part in determining the student's musical level. Most average, or better, second year students will be ready for easy classical repertoire near the end of the second year. Younger students, or those of less ability, may not be ready for "serious" literature until the third year of lessons.

There is no need to rush into music by the master composers just for the sake of getting there. Too many teachers assign difficult music too soon, and do not allow their pupils to develop gradually from level to level with sufficient material for reinforcement. The result of assigning difficult music too soon can be a general breakdown in the natural development process.

Suggestions in this chapter for repertoire, sight-reading, etc., are designed for students of average ability. The following three albums contain literature accessible to most second year students. The contemporary pieces are generally a little easier than the others in each collection. They should be assigned before the pieces from the Baroque, Classical, and Romantic composers.

Bastien, James (ed.) **First Piano Repertoire Album** Neil A. Kjos Music Company (1981).

This book contains easier pieces by J.S. Bach, Mozart, Haydn, Beethoven, Schumann, and includes sixteen pieces by James Bastien in Baroque, Classical, Romantic, and Contemporary styles.

Bastien, Jane Smisor (ed.) **Piano Literature, Volume One** Neil A. Kjos Music Company (1966).

Included are easier pieces by J.S. Bach, Spindler, Mozart, Beethoven, Schumann, Kabalevsky, Shostakovich, and Bartók.

Sheftel, Paul (ed.) **Beginning Piano Solos** Carl Fischer (1984).

This volume has an excellent selection of music from four periods. Composers include J.C.F. Bach, J.S. Bach, W.F. Bach, Bartók, Beethoven, Burgmüller, Couperin, Diabelli, Duncombe, Haydn, Kabalevsky, Milhaud, Moore, L. Mozart, W.A. Mozart, Rameau, Schumann, Tchaikovsky, Telemann, and Türk.

Practice Suggestions

The mechanics of hand coordination, phrasing, delineation of linear lines, gradation of dynamics, etc., must be at a sufficient level to play pieces convincingly. Only with careful and correct practice will students begin to develop the equipment that is necessary for projecting the style and mood to perform music in a convincing manner. A few general practice suggestions are:

1. hands separate practice
2. slow practice
3. paying careful attention to the correct fingering
4. using the correct hand motions needed for phrasing
5. tapping one hand like a metronome while playing the other hand
6. using a metronome and counting aloud while practicing

Contemporary Collections

There are a number of contemporary collections by composers of educational piano music that contain suitable music for study and performance that are slightly less difficult than works in easy classical collections. The following list gives some suggested second year collections written by composers who have lived in this century and write attractive pieces for children.

Bastien, James   Dinosaur Kingdom Neil A. Kjos Music Company (1988).
This volume provides a brief history of dinosaurs and eleven contemporary sounding pieces. Most of the pieces use slight dissonances to portray the sounds of the pre-historic, extinct creatures. Text about various dinosaurs is included. The level of difficulty is second and third year.

Bastien, James   Indian Life Neil A. Kjos Music Company (1987).
The historic customs of North American tribes are portrayed in this book. The descriptive text for each piece tells about various functions of tribal life. Even though each piece has the expected fifths in some form, there are many different compositional styles represented.

Bastien, Jane Smisor   Performance, Levels 2, 3 Neil A. Kjos Music Company (1985).
These two books contain an enjoyable variety of original works, folk songs, and popular styles, These pieces are designed for study as well as performance in recitals, auditions, and contests.

Clark, Mary Elizabeth (ed.)   **Contempo 1, Contempos in Crimson, Contempos in Jade, Contempos in Orchid, Contempos in Sapphire** Myklas Press (1972-73).
This series is designed to introduce the young pianist to twentieth-century idioms such as polytonality, whole-tone and twelve tone scales, clusters, ostinato, etc. *Contempo 1* contains a brief informative text for each compositional device with a musical example. New idioms are described as used in succeeding books. The music is by various composers. Generally, the level of difficulty ranges from early second year to third year.

George, Jon   A Day in the Jungle Birch Tree Group Ltd. (1968).
Twelve little pieces comprise this collection of imaginative, one-page pieces. The teaching features of the compositions are described in the contents. This is a superior set of elementary descriptive pieces, tastefully illustrated and annotated by the composer.

Gillock, William   Accent on Solos, Levels 2, 3 Willis Music Company (1969).
Both books contain well-written original solos. Baroque style is represented in both the "Gavotte" and "Musette" in Level 2. Sonatina style is used in "Sliding in the Snow," and Classical style is featured in "The Queen's Minuet" in Level 3.

Second Year Students

Last, Joan   Cats Oxford (1964).

Joan Last has written extensively for children and produced some excellent music—*Cats* is a good example of her style. Written in suite form as ten little piano solos, this collection contains attractive music at about the late second year level. Some excellent teaching features are phrasing, pedal, quickly changing positions and registers, and a variety of styles and moods. Attractive illustrations enhance this collection.

Noona, Walter and **Carol   The Contemporary Performer, Level 2** Heritage Music Press (1975).

This series (four books) is designed to introduce youngsters to idioms of twentieth-century styles such as polyrhythms, clusters, polytonalities, twelve-tone rows, and ostinato patterns. The information about the compositional devices is concise and informative.

Olson, Lynn Freeman   Pop! Goes the Piano, Book 1 Alfred Publishing Company (1985).

This series (three books) is comprised of pieces in a lighter mood such as jazz, blues, country, ballads, and Latin styles.

SECOND YEAR TECHNIQUE

Technique is an amalgamation of a number of skills that form a suitable background enabling students to perform piano literature in a musical fashion. When problems are encountered in the student's music, the teacher should invent little exercises to overcome these difficulties, or use a book that has exercises designed to meet the needs of the student.

Second year students should have developed individual finger coordination sufficiently to allow concentration on hand coordination drills. Phrasing, dynamic shading, balance between hands, etc., now can be studied in more depth. Technical drills should be constructed to assist students in playing music that is more difficult than first year pieces.

Some of the following technical skills were begun during the first year of lessons; others are new for second year students.

1. phrasing
2. legato and staccato combined
3. balance between hands
4. dynamic shading
5. part-playing
6. scales
7. triads and inversions
8. Alberti bass

Phrasing

Good phrasing habits do not come easily and naturally, even to gifted students. Teachers must constantly show pupils how to drop on the beginning of a phrase and lift the wrist at the conclusion of the phrase. For clear examples of phrasing in both photos and music examples, read Gyorgy Sandor's book *On Piano Playing* (Schirmer Books/Macmillan, 1981). Chapter 5 clearly defines motions used in phrase groups.

Phrasing is best taught by beginning with short slurred groupings. As discussed in the previous chapter, it is advisable to instruct students to employ a "down-up" wrist movement, the down movement being on the first note (usually a strong beat), and the up movement on the last note (often a weak beat).

Example 1 Phrasing exercises.

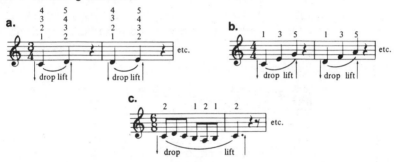

c.

Second year students will encounter a variety of phrases that will include combinations of slurred and staccato groups. It is helpful to assign studies for practicing these combinations.

Example 2 Exercise for slurred and staccato groups.

Say: down up up up down off

As indicated in Example 2 the student should "say" the phrasing aloud: "down up" for slurs, and "up" for all staccato notes. By saying the phrasing aloud the student will become aware of the correct hand motion.

Legato & Staccato Touches Combined

Many second year pieces require legato-staccato combinations. This combination requires careful hand coordination. Because both hands "want" to do the same thing at the same time, each hand must be trained to function independently.

Example 3 Exercise for the combination of legato and staccato touches.

Balance Between Hands

Most pieces contain a melody and accompaniment, or two-voice counterpoint. Each style requires stressing one hand and playing the other softer. The main difficulty for combining "loud and soft" is coordination between the hands. Studies can be designed to develop a balance of tones (voicing) and to prepare students for this situation when encountered in their music.

Example 4 Exercise for balance between hands.

Dynamic Shading

First year students usually do not have sufficient control over their fingers to warrant a great deal of emphasis on shaping melodies using sophisticated dynamic colorings. However, within the second year emphasis should be given to dynamic shading. A few exercises may be devised for crescendo and decrescendo extending over several measures.

Example 5 Exercises for crescendo and decrescendo.

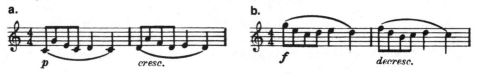

Part-Playing

The ability to hold one finger down while playing others in the same hand is difficult for students at first, but with some preparatory drills, the difficulties can be overcome.

Pedagogical Techniques

Example 6 Part-Playing.

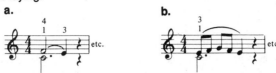

Numerous second and third year pieces require the mechanics of part-playing. In measure four of Example 7, the G in the right hand must be sustained while playing the upper notes.

Example 7 Right hand with sustaining and moving voices at the same time.

Caravan

James Bastien

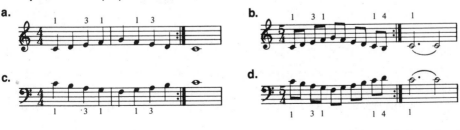

"Caravan" from *First Piano Repertoire Album* by James Bastien (Neil A. Kjos Music Company 1981).

Scales

During the first year of lessons, scale playing is minimal for most students. The reason is because few, if any scale passages are used in first year literature. However, most teachers generally agree that some exposure to scale patterns will benefit first year students—tetrachord scales, and scales in one octave. Although scale presentation is a highly individual matter, it is logical to conclude that the presentation of scales is more easily handled in the second year. This is especially true of parallel scale playing which requires more control and coordination.

Scale preparation exercises will be of benefit to students. Explain how to turn the thumb under and how to cross over the thumb.

Example 8 Scale preparation exercises.

a.

b.

c.

d.

Second Year Students

For one-octave scale fingerings there are two approaches about how to play the top note in the right hand, and the bottom note in the left hand. Some teachers prefer not to use the fifth finger at all. While fifth finger substitutes (thumbs) may be helpful for students to play scales two octaves or more, they are not ever used this way in compositions, and it seems awkward to play them in this manner. The two following fingering systems show the differences mentioned with a C major scale:

```
1. RH   1 2 3 1 2 3 4 5
   LH   5 4 3 2 1 3 2 1
2. RH   1 2 3 1 2 3 4 1
   LH   1 4 3 2 1 3 2 1
```

Scale fingerings should be *memorized*. Teachers may or may not choose to use a published book of scales. The few scale books suggested are suitable for second or third year students.

Bastien, James Major Scales & Pieces, Minor Scales & Pieces Neil A. Kjos Music Company (1966).
Includes all major and minor scales with related exercises and a piece in each key. Late second or early third year level.

Bastien, James Scales, Chords & Arpeggios Neil A. Kjos Music Company (1988).
Contains all the major and minor scales, plus cadence chords, and arpeggios. These materials may be used for study and for auditions such as the National Guild of Piano Teachers.

Brown Scale Book, The Frederick Harris Music Company (1948).
Includes all major and minor scales, triads and inversions, dominant seventh chords, diminished seventh chords, and the chromatic scale.

Pace, Robert Finger Builders, Book 3 Lee Roberts Music Publications (1981).
Includes all parallel major and minor scales and a variety of five-finger exercises and some Hanon studies.

Palmer, Willard, Morton Manus and **Amanda Vick Lethco Elementary Musicianship, Book 1** Alfred Publishing Company (1987).
Includes all major and minor scales, triads, arpeggios, and cadences. Appropriate for first, second, or third year students.

Triads & Inversions

Triad studies serve two purposes—technical and theoretical. Triad drills are an important part of a student's technical program to aid in developing a good hand position, and to develop ease and control over the keyboard.

Example 9 Triads and inversions.

Sometime during the second year of lessons students should be taught triads and inversions in both blocked and broken styles as shown in Example 9. Students should memorize the correct fingering for each inverted chord. To make students aware of the different fingering for inverted chords, it is helpful to circle the fingering that is *different.*

Triads and inversions should be studied ascending and descending. Since fingering is an important aspect with learning triads and inversions, sufficient drill should be assigned so that the correct fingering will become automatic. It is helpful to have the student say aloud the fingering for the *middle* note of each triad, as this is the finger that will be changed in the inversions, such as for the right hand "3 2 3 3," and for the left hand "3 3 2 3."

The student should learn the triads and inversions for *each* scale studied—major and minor. This will prepare the student to play pieces in various keys requiring broken chord patterns.

Alberti Bass

The Alberti bass pattern should be studied in preparation for sonatinas and other pieces that use this style of accompaniment. First have the student play the left hand alone saying the "position" of the notes aloud: "bottom top middle top" as shown in Example 10a. Next, the student

Second Year Students

Example 10   Alberti bass studies.

Say: bottom top middle top

should play the Alberti bass in the left hand and blocked chords in the right hand as in Example 10b. The student should learn to play the Alberti bass in the keys which will be used in easy sonatinas—C G F. Other more difficult keys can be practiced at the teacher's discretion.

Examples of compositions using the Alberti bass in sonatinas include Attwood's *Sonatina in G;* Beethoven's *Sonatina in G;* Clementi's *Sonatina in C*, Op 36 No. 1; and Haslinger's *Sonatina in C*, second movement.

Suggested Technique Books

In addition to any exercises the teacher might invent for individual drill, the following books will be beneficial for second (or third) year students.

Bastien, James   Technic, Levels 2, 3 Neil A. Kjos Music Company (1986).
These two books contain short exercises using scales, phrasing, triads and inversions, legato thirds, chromatics, and the Alberti bass.

Clark, Frances, Louise Goss and **Sam Holland   Musical Fingers, Books 1, 2** The New School for Music Study Press (1983).
These books provide exercises for the development of phrasing, chromatics, scales, hand crossings, legato thirds, part-playing, triads and inversions, and accompaniment patterns.

Last, Joan   Freedom Technique, Book 1 Oxford (1971).
The brief studies in this twelve-page book provide a variety of exercises such as rotary patterns, slurred groups, arm weight, scale preparation, scales, arpeggios, chromatic scale, and one pedal exercise. Each example is purposely short to allow several to be played in each practice session.

Palmer, Willard, Morton Manus and **Amanda Vick Lethco   Technic Book, Levels 2, 3** Alfred Publishing Company (1984).
These books contain exercises using intervals, phrasing, scales, triads, and chromatics.

Pedagogical Techniques

SECOND YEAR THEORY

In the previous chapter the importance of including theory and keyboard harmony as an integral part of piano lessons was discussed. Students must understand what they are doing regarding various phases of theory—key signatures, harmonic structures, etc. The teacher should set a goal to make students musically literate in every aspect of music.

Theory and keyboard harmony may be included in the private lessons, or taught in a separate theory class. The second year theory program is a continuation of concepts already introduced. Review at the start of the second year is essential.

New theoretical concepts in the second year are:

1. primary chords
2. chord progression I IV$^6_4$ V$^6_5$
3. the order of sharps and flats
4. major scale pattern
5. minor key signatures
6. minor scales

Primary Chords

Primary chords may be explained as chords built on the first, fourth, and fifth degrees of the scale. Each chord has a name: I chord = tonic, IV chord = subdominant, V chord = dominant.

Example 11 Primary chords in C major.

Primary chords form the basic harmony in music. It is important for students to write and play these chords until they have learned them. In addition, students should be able to identify the primary chords used in pieces they are playing. Primary chords may also be used for ear training activities.

Chord Inversions

Since only the tonic chord is used in root position, it is important to give students clear explanations of inverted chords. First inversion chords are shown as $^6_3$ chords (the 6 indicates a sixth above the bottom note, the 3 indicates a third above the bottom note); second inversion chords are shown as $^6_4$ chords (the 6 indicates a sixth above the bottom note, the 4 indicates a fourth above the bottom note).

Example 12 Primary chords and inversions.

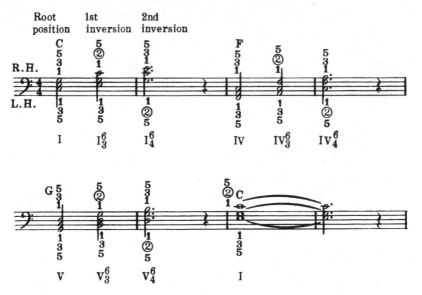

Have students play the tonic and second inversion subdominant chord in succession to experience moving the thumb *up* a whole step.

Example 13 Tonic and second inversion subdominant chords.

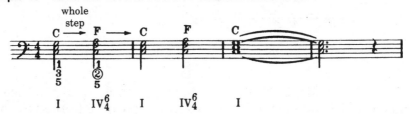

When explaining the dominant seventh chord it is helpful to first show that it is built on the fifth scale degree (Example 14a). Explain that this chord has *three* inversions. This chord is easier to play in first inversion with only three notes—omitting the fifth of the scale. Have the student practice changing from tonic to the first inversion dominant until it is easy to play.

After the student has played the tonic-subdominant chords and the tonic-dominant seventh chords, they should now be combined for practice as shown in Example 15. This pattern should be learned for each new key.

Pedagogical Techniques

Example 14   Dominant seventh chord and inversions.

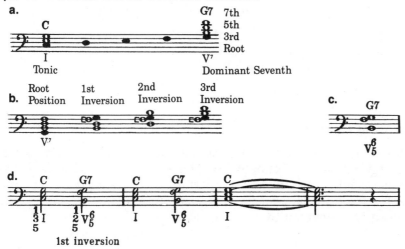

Example 15   I IV$^6_4$ V$^6_5$ chords.

The Order of Sharps & Flats

The order of sharps and flats should be taught in preparation for naming key signatures and for playing and writing scales. Arrows in the score showing the direction of the next sharp or flat is a good learning aid.

Example 16   The order of sharps and flats.

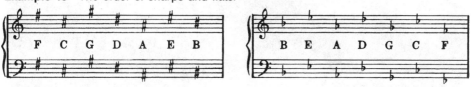

It is helpful for students to write the order of sharps on blank music paper several times a day. They should be written exactly as shown in Example 16.

When teaching flats, point out that the sequence uses the same letters as sharps, but in reverse order. In addition to writing sharps and flats, they may be played on the piano while singing their names in the following manner.

Second Year Students

Sharps
RH   F   G   A   B

Flats
RH   E   D   C

LH   C   D   E

LH   B   A   G   F

Major Scale Pattern

Major scales may be explained as having eight tones in a pattern of whole and half steps (Example 17). The scale is divided into two equal parts, each having four notes. Each part is called a *tetrachord*. The pattern for each tetrachord is *whole step* (1), *whole step* (1), *half step* (½). Each tetrachord is connected by a whole step.

Example 17   Major scale pattern.

When first teaching scales, it is important to explain and demonstrate how the thumb turns under, and how to cross a finger over the thumb. The thumb should be turned under smoothly without twisting the hand and arm out of shape.

Example 18   Correct hand position for turning the thumb under.

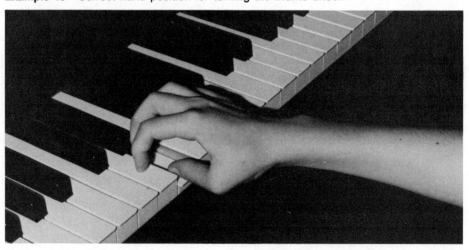

Pedagogical Techniques

The following exercises will help the student understand the "crossing" and "turning" principles.

Example 19 Scale preparation exercises.

Minor Key Signatures

For most students, minor key signatures and scales can be assigned about midway through the second year of lessons. However, for students of less than average ability, it would be better to wait until the third year of lessons.

Explain that the *same* key signature is used for relative major and minor keys. There are two methods of determining the minor key name. To avoid confusion, have the student choose one method that is easier to understand, and use that procedure for determining the minor key name.

Example 20 Methods of determining minor key signatures.

1. From the tonic note, count up to the sixth note of the major scale; that tone is the name of the relative minor key.

2. From the tonic note, count down three half steps on the keyboard; that tone is the name of the relative minor key.

Minor Scales

There are three forms of minor scales: *natural, harmonic,* and *melodic.* The harmonic minor scale should be stressed more than the other two because it is used more frequently.

Second Year Students

Example 21 The three forms of minor scales.

1. The minor scale that starts on the sixth tone of a major scale is called *natural* minor; it has the same key signature as the major scale referred to.

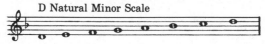

D Natural Minor Scale

2. To construct the *harmonic minor* scale, raise the seventh tone of the natural minor scale one half step.

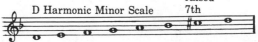

D Harmonic Minor Scale   raised 7th

3. The *melodic minor* scale consists of two parts: one form is used ascending, and another is used descending. To construct the melodic minor scale, raise the sixth and seventh tones of the natural minor scale one half step ascending, and lower them descending.

D Melodic Minor Scale

raised 6th & 7th   lowered 7th & 6th

Theory Books

Theory books are designed to follow the concepts presented in the student's method book at each level. Theory books that include considerable playing are essential for students. Recommended theory books stressing keyboard harmony are:

Bastien, James   Theory, Levels 2, 3   Neil A. Kjos Music Company
Pace, Robert   Theory Papers, Book 2   Lee Roberts Music Publications, Inc.
Palmer, Willard, Morton Manus and **Amanda Vick Lethco**   Theory Book, **Levels 2, 3**   Alfred Publishing Company

SECOND YEAR SIGHT-READING

A reading program should be designed for each student based on a level that is slightly below the assigned repertoire given. Most piano methods consist of a basic reading program that is progressive. However, additional books need to be assigned for sight-reading practice.

A good way to develop reading skills is to use flashcards. They may be made by the teacher for use in individual lessons or in group lessons. Short musical phrase flashcards are most effective for drills in sight-reading.

Example 22 Sight-reading flashcard.

As the card is held up the student should perceive the clef signs, key signature and meter signature; the correct position for both hands; the rhythm (the note values may be tapped before beginning to play); and any changes in hand position that might occur (crossing 2 over 1 in the left hand, third measure). While playing, the student should say the counts aloud (or sing note names), and look far enough ahead to keep going in tempo, and play slow enough to be able to play straight through without stopping.

A series of sight-reading cards may be made in a progressive order to become gradually more difficult in melody, rhythm, and harmony. These sight-reading cards can be effectively used in group lessons. Have one student read a card with the others observing to see if the student makes any mistakes. The student who reads perfectly (correct notes, rhythm, phrasing, fingering, etc.) gets to keep the cards; the student who has the most correct cards wins the game.

Several useful sight-reading books for average second year students are:

Bastien, James Sight Reading, Levels 1, 2 Neil A. Kjos Music Company
Bastien, Jane Smisor Performance, Level 2 Neil A. Kjos Music Company
Johnson, Thomas Hands Together Hinrichsen/Peters
Palmer, Willard, Morton Manus and **Amanda Vick Lethco Fun Book, Level 2** Alfred Publishing Company
Palmer, Manus and **Amanda Vick Lethco Recital Book, Level 2** Alfred Publishing Company
Waxman, Donald First Folk Song Pageant Galaxy

SECOND YEAR MATERIALS

Second year material should be planned to introduce the student to new elements while at the same time providing review drills for reinforcement. New items should be spaced evenly to allow time for absorption. The following general guide lists objectives for second year students based on the school year.

Second Year Students

Example 23 Approximate sequence of second year students.

	REPERTOIRE	RHYTHM	TECHNIQUE	KEYBOARD HARMONY
Sept.–Oct.	General review. Begin playing pieces with scale passages, primary chords, triads and inversions.	Review.	Review 5-finger patterns. Contrary and parallel scale studies. Primary chord drills. Triad and inversion exercises.	Major scales. Harmonize melodies with I IV V^7 chords.
Nov.–Dec.	Note-against-note style.	$\frac{6}{8}$ meter.	Dynamics. Interval exercises. Legato note exercises.	
Jan.–Feb.	Minor scale pieces. Broken chord bass patterns.	Triplets.	Minor scale studies. Contrary and parallel motion. Primary chord drills in minor. Minor triads and inversions.	Harmonize melodies using broken bass patterns and Alberti bass.
Mar., April, May	Easy piano literature. Easy sonatinas.		Chromatic scale.	

Pedagogical Techniques

THEORY	EAR TRAINING	OTHER ELEMENTS
Review with flashcards: note names, intervals, key signatures. Half and whole steps. Tetrachords in major scales.	Review question and answer phrases, singing intervals, identifying I IV V^7 progression. Identify major and minor triads.	New repertoire. Crossing fingers over or turning the thumb under. Sight-reading.
Order of sharps. Group 2 keys (D A E).		Subtle dynamics— crescendo, decrescendo. Develop tempo consistency by using metronome; give tempo markings for home practice.
Minor key signatures. Order of flats. Group 3 keys (D♭ A♭ E♭).	Identify i iv V^7 in minor keys. Question and answer phrases in minor keys.	

Second Year Students

FOR DISCUSSION & ASSIGNMENT

1. Discuss your philosophy concerning repertoire and sight-reading. At the second year level, which do you consider more important. Why?
2. Use a second year student(s) to demonstrate phrasing, legato and staccato combinations, voicing, dynamic shading, part-playing, scales, triads and inversions, and the Alberti bass. Which items do you consider most important? Why? List other second year technical considerations.
3. How much theory is necessary for second year students? Should it be taught along with the private lessons, or apart from the private lessons? Why?
4. At a music store or pedagogy reference library make a survey of second year supplementary books and solos. Present several books and solos and tell why they would be useful for second year students.
5. From your experience of examining second year literature, compose a second year solo and point out the teaching features.
6. Outline a second year program for repertoire, technique, and theory.

Third Year Students 8

In teaching students at the third year level, one should carefully consider their age. If they begin lessons at the age of seven or eight, they will now be about ten or eleven—pre-adolescents. The teacher should provide incentives such as auditions, contests, recitals, and group participation.

Parents should be reminded that they still need to provide encouragement and help their children find sufficient time for practice. The repertoire in the third year is more demanding, compositions are now longer and more involved, so more practice is required. Approximately forty-five minutes to an hour of practice time is needed for students in their third year of lessons.

At this age sports play an increasing role in boys' and girls' lives. Many students are able to combine piano lessons with various seasonal sport activities. However, the teacher must be prepared for somewhat less practice time due to outside interests. If sufficient motivation is provided by the teacher, students will be able to move ahead and make progress.

THIRD YEAR MUSIC PROGRAM

In a continuous program of study the materials covered in successive years will gradually broaden and expand and become progressively more complex. The key to successful learning is to pace the rate of advancement gradually. Some students may require further drill at a particular level before proceeding to more complex material. Others may be quick to catch on, and can be pushed ahead more rapidly. The gulf between those who remain at the same level and those who progress at an accelerated rate becomes more pronounced for each year of study.

Most third year students will be ready for music by the master composers. Some will have already begun easy literature in the second year. There is a wealth of fine material available by master composers from the seventeenth, eighteenth, and nineteenth centuries, and there is an abundance of outstanding music written by twentieth-century composers.

There are many good editions of works of individual composers—all Bach, all Schumann, etc., as well as editions of collected works by several composers. Generally the level of difficulty varies widely in collections of works by individual composers, therefore it appears to be more practical to buy one volume that contains graded works by several composers.

Consideration should be given to the simplification or omission of ornaments in Baroque music. Some teachers prefer to omit ornaments if they are too difficult for students to play. The "Minuet in G" from *The Notebook for Anna Magdalena* may be too difficult for young students to play with the indicated mordents and trills. However, for older students with good facility, the ornaments may be learned as printed in the score. Discretion should be used by the teacher in the use of ornaments.

Repertoire Collections

The following collections of easy classics are suitable for study and performance by third year students. There are many more collections than what is listed.

Alternatives to the following collections are collections representing just one composer. A useful series is the *Easiest Piano Selections* of Bach, Bartók, Beethoven, Kabalevsky, Schumann, etc., published by the Alfred Publishing Company. The level of the pieces often progresses quite rapidly within each book. Therefore, it would serve most students better to play a variety of music in a collection, rather than playing many pieces from single-composer albums.

Agay, Denes (ed.) **Easy Classics to Moderns** Consolidated Music Publishers (1956).

This collection of 142 compositions contains piano literature dating from the second half of the seventeenth century to the present time. The compositions range in difficulty from easy level (late second year, or early third year) to more difficult levels (fourth year and beyond).

Bastien, James (ed.) **First Piano Repertoire Album** Neil A. Kjos Music Company (1981).

This collection includes pieces by Türk, Diabelli, Hook, Hässler, Schein, Telemann, J.S. Bach, Haydn, Mozart, Beethoven, Schumann, and various pieces by James Bastien. Included are practice suggestions as well as short biographies about each composer.

Bastien, Jane Smisor (ed.) **Piano Literature, Volumes 1, 2** Neil A. Kjos Music Company (1966). Compact discs are available for the complete series.

Volume 1 may be given to better than average late second year students, but a number of the pieces are more suited to the third year level. This collection contains short pieces by J.S. Bach, Spindler, Mozart, Beethoven, Schumann, Kabalevsky, Shostakovich, and Bartók. *Volume 2* contains pieces at about late third year level and beyond. Included are works by J.S. Bach, Clementi, Beethoven, Schumann, Kabalevsky, Rebikoff, and Bartók.

Goss, Louise (ed.) **Piano Literature, Book 2** Birch Tree Group Ltd. (1954).
This collection includes pieces by J.S. Bach, Mozart, Haydn, Beethoven, and Schumann. The selections are appropriate for third year students to study and perform.

Popular Collections

Most students enjoy playing some popular styles. The following list contains only a few suggested titles. If students request current hit selections, those can be chosen from arrangers such as Dan Coates (Warner Bros. Publications), Pamela and Robert Schultz (Columbia Pictures Publications), and others.

Bastien, James **Boogie, Rock & Country, Level 3** Neil A. Kjos Music Company (1987).
Eleven pieces in various styles (boogie, blues, rag, country, rock) are contained in this collection for third year students.

Bastien, Jane Smisor and **James Bastien** **Pop Piano Styles, Level 3** Neil A. Kjos Music Company (1980).
Boogie, blues, rock, rag, and disco styles are included in this volume.

Guaraldi, Vince **Charlie Brown's Greatest Hits** Hal Leonard (1984).
For Peanuts fans this collection features arrangements, by Bill Boyd, of popular television specials.

King, Sanford **I'm Playing Ragtime** Carl Fischer (1975).
Twelve one-page originals with real rag style flavor are contained in this sixteen-page collection. Mostly two-part style writing is used. Syncopation abounds in these catchy pieces.

Olson, Lynn Freeman **Pop! Goes the Piano, Book 2** Alfred Publishing Company (1985).
An excellent cross-section of popular styles is in this well-written volume.

Contemporary Collections

There are numerous collections of music by composers who write educational piano music. These pieces often do not sound "contemporary" (twelve-tone style, use of dissonance, etc.). The following list contains a selection of twentieth-century composers who write music in a variety of styles.

Agay, Denes (ed.) **The Joy of Bartók** Yorktown/Music Sales (1984).
The works in this collection are in a graded sequence enabling students to use this volume for several years. The edition is first-rate, easy to read, and is well-spaced on the page.

Third Year Students

Album of Easy Pieces by Modern Composers
Kalmus/Belwin/Columbia Pictures Publications (no date available).
This volume contains an excellent selection of contemporary pieces by Bartók, Kabalevsky, Shostakovich, Prokofiev, and Stravinsky. This is an excellent collection.

Anson, George   New Directions Willis Music Company (1961).
New sounds explored include polytonality, tone clusters, twelve-tone row, and experimental harmonies. The sampling of styles would assist students in a better understanding of contemporary music. This book is appropriate for late third year or early fourth year students.

Anson, George (ed.)   **Survey of Piano Literature, Book 3—The Contemporary Scene** Elkan-Vogel/Presser (1960).
This is a choice collection of contemporary favorites. Composers include Bartók, Kabalevsky, Stravinsky, Shostakovich, Phillips, Ornstein, and Persichetti.

Bartók, Béla   Young People at the Piano, Books 1, 2 Boosey & Hawkes (1950).
These two twelve-page volumes provide easy selections for third year students. Some pieces are written in two-voice style, others have melody and accompaniment. Hungarian music requires accents and stress marks, and Bartók has written these where needed.

Bastien, Jane Smisor   2nd Parade of Solos Neil A. Kjos Music Company (1988).
The pieces in this collection are written in a variety of styles. The book is divided into sections with original solos, seasonal pieces, and pieces written by Mrs. Bastien in classic styles.

Bastien, James   Space Adventures Neil A. Kjos Music Company (1987).
The music is written in slightly contemporary styles depicting various elements of outer space. There are brief paragraphs about each space adventure.

Clark, Frances and **Louise Goss** (eds.)   **Contemporary Piano Literature, Book 2** Birch Tree Group, Ltd. (1955).
This volume has standard contemporary music by Bartók, Kabalevsky, and Shostakovich, as well as some excellent compositions commissioned for this series by Sigmeister, Tansman, and Tcherepnin.

Dello Joio, Norman   Suite for the Young Marks/Hal Leonard (1964).
This superb collection of ten imaginative pieces rates at the top of the scale in contemporary educational music. All the pieces contain special mildly contemporary flavors, and some utilize didactic devices: "Invention" uses major and minor triadic melodies; "A Sad Tale" uses an ostinato

bass. Favorites are "Bagatelle" (staccato touch), "Small Fry" (wonderfully jazzy), and "Little Brother" (staccato and syncopated cross accents). The compositions are about late third year; some are fourth year in difficulty.

George, Jon   A Day in the Forest Birch Tree Group Ltd. (1973).
Consisting of eight pleasant vignettes seen on a country outing, these imaginative pieces are a sure delight to teach.

George, Jon   Kaleidoscope Solos, Books 4, 5 Alfred Publishing Company (1974).
Many of these pieces involve such teaching techniques as sustained and moving voices in one hand, complex rhythms, irregular meters, asymmetrical phrase lengths, and chromaticism. *Book 4* is mid to late third year; *Book 5* is late third year and beyond.

George, Jon   Medieval Pageant Oxford (1972).
The eight attractive pieces in this book create a marvelous atmosphere of "once upon a time" and delve into the storybook land of long ago. Modes and ostinatos used in the pieces maintain a strong medieval flavor. A brief "Fanfare" is the curtain raiser for the ensuing "Processional" which is followed by "The Troubador Sings" and "The Jester Performs." The concluding pieces are "Branle," "Air," and "Gigge."

Gillock, William   Accent on Rhythm and Style Willis Music Company (1962).
Flair and taste are portrayed in this superb collection of seven pieces. These pieces span four style periods. Favorites are "Sonatina" written in classical style, and "Spanish Gypsies" written in contemporary style. The level of difficulty is about third year, some are fourth year level.

Gillock, William   Fanfare Birch Tree Group Ltd. (1957).
Written as little suites in imitative Baroque style, this book is a gem. Descriptive titles, imaginative music, and a variety of moods are found throughout. The level of difficulty is about mid to late third year.

Kabalevsky, Dmitri   24 Pieces for Children, Opus 39 Alfred Publishing Company, MCA/Hal Leonard, G. Schirmer, others.
Some of these well-known pieces are accessible to third year students. Many of the easier compositions appear in anthology collections.

Noona, Walter and Carol   The Contemporary Performer, Level 3 The Heritage Music Press (1975).
This series of four books is designed to introduce youngsters to twentieth-century styles such as modes, polyrhythms, clusters, polytonalities, twelve-tone rows, and ostinato patterns. The information about the compositional devices used is concise and informative.

Third Year Students

Olson, Lynn Freeman   Piano Favorites Carl Fischer (1987).

These fifteen pieces provide an excellent variety of original compositions. Favorites are "Make It Snappy!," "Secret Mission," "Midnight
Express," and "Rhythm Machine." The pieces were originally published as
single sheets. The level ranges from second year to late third year.

Persichetti, Vincent   Little Piano Book Elkan-Vogel/Presser (1954).

Fourteen pieces containing representative contemporary styles can
serve as preparation for larger works. The music looks easy, but the level
of difficulty is at least mid to late third year level. The writing is first-rate,
and the pieces are a delight to teach.

Rowley, Alec   Five Miniature Preludes and Fugues Chester/Belwin/ Columbia Pictures Publications (1946).

Only rarely does one come across such a delightful collection of exceptional pieces. The contrapuntal melodies are valuable for practice in bringing out voices in either hand.

Waxman, Donald   First Recital Pageant Galaxy (1962).

The compositions in this sixteen-page book are at least mid to late third
year level for most students. The writing is first-rate and is suitable for both
study and recital use. Two duets are also included.

Zeitlin, Poldi and **David Goldberger** (eds.)   **Russian Music, Book 2** MCA/
Hal Leonard (1967).

This is the second book in a six-book series divided into three grades
(elementary, intermediate, and advanced) with two levels in each grade. All
the books have outstanding contemporary music by Russian composers,
as well as some compositions by Glinka, Tchaikovsky, Prokofiev, Kabalevsky, and others. Several duets are included in each volume.

Sonatinas

Sonatina literature is replete with rich resources for pianistic development. Phrasing, voicing (balancing of tones), scales, graded dynamics,
moods and tempos constitute basic elements for interpretation. Also, form
and style are two aspects for study.

Most sonatinas stem from the Classical period (1750-1830). Sonatina
form is basically that of a diminutive sonata; the study of sonatinas will
acquaint the student with the general musical form that is characteristic
of the classical sonata.

A sonatina usually has three movements (sometimes two) of contrasting
moods and tempos. The first movement usually contains two themes.
Sonatinas in major keys have the second theme in the dominant key;
sonatinas in minor keys have the second theme in the relative major key.
Most first movements of classical sonatinas are in major keys. The following outline is called *sonatina form*.

First section:	1. A theme (tonic key)
	2. B theme (dominant key)
Second section:	1. Brief development section
	2. A theme (tonic key)
	3. B theme (tonic key)
	4. Optional codetta (tonic key)

For an example of a model sonatina form, analyze the first movement of Clementi's *Sonatina in C*, Op 36 No. 1:

First section:	1. A theme in C (measures 1-8)
	2. B theme in G (measures 9-15)
Second section:	1. Brief development of the A theme (measures 16-23)
	2. A theme in C (measures 24-31)
	3. B theme in C (measures 32-38)

Some second year students will have already played easy first sonatinas and will now be ready for works that are more difficult. The following list provides suitable sonatinas for third year students.

Agay, Denes (ed.) **Sonatinas, Volume A** Witmark/Warner Bros. Publications (1960).

The sonatinas in this collection are by André, Biehl, Clementi (Op. 36 No. 1), Duncombe, Beethoven (*Sonata in G Major*), Agay, Koehler, Latour, Salutrinskaya, and Schmitt. This book includes a nice cross-section of sonatinas by composers from many periods.

Bastien, James and **Jane Smisor Bastien** **First Sonatina Album** Neil A. Kjos Music Company (1984).

The standard sonatinas by Duncombe, Attwood, Spindler, Beethoven (*Sonatinas in G* and *F Major*), Clementi (Op. 27 No. 11), Lynes, and Haslinger. Also included are original sonatinas by the Bastiens (*Sonatina in Classic Style, Sonatina in Romantic Style, Winter Sonatina*).

Bastien, James (ed.) **Sonatina Favorites, Book 1** Neil A. Kjos Music Company (1977).

This series of three books contains a representative sampling of sonatinas by various composers. Book 1 has sonatinas by Duncombe, James Bastien (*Sonatina in Classic Style*), Attwood, Spindler, Beethoven (*Sonatina in G Major*), Lynes, and Clementi (Op. 16 No. 1). An explanation of sonatina form is provided, and themes are identified in the sonatinas.

Bastien, Jane Smisor **Two Sonatinas** Neil A. Kjos Music Company (1987).

These two sonatinas are clear and concise in form and content. Each has three movements. Explanations of sonatina form and practice directions are provided for students.

Cobb, Hazel **Sonatina Album** Belwin/Columbia Pictures Publications (1959).

Miss Cobb had an affinity for writing first-rate little versions of classic

Third Year Students

sounding sonatinas. This album of four sonatinas is just the right level for third year students.

Gillock, William   Accent on Analytical Sonatinas Willis Music Company (1964).

This superb collection contains three sonatinas. Each has first-rate melodic invention, logical phrasings, appropriate dynamics, and authentic imitative classic style. They are excellent study pieces to bridge the gap between easy level sonatinas and those of more complexity.

Glover, David Carr, and **Maurice Hinson   Sonatinas for Piano, Book 1** Belwin/Columbia Pictures Publications (1982).

Included are sonatinas by Biehl, Attwood, Haslinger, Wanhal, Latour, Beethoven (*Sonatinas in G* and *F Major*), Koehler, Gurlitt, Wilton, Benda, Schmitt, and Hook. This is a nice mixture of familiar and unfamiliar sonatinas.

Hinson, Maurice   Masters of the Sonatina Alfred Publishing Company (1986).

This well-edited book provides sonatinas by Bertini, Biehl, Diabelli, Duncombe, Gurlitt, Kabalevsky (Op. 27 No. 11), Le Couppey, Pleyel, Reinecke, Spindler, Steibelt, Vanhal, and Wesley. A teacher looking for seldomly taught sonatinas will find mostly those in this collection.

THIRD YEAR TECHNIQUE

Third year students are at a juncture between elementary and intermediate levels. Technical drills will enable students to bridge the gap between the first two years spent learning fundamentals and the fourth year—intermediate level. The transition will be made smoothly if playing ability can be developed sufficiently to meet new challenges in repertoire.

Considerable emphasis should be placed on the following five areas:

1. finger patterns
   a. hand position shifts
   b. finger crossings
   c. broken chord patterns
   d. legato thirds patterns
   e. arpeggio preparation
2. finger independence studies
3. forearm rotation
4. pedaling
5. technical studies
   a. exercises
   b. études

Pedagogical Techniques

Finger Patterns

Early elementary piano music (first year and part of the second year) is based essentially on five-finger patterns. Within that context there is little room for error in choice of fingerings. However, even in simple music, the teacher must make sure that good "finger-conscious" habits are formed from the beginning.

Whether the student responds correctly to a variety of patterns (hand shifts, finger crossings, extended and contracted position, etc.) will depend on the muscular (kinesthetic) reflexes that should have been trained to meet a variety of keyboard patterns.

As the student's music becomes more complicated, it is essential to choose the correct fingering. The student should not be "left to his own devices" in choosing fingering, for awkward unpianistic fingerings may occur. The teacher must lead the student to the correct choice, and in many instances support the choice of fingering with reasons why.

Hand Position Shifts

A shift from one hand position to another is one of the most basic keyboard patterns. First and second year pieces require hand position shifts with increasing degrees, and by the third year this method of operation is standard fare. The teacher should point out new positions so students will learn to think ahead and perceive shifts *before* they occur.

The first four measures of the "Minuet in G" from *The Notebook for Anna Magdalena* uses a hand shift which is representative of this type of pattern. The student should be taught to prepare ahead at the end of the second measure and then move quickly to the third measure so the first beat can be played in time.

Example 1 From " Minuet in G."

Be specific with directions. Draw an arrow, or circle the finger that begins a new hand position in the score as shown in Example 2 (Clementi's *Sonatina*, Op. 36 No. 1).

Example 2 Arrow and circle indicate a hand shift.

Preparing a new hand shift during rests is another essential. While one

Third Year Students

hand plays, the other hand must prepare ahead and be ready to play. Students often hesitate at the end of measure 8 of Clementi's *Sonatina*, Op. 36 No. 1 because the left hand was not prepared early enough (Example 3). It must be ready to play *before* measure 9 is reached. This is an essential aspect of piano playing that should be taught.

Example 3   Large shift for the left hand.

Students should be made to realize that being aware of hand position shifts and preparing ahead will aid them in reading and memorizing. These important elements should be taught within the first three years of lessons.

Finger Crossings

Students will encounter scale type passages more frequently in the third year. In the previous chapter, Example 8 gave four scale preparation exercises specifically for turning the thumb under a finger or crossing a finger over the thumb.

The sixth measure of the "Minuet in G" from *The Notebook of Anna Magdalena* contains a representative example of a finger crossing in a descending figure.

Example 4   Finger crossing in a descending line.

The tenth measure of Clementi's *C Major Sonatina* contains a representative example of a thumb tucking under in an ascending figure.

Example 5   Tucking thumb under in an ascending line.

It is advisable to have students look through an entire piece and circle all the places where finger crossings occur.

Broken Chord Patterns

Easy sonatina literature contains a variety of broken chord patterns. In the previous chapter (7) two preparatory Alberti bass exercises were given in Example 10. These should be practiced *before* playing music with figures of this type.

Measures 5 and 6 of Beethoven's *Sonatina in G* (Example 6) contain examples of Alberti bass figures. The key to the fingering of such broken chord figures lies in the shape of the chordal outline. The student should play the notes as solid chords to discover the correct fingering and also to determine the names of the chords. A group of notes should be perceived as a whole rather than individual notes in a series. Both reading and memory will be improved by careful analyzation.

Example 6 Seeing an Alberti bass as solid chords.

Unfortunately, a legato line can easily be broken by using incorrect fingering. The following passage shows both incorrect and correct fingerings.

Example 7 Achieving a legato line: incorrect and correct fingerings.

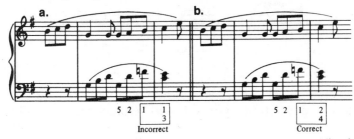

Third Year Students

Legato Double Note Patterns

In double note passages the legato effect is dependent upon connecting one or more of the notes in the figure as shown in Beethoven's *Sonatina in G*. If both notes move by step, both notes can be connected.

Example 8 Legato line is possible in left hand.

However, if only one note moves by step and the other is repeated, only the *moving* note can be made legato.

Example 9 Bottom line of left hand cannot be completely legato.

Since the latter figure (Example 9) is more difficult to execute, studies like those in Example 10 should be devised for practice. The coordination required to hold one finger down while moving another in the same hand is difficult, but with sufficient drill the difficulties can be overcome.

Example 10 Exercises to develop independent use of fingers.

Chords in a cadential passage frequently have only one or two notes to give the legato sound. These figures should be practiced in a variety of keys.

Pedagogical Techniques

Example 11 Chords with one or two legato notes.

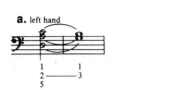

Arpeggio Preparation

Students probably will have played arpeggio figures hand-over-hand style within the first two years and will be acquainted with the sound. Sometime within the third year (or early fourth) it is likely that a broken chord figure for one hand will be encountered as shown in the "Minuet in G" from *The Notebook for Anna Magdalena.*

Example 12 Broken chord figure.

Exercises can be devised for the extended reaches required in broken chord figures as shown in Example 13.

Example 13 Arpeggio preparation exercises.

It is important to use the *correct fingerings* for arpeggio figures; the fingering is based on the shape of the chord. The general rule for either blocked or broken chord depends on the spacing:

Third Year Students

Right Hand
When there is an interval of a *fourth* between the top two notes, use the *third* finger for the third note of the chord.

When there is an interval of a *third* between the top two notes, use the *fourth* finger for the third note of the chord.

Left Hand
When there is an interval of a *fourth* between the bottom two notes, use the *third* finger for the second note of the chord.

When there is an interval of a *third* between the bottom two notes, use the *fourth* finger for the second note of the chord.

Although most third year students will not be confronted with two-octave arpeggios in their music, it is helpful to give some preliminary exercises. These may be given to students whose fingers are long enough to turn the thumb under without straining.

Example 14   Preparatory arpeggio exercises.

Finger Independence Studies

Finger independence studies can be given to develop the ability to hold some notes while playing others. These studies may be written by the teacher (Example 15), or a book such as Schmitt's *Preparatory Exercises*, Op. 16 may be assigned.

Pedagogical Techniques

Example 15 Exercises for finger independence.

a. Hold down all fingers except the one playing.

b. Hold down 1 and 2 throughout.

Forearm Rotation

Forearm rotation requires a special motion. The rotary movement is used whenever notes in a series move back and forth: Alberti bass, broken octaves (sevenths, sixths, fifths, fourths, thirds, seconds), trills, etc.

The rotary movement may be explained by demonstrating how one turns a door handle: the forearm rotates (turns) either left or right as shown in Example 16. Make sure that *only* the forearm rotates; the upper arm should not move about. Also explain that the forearm will rotate in the direction of the next note to be played.

Example 18 may serve as an introductory study in forearm rotation. An excellent description of rotation is given in Gyorgy Sandor's book *On Piano Playing* (Schirmer Books/Macmillan, 1981).

Pedaling

The damper pedal is rarely used in beginning lessons because most young children cannot easily reach the floor with their feet. However, most children like the sounds the pedal creates. Within the first two years, the pedal may be used at the end of a piece, with chords, with hand-over-hand arpeggios, etc.

Third Year Students

Example 16 Rotary motion.

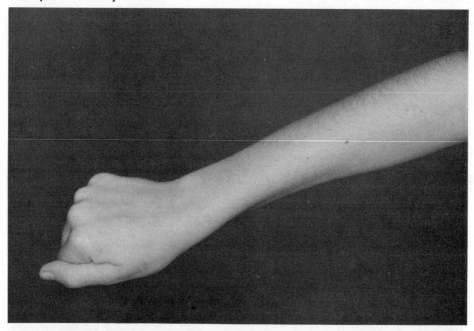

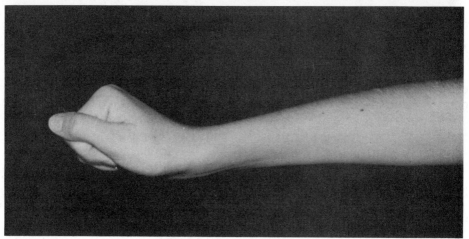

Explain what happens when the foot presses the damper pedal. Let the child look into the piano and see the dampers lift from the strings and

Example 17 Rotation at the keyboard.

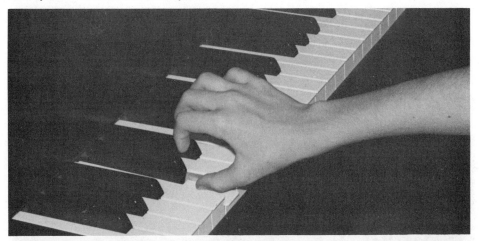

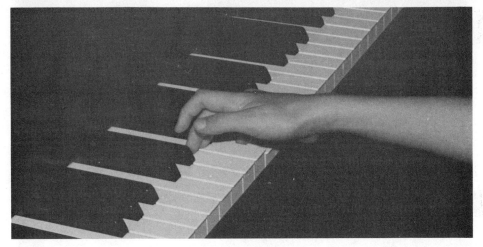

Example 18 Forearm rotation exercise.

then rest on the strings to "dampen" the sound. Do *not* refer to the damper pedal as the "loud pedal." The pedal gives a harmonic effect; it does not really make the sound louder.

Third Year Students

When using the damper pedal, the heel should remain on the floor as shown in Example 19. The young child will have to sit near the front of the chair or bench so the pedal can be reached.

Example 19   Foot on the pedal.

a. Incorrect

b. Correct

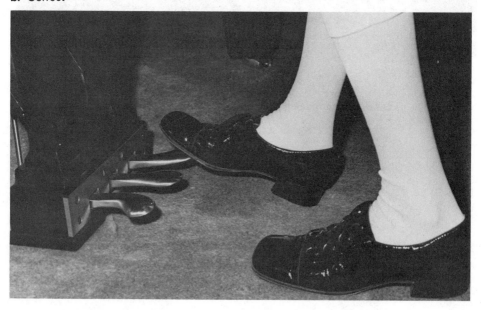

Pedagogical Techniques

At first the damper pedal will be used in a simple way to connect notes of a chord as shown.

Example 20 Pedal held for arpeggio.

"Tiger Chase" from *Performance, Level 2* by Jane Smisor Bastien, Neil A. Kjos Music Company (1985).

After the basic use of the pedal has been experienced, *syncopated pedaling* (or "overlapping" pedal) may be taught. This type of pedaling is difficult and should not be taught too early. However, it is one of the most essential elements of good playing and should be presented carefully.

The most important factor in using the syncopated pedal is to use a quick down-up motion. If the pedal is changed too late, a blurred sound will result. Example 21 will help students get started correctly.

Example 21 Syncopated, or "overlapping," pedal exercise.

If a student has difficulty in changing the pedal after the beat, use the rhythmic presentation in Example 22. The arrows indicate exactly when to depress the pedal. The pedal should be changed evenly, allowing time for the harmonic changes.

Example 22 Arrows indicate when to pedal.

Joseph Banowetz's book *The Pianist's Guide to Pedaling* (Indiana University Press, 1985) is an outstanding reference on pedaling. Included is a history of pedals, pedaling techniques, and examples of how to pedal specific works of selected composers.

Third Year Students

Technique Books

Teachers vary in their approach to technical drills. Some give Hanon studies to young children on a regular basis, while others treat the studies like the plague and never teach them. Some teachers prefer to give scales to beginners, others prefer to wait until some basic fundamentals have been learned. Hanon, Schmitt, Czerny, Beringer, Pischna, Philipp, and numerous others have written volumes of exercises at all levels. The whole realm of technical emphasis is essentially left to the teacher.

The entire matter of exercises versus pieces should be seriously considered. Lesson and practice time should be divided to include both pieces and technique, as well as theory and sight-reading.

When playing technical studies, musical qualities should always be considered. Tone, melodic line, voicing (balancing of melody and accompaniment), phrasing, etc. are all necessary components of a technical program.

The teacher may select technical studies from a variety of books. The following list is suitable for most third year students.

Hanon Studies

Bastien, James (ed.) **First Hanon Studies** Neil A. Kjos Music Company (1976).

This volume contains the first twenty studies, written in eighth notes, hands one octave apart. Practice suggestions are provided on the first two pages for varying the touch, phrasing, rhythm, tempo, dynamics, and key changes.

Dexter, Harry (ed.) **Hanon: The Virtuoso Pianist** Shattinger/Hansen (1972).

This volume contains the complete sixty exercises.

Ferté, Armand **The Young Pianist Virtuoso** Schott (1963).

Thirty-seven Hanon studies are included, as well as all major, minor, and chromatic scales.

Palmer, Willard (ed.) **Hanon: The Virtuoso Pianist** Alfred Publishing Company (1971).

All sixty exercises are included in this beautifully printed edition.

Exercise Books

Bastien, James **Magic Finger Technique, Books 2, 3** Neil A. Kjos Music Company (1966).

These two books include exercises in all keys for phrasing, legato and staccato touch combined, balance between hands, chromatic scale exercises, finger independence exercises, chords and inversions, scales, double note exercises, Alberti bass patterns, and wrist staccato exercises.

Bastien, James **Technic, Levels 3, 4** Neil A. Kjos Music Company (1986).

Pedagogical Techniques

Included are exercises for wrist staccato, overlapping pedal, scale practice, triads and inversions, sixteenth note studies, and double notes. Also included are exercises by Gurlitt, Schmitt, Lemoine, and Czerny.

Clark, Frances, Louise Goss and **Sam Holland Musical Fingers, Book 3** The New School for Music Study Press (1985).
This book has exercises using sixteenth notes, five-finger positions, scales, arpeggios, double notes, rotation, part-playing, and chords.

Olson, Lynn Freeman (ed.) **The Best Traditional Piano Etudes, Books 1, 2** Alfred Publishing Company (1984).
These two books have a wide variety of exercises by Berens, Gurlitt, Köhler, Schytte, Le Couppey, Streabbog, Beyer, Czerny, Concone, and others. The exercises are arranged in a progressive order of difficulty.

Palmer, Willard, Morton Manus, and **Amanda Vick Lethco Technic Book, Level 4** Alfred Publihing Company (1986).
Included are exercises for triplets, inverted chords, part-playing scales, and sixteenth notes.

Etude Books
Bastien, James (ed.) **Czerny and Hanon** Neil A. Kjos Music Company (1970).
Twenty studies by Czerny and the first twenty Hanon studies are included in this book. Also included are major and minor arpeggios, and melodic minor scales.

Czerny, Carl The Little Pianist, Book 1, Op. 823 G. Schirmer (1902).
For Czerny enthusiasts this collection contains little study pieces at about late second and third year levels.

McArtor, Marion Piano Technic, Books 1, 2 Birch Tree Group Ltd., (1954, 1955).
These books from the Frances Clark Library are written according to a planned program for developing facility and control. The short etudes are based on five-finger patterns, extended and contracted patterns, scale patterns, slurred groups, arpeggio patterns, and chord patterns.

Palmer, Willard (ed.) **Köhler Twelve Easy Studies,** Op. 157 Alfred Publishing Company (1972).
This book has exercises for phrasing, scales, and part-playing.

Palmer, Willard (ed.) **Schmitt Preparatory Exercises,** Op. 16 Alfred Publishing Company (1977).
These short exercises provide a variety of drills for five-finger studies. Also included are all major and minor scales, major and minor arpeggios, and the chromatic scale.

Third Year Students

THIRD YEAR THEORY

The main function of a theory program is for the basic understanding of harmonic materials in the student's repertoire. The student should be able to discern chordal outlines and progressions, interval relationships, key, etc. The teacher must constantly strive to make the student musically literate in every aspect of music.

Recognition of basic harmonic patterns is helpful in sight-reading, learning new music, and in memorizing. Students often have difficulty in memorizing simply because they do not understand what they are playing. They play a piece over and over without comprehension and depend on motor reflexes to learn the piece.

The third year theory program should provide a review of items already introduced: intervals, key signatures, chords, scales (major and minor), etc. There will be fewer new elements learned in the third year because a great deal of basic theory has already been presented. New information includes:

1. altered intervals
2. augmented triads
3. diminished triads
4. scale degree names
5. primary and secondary triads

Altered Intervals

Any interval can be made larger or smaller. Students should learn the altered intervals shown in Example 23 for a better understanding of harmonic "discrepancies" used in repertoire being studied. Altered intervals should also be included in ear training activities.

Example 23 Altered intervals.

min 3rd   Aug 4th   dim 5th Aug 5th   min 6th   min 7th

Augmented Triads

An augmented triad consists of a major third and an augmented fifth. Thus, to form an augmented triad, the top note of a major triad is raised one half step.

Pedagogical Techniques

Example 24 Major and Augmented triads.

Diminished Triads

A diminished triad consists of a minor third and a diminished fifth. Thus, to form a diminished triad, the top note of a minor triad is lowered one half step.

Example 25 Minor and Diminished triads.

Scale Degree Names

The scale degree names—tonic, subdominant, and dominant—have already been learned. Students should now learn all the names.

Example 26 Scale degree names.

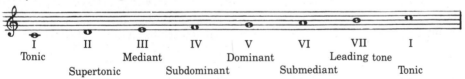

1. tonic (the key note)
2. supertonic (one step above tonic)
3. mediant (midway from tonic to dominant)
4. subdominant (one step under the dominant)
5. dominant (a major, or dominant, element in the key)
6. submediant (midway down from tonic to subdominant)
7. leading tone ("leads" to the tonic)

Primary & Secondary Triads

Triads may be built on each tone of the scale. I, IV, and V are always major (primary); ii, iii, and vi are always minor (secondary); and vii is always diminished.

Third Year Students

Example 27 Primary and secondary triads in a scale.

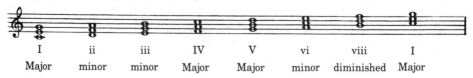

I	ii	iii	IV	V	vi	viii	I
Major	minor	minor	Major	Major	minor	diminished	Major

THIRD YEAR SIGHT-READING

Students should be provided with reading music that is slightly below the assigned repertoire level: the music should not be too difficult for easy comprehension.

While reading, students should:

1. keep their eyes on the music book
2. pay attention to the dynamics
3. read the rhythm correctly paying careful attention to the pulse in each measure
4. read horizontally and vertically
5. pay attention to the correct fingering

The following books contain practical sight-reading music at the third year level. Additional reading books may be assigned by the teacher.

Bastien, James   Sight Reading, Level 3 Neil A. Kjos Music Company (1976).
Deutsch, Leonard   For Sight Reading, Book 1 The Heritage Music Press (1950).
Johnson, Thomas A.   Moving Forward Hinrichsen/C.F. Peters (1964).

FOR DISCUSSION & ASSIGNMENT

1. Discuss your philosophy concerning repertoire collections. Do you favor one-composer volumes (all Bach, all Kabalevsky, etc.)? Do you favor multi-composer collections?
2. Would you use an urtext or edited collection for third year students?
3. Should popular music be given to youngsters? Why or why not?
4. What teaching purpose is served by assigning sonatinas?
5. Use a third year student(s) to demonstrate finger patterns (various types described in this chapter), finger independence studies, forearm rotation, and syncopated pedaling. Which items do you consider most important? Why? List other third year technical considerations.
6. In addition to the theory items discussed in this chapter, what others would you include for third year students?

7. Make a survey of third year repertoire books and solos at a music store or pedagogy reference library. Present several books and solos and tell why they would be useful for third year students.
8. From your experience in examining third year literature, compose a third year solo, point out the teaching features, and perform it.

FOR FURTHER READING

Banowetz, Joseph. *The Pianist's Guide to Pedaling*. Bloomington: Indiana University Press, 1985. The author clearly presents a history of the pedals, pedaling techniques, and examples of pedaling the works of selected composers. A useful bibliography of sources is also included. This is a first-rate reference.

Intermediate Students 9

The intermediate student is one who has the facility to play sonatinas, Bach's *Two-Part Inventions*, Kabalevsky's *Toccatina*, and other works of similar difficulty. The age of the student at the intermediate level will vary according to when lessons were first begun; most intermediate students are between ten and thirteen years of age.

Within intermediate music there is a wide range of levels. Contest and audition music is frequently qualified by such terms as *early intermediate, intermediate,* and *upper intermediate*. This degree of latitude within the intermediate period indicates that most students will advance slowly. The time span for average students is about three years.

One of the problems in teaching the intermediate student is to keep all levels of musicianship moving ahead at a similar pace. When the transition from method book pieces to piano literature has been made, the tendency is to concentrate on a few compositions and neglect other teaching elements. This could soon lead to a deficiency in one of the basic musicianship areas.

One such area is technique. The study of repertoire alone probably will not be sufficient to develop the playing skills needed.

The rate of advancement during the intermediate period should be carefully regulated. Sometimes the student should be pushed ahead by assigning more difficult music; but the reverse is more often true. Frequently there is an inclination for the teacher to push the student too fast through this stage of development. The teacher may assign material that is too difficult for the student to perform musically and technically. This often leads to frustration and defeat. Rather than discouraging the student and causing a loss of interest, time should be given to allow development at a realistic rate.

One of the main problems confronting intermediate students is the demands made on their time from outside activities. If conflicts become too pressing, many will become piano dropouts. Usually, the less interested or less gifted are the first to go. If their musical ability is modest, the time needed for practice is often the "straw that breaks the camel's back." Those who find it necessary to quit should be allowed to do so without recriminations from either the parents or the teacher. Encouraging an interested student is beneficial, but *forcing* an uninterested student generally does not produce successful results.

The intermediate student can be guided through this period successfully if the teacher sets realistic goals. Adequate time must be given for development, and the teacher may have to hang on for a while before pushing ahead. This is a crucial point in the student's development to make it through this stage and progress to higher levels of piano playing.

INTERMEDIATE REPERTOIRE

Although emphasis will focus on literature, a broad-based program must be maintained to ensure continued development in all musicianship phases.

Students at this level vary widely in aptitude and interest; it is therefore impossible to outline a program that will serve the needs of all students. The general information outlined in this chapter is intended for students of average ability. Four areas of study will be discussed: repertoire, technique, theory, and sight-reading.

The intermediate repertoire is generally divided into three levels:

1. early intermediate (for about fourth year students)
2. intermediate (slightly more difficult—late fourth or fifth year)
3. upper intermediate (more difficult—about fifth or sixth year)

It is important to choose music that is not too difficult for students to play. In competitions one frequently hears a piece played by a student who does not yet have the technical capabilities to perform it effectively: the tempo is too slow (or too fast), the runs are not even, or the character and mood of the piece is not evident in the student's performance. In this case the teacher should have chosen an easier piece.

For teachers who would like to use an intermediate method, the *Intermediate Piano Course* by James and Jane Smisor Bastien (Neil A. Kjos Music Company, 1982) is a well-written series. This method consists of repertoire, theory, technique, and multi-key solo books divided into three levels. The first level may be assigned after the completion of any beginning method. For a complete description of each book, refer to Chapter 4.

Collections

There are numerous collections of classical music at the intermediate level. A few titles are:

Agay, Denes (ed.)   **The Joy of Baroque** (1974); **The Joy of Classics** (1965); **The Joy of Romantic Piano, Books 1, 2** (1976-77) Yorktown Music Press/Music Sales.

These eighty-page books contain interesting intermediate selections, many of which are unfamiliar. *The Joy of Baroque* has only music from that period. *The Joy of Classics* gives a cross-section of composers from the Baroque through the Romantic period. *The Joy of Romantic Piano* contains works mostly by infrequently taught composers: Arensky, Moscheles, Rimsky-Korsakov, Maykapar, Bizet, etc.

Bastien, James and **Jane Smisor Bastien** (eds.)   **Intermediate Repertoire, Books 1, 2, 3** Neil A. Kjos Music Company (1982).

These three books include works by master composers from each period and original works by the Bastiens in imitative period styles. Each era is clearly explained in pictures depicting the style of the period, as well as information on compositional style, form, keyboard instruments, and composers.

Bastien, James (ed.)   **Piano Literature, Volume 3 for the Intermediate Grades** Neil A. Kjos Music Company (1968).

A cross-section of music from the Baroque, Classical, Romantic, and Contemporary periods is represented by composers J.S. Bach (three inventions), Kirnberger, Haydn, Clementi, Beethoven, Kuhlau (two sonatinas), Schubert, Burgmüller, Heller, Elmenreich ("Spinning Song"), Spindler, Tchaikovsky, Grieg ("Elfin Dance, "Puck," "Sailor's Song"), Schumann, Rebikoff, Kabalevsky, Khachaturian, and Bartók ("Evening in the Country"). The level of difficulty ranges from early intermediate to upper intermediate.

Hinson, Maurice (ed.)   **Dances of Beethoven** Alfred Publishing Company (1986).

This collection provides a definition of dance forms, a guide to pedaling, explanation of ornaments, and information about tempo, dynamics, and articulation. The pieces are "limited" to the allemande, country dance, ecossaise, German dance, minuet, and waltz.

Olson, Lynn Freeman   Applause! Book 1 Alfred Publishing Company (1986).

An excellent collection of showy pieces from all periods include works by C.P.E. Bach, J.S. Bach, W.F. Bach, Bartók, Beethoven, Debussy, Grieg, Heller, Kabalevsky, Khachaturian, Schumann, and Tcherepnin. The level is about early to mid intermediate.

Palmer, Willard and **Amanda Vick Lethco   Introduction to the Masterworks** Alfred Publishing Company (1976).

A useful explanation of style, ornaments, dynamics, and form is provided for the four periods represented in this collection. Composers include J.S. Bach, Couperin, Scarlatti, Handel, Haydn, Mozart, Clementi, Beethoven, Chopin, Schumann, Grieg, Bartók, Satie, and Prokofiev. The music is well-edited and is about right for the early to mid intermediate student.

Editions

Even at the intermediate level the music from the four historical eras (Baroque, Classical, Romantic, Contemporary) is so vast that the discussion of editions can only be dealt with in a cursory manner in this book. J.S. Bach left most of his keyboard music unedited as to tempo, phrasing, and dynamics. Ornamentation was not written out in Baroque music. Therefore, the teacher should make an effort to use reliable editions for music from this period. For further information about editions, see Chapter 19.

The two most frequently studied works by Bach at the intermediate level are the *Twelve Little Preludes* and the *Two-Part Inventions*.

Twelve Little Preludes: Three excellent editions of the preludes are worthy of consideration. The first, titled *18 Short Preludes*, is edited by Willard Palmer (Alfred Publishing Company, 1971) and includes six other preludes. This edition provides an excellent discussion of ornamentation as well as an authentic representation of the music as the composer left it. Editorial suggestions are in light gray print, called a "screen." The second, titled *Kleine Präludien und Fughetten* (Wiener Urtext Edition, 1973) is edited by Walther Dehnhard and is tastefully done with minimal editorial additions. The third, titled *Kleine Präludien Fughetten* (Henle, 1975) is edited by Rudolf Steglich. This edition has a nice clean look with fingering being the only editorial addition. In the last two urtext editions the teacher must be prepared to add dynamics, tempo and phrasing, as well as to supply the realization of the ornaments.

Two-Part Inventions: The popularity of the *Inventions* has led to a profusion of editions. Teachers should compare several of these to discover which one(s) best suits the needs of students. The editions for consideration are those by the following publishers: Alfred Publishng Company (edited by Willard Palmer), Henle (edited by Walther Lampe), C. F. Peters (Ludwig Lanshoff), Kalmus/Belwin/Columbia Pictures Publications (Hans Bischoff), and the Wiener Urtext Edition (Erwin Ratz). It is also useful to consult the original version, which may be obtained in both the Lea Pocket Scores/Belwin/Columbia Pictures Publications and the Dover reprint series.

Sonatina Collections

In teaching sonatinas from the Classical period, the teacher should use reliable editions—ones that are not over-edited. Editions published around the turn of the century tend to place staccato marks at the ends of phrases. In most cases composers did not put these marks in their music. The ends of the phrases should be released smoothly, not in a clipped manner. Editions by Alfred Publishing Company, Henle, C.F. Peters, and Schott are more accurate than some of the others available.

There are many intermediate sonatinas from which to choose. Muzio Clementi (1752-1832) and Friedrich Kuhlau (1786-1832) are two masters who stand out as being the most significant composers of student sonatinas. Other composers include Johann Dussek (1761-1812), Anton Diabelli (1781-1858), Cornelius Gurlitt (1820-1901), and Heinrich Lichner (1829-98).

Although Clementi was a prolific composer who wrote approximately sixty-four piano sonatas and other serious works, he is best remembered for his didactic works, the set of studies called *Gradus ad Parnassum*, and his many sonatinas. The sonatinas are listed as Opus 36 (six sonatinas), Opus 37 (three sonatinas), and Opus 38 (three sonatinas). Because of the easy grade level (early intermediate), Opus 36 is the most frequently studied of the group. The first sonatina in this set is the immensely popular C major.

The sonatinas by Kuhlau are played less than those of Clementi, but they are of comparable quality. The best known Kuhlau sonatinas are Opus 20 (three sonatinas), Opus 55 (six sonatinas), and Opus 88 (two sonatinas).

In addition to individual composer sonatina volumes (all Clementi, etc.), there are numerous sonatina collections available. The complete array of sonatina literature may be seen at a sheet music store, but for quick reference, a few volumes of sonatina collections are listed.

Agay, Denes (ed.) **The Joy of Sonatinas** Yorktown/Music Sales (1972).

The nineteen works in this volume present a sampling of sonatinas from the Classic through Contemporary periods, plus two original works by Mr. Agay. The first half of the book contains sonatinas at about the third year level; the second half contains intermediate level sonatinas by composers Latour, Gurlitt, Beethoven, Kuhlau, Benda, Mozart, and others.

Bastien, James (ed.) **Sonatina Favorites, Books 2, 3** Neil A. Kjos Music Company (1977).

This three-book series contains a representative sampling of sonatinas by various composers. An explanation of sonatina form is provided, and the themes are identified in the sonatinas. Book 2 contains sonatinas by Haslinger, Lichner, Beethoven (F Major), Clementi (Op. 36 No. 2), and Bastien (*Sonatina in Romantic Style*). Book 3 contains works by Clementi, Kuhlau, and Bastien (*Sonatina in Contemporary Style*). The level of difficulty ranges from early intermediate to upper intermediate.

Frey, Martin (ed.) **The New Sonatina Book, Book 1** Schott (Edition 2511; no date given).

This volume contains an excellent cross-section of sonatinas by Haslinger, Schmitt, André, Clementi, Kuhlau, Dussek, and others. The sonatinas are arranged in order of difficulty from early intermediate to upper intermediate and beyond.

Intermediate Students

Glover, David and **Maurice Hinson** (eds.) **Sonatinas for Piano, Book 2** Belwin/Columbia Pictures Publications (1982).

This album contains sonatinas by Benda, Pleyel, Kabalevsky (Op. 27 No. 11), Clementi (Op. 36 Nos. 2 and 3), Cimarosa, Reinecke, Mozart, Diabelli, Haydn, Kirchner, and Handel.

Hinson, Maurice (ed.) **Masters of the Sonatina, Volumes 2, 3** Alfred Publishing Company (1986).

This three-volume series contains a wide selection of sonatinas by well-known composers and others who are more obscure. Volume 2 includes sonatinas by C.P.E. Bach, Beethoven (F Major), Benda, Camidge, Cimarosa, Czerny, Haslinger, Khachaturian (A minor), and Paganelli. Volume 3 contains more difficult sonatinas by Bartók, Cimarosa, Clementi, Handel, Haydn (C Major), Hewitt, Jones, Kabalevsky, Mozart, Myslivecek, and David Wagner.

Köhler, Louis and **Adolf Ruthardt** (eds.) **Sonatina Album, Volumes 1, 2** C. F. Peters (Editions 1233a, 1233b; no date given).

These two large volumes (130 pages, 116 pages) have most of the standard sonatina literature by such composers as Clementi, Diabelli, Dussek, Kuhlau, and others. The music is well-spaced on the page and is well-edited. The level of difficulty ranges from early intermediate to upper intermediate and beyond.

Small, Alan **Sonatina Album** Alfred Publishing Company (1977).

This spiral bound volume contains sonatinas by Beethoven, Clementi (complete Opus 36), Diabelli, Dussek, Haydn, Kuhlau (Op. 20 Nos 1, 2, 3; Op. 55 Nos. 1, 2, 3) and Mozart (K.545).

Although collections provide standard sonatina literature, there are many fine intermediate sonatinas published either in small volumes or as individual sheet music. The following list contains a representative number of these.

Agay, Denes **Sonatina No. 3** Sam Fox (1962).

This three-movement work is written in a mildly contemporary style similar to Kabalevsky. The first movement, *Allegro giocoso*, is an exciting, spirited piece that gains momentum throughout. The second movement, *Andante delicato*, is a stately song. The last movement, *Allegro con brio*, is a spirited rondo which is the most difficult of the three movements. Upper intermediate level.

Agay, Denes **Sonatina Toccata** Boosey & Hawkes (1964).

This whimsical, dashing one-movement piece creates a perpetual motion effect by the rapid eighth note figures that run throughout. Rhythmic variety is achieved by the melodic line composed in varying phrase lengths. Teaching features include balance of melody and accompaniment and varieties of touch. Intermediate level.

Bastien, James   Sonatina in Classic Style, Sonatina in Romantic Style, Sonatina in Contemporary Style   Neil A. Kjos Music Company (1977).

Each sonatina has three contrasting movements. The first movement of *Sonatina in Classic Style*, marked *Allegro moderato*, is useful for teaching phrasing, balance of melody and accompaniment, and rhythmic precision. The second movement, "Arioso," sings a plaintive melody above a simple accompaniment. The third movement, "Rondo," is in $\frac{6}{8}$ meter and uses running eighth and sixteenth notes. Early intermediate level.

The first movement of *Sonatina in Romantic Style*, marked *Allegro moderato*, features a lyrical melody for the A section, and a march-like melody for the B section and closing section. The second movement, "Interlude," sings a plaintive melody with legato accompaniment. The third movement, "Rondo," is spirited and rhythmic in A B A Coda form. Intermediate level.

The first movement of *Sonatina in Contemporary Style*, marked *Allegro con brio*, begins and ends in the E tonality. The repeated notes must be crisp, and played with good facility. The second movement, "Canzonetta," sings a flamenco melody for the A section and has a recitative-like effect in the B section. The third movement, "Tarantella," is the most difficult, requiring clarity and evenness in the running notes and the ability to sustain the energetic pulsation throughout. Upper intermediate level.

Clark, Mary Elizabeth (ed.)   Sonatinas from Myklas, Volumes 1, 2; Second piano parts for Sonatinas, Volumes 1, 2   Myklas Music Press (1977).

These two volumes contain new sonatinas by various composers. Most are written in imitative classic style, others are somewhat romantic or contemporary sounding. All have three movements. The second piano parts (separate publications) provide useful ensemble opportunities. Volume 1 is early intermediate level; Volume 2 is intermediate level.

Gillock, William   Sonatina in Classic Style   Willis Music Company (1959).

Excellent melodic invention, pulsating rhythms, and a fine imitative Classic style have made this a study, recital, and contest favorite. The first movement, *Allegro deciso*, is effective for teaching phrasing, balance of tone (voicing), scales, and rhythmic precision. The second movement, *Andante con espressione*, features written-out turns in the melody line. The last movement, *Allegro vivace*, is a spirited rondo comprising scales, terraced dynamics, and inventive melodic lines. Intermediate level.

Gillock, William   Sonatine   Willis Music Company (1963).

Reminiscent of Debussy and Ravel, this piece sparkles with lyrical melodies and first-rate harmonic progressions. The first movement contains scale passages, chromatic harmonies, and effective phrase structures. The second movement has a dream-like quality with lilting melodies. The last movement is a lively rondo with an exciting ending. Upper intermediate level.

Intermediate Students

Kabalevsky, Dmitri Sonatina, Op. 13 No. 1 Alfred Publishing Company, Kalmus/Belwin/Columbia Pictures Publications, others.

Kabalevsky's prolific student works are among the most useful teaching material; this sonatina is one of his best known and most frequently performed works. The first movement, *Allegro assai e lusingando*, requires articulation and clarity to present a convincing performance. It is comprised of irregular phrase lengths which must be phrased carefully as indicated. The second movement, *Andantino*, requires careful balance of melody and acompaniment. The last movement, *Presto*, is a running toccata-like piece in $\frac{9}{8}$ meter reminiscent of a gigue. The problems of articulation and clarity are present in all movements, and facility and control are required for a convincing performance. Upper intermediate level.

Vandall, Robert Jazz Sonatina Bradley Publications (1984).

This is an exciting three-movement work featuring dashing melodies and dramatic harmonies. The first movement has short right hand melodies accompanied by harmonic fifths in the bass for the A section; the B section is marked *cantabile* and provides an excellent lyrical contrast. The second movement, titled "Blues Plus," has second inversion chords in the right hand and single and double notes in the bass. The third movement, titled "Rondo," has a driving beat and rhythmic vitality. This piece, played whole or in part, makes an outstanding recital, audition, or contest piece. Upper intermediate level.

Contemporary Collections

Contemporary collections frequently contain standard works by such composers as Bartók, Kabalevsky, Tansman, Prokofiev, and Stravinsky. In addition to these there are many individual works by contemporary composers at the intermediate level.

The following list gives a selection of music by contemporary composers. Most of the music is at least mildly contemporary sounding. The list is not intended to be extensive; it merely provides a representative sampling of some of the less frequently taught music by contemporary composers.

Bartók, Béla For Children Boosey & Hawkes (1947), others.

These two volumes consist of eighty-five pieces based on Hungarian and Slavonic children's folk songs. The music is written without octaves and is graded from about late second year through the early advanced level. Many of the pieces appear in collections.

Bloch, Ernest Enfantines Carl Fischer (1934).

These ten pieces rank among the best for teaching children. The music is on the sophisticated side stressing mood, color, and imagination. Favorites are "Lullaby," "Joyous March," and "Teasing." Intermediate to upper intermediate levels.

Clark, Frances and **Louise Goss** (eds.) **Contemporary Piano Literature, Books 3, 4** Birch Tree Group Ltd. (1957).

These two books contain standard contemporary music by Gretchaninoff, Kabalevsky, Bartók, Prokofiev, and Stravinsky, as well as some excellent compositions commissioned for this series by Tcherepnin, Scott, Moore, and Finney. Book 3 is about early intermediate; Book 4 is approximately intermediate level.

Clark, Mary Elizabeth (ed.) **Contempo 2** Myklas Music Press (1974).

This book is a sequel to *Contempo 1* (1972). The idioms introduced include new modes, Japanese scale, and pandiatonic music. Intermediate to upper intermediate levels.

Clark, Mary Elizabeth (ed.) **In the Mode** Myklas Music Press (1974).

Twelve pieces, by various composers, are based on the seven modes that are briefly described on the last two pages of the book. Two duets are included. Intermediate to upper intermediate levels.

Creston, Paul Five Little Dances, Op. 24 G. Schirmer/Hal Leonard (1946).

This little suite of mildly contemporary pieces is appealing in style and mood, and the music is attractively written. Intermediate level.

Dello Joio, Norman Diversions Marks/Hal Leonard (1975).

The five beautifully written pieces in this collection are of varying styles and levels. The "Preludio" opens the suite using linear style and pedal point effects. "Arietta" is a lovely song using a singing melody over a constant pedal point bass. "Caccia" is a bright, animated, dance-style piece using catchy rhythms and fanfare melodies. "Choral" develops from a single line melody into two voices, and ends with four voices. "Giga" is a rollicking dance, starting with thin texture and building to a stunning finish. Mostly upper intermediate or early advanced levels.

Dello Joio, Norman Lyric Pieces for the Young Marks/Hal Leonard (1971).

This distinguished American composer has created a sequel to his popular *Suite for the Young. Lyric Pieces for the Young*, however, does not have the immediate appeal and spontaneity of the earlier collection. Included in this volume are six pieces; the favorite is "Prayer of the Matador." Upper intermediate level.

Diemer, Emma Lou Sound Pictures Boosey & Hawkes (1971).

Comprising ten one-page pieces, this collection explores the realm of contemporary music using such devices as tone-clusters, parallel fourths and fifths, pedal effects, and glissando effects. These sound samplings will give students and teachers a better understanding of music today. Early intermediate level.

Intermediate Students

Dutkiewicz, Andrzej The Puppet Suite Neil A. Kjos Music Company (1984).

This collection of fifteen pieces is a welcome addition to collections of contemporary music. Most of the pieces are in two-part style, some have melody and harmonic accompaniment. Intermediate to upper intermediate levels.

Gillock, William   Lyric Preludes in Romantic Style Birch Tree Group Ltd. (1958).

In the same manner as *Fanfare* (written in Baroque style), these preludes serve as an introduction to the Romantic period. The mostly one-page compositions explore the twelve major and minor keys using parallel relationships. The music is colorful and imaginative. Intermediate to upper intermediate levels.

Kabalevsky, Dmitri   Four Rondos, Op. 60 MCA/Hal Leonard (1960).

This is a superb collection of four contrasting pieces, each depicting a different mood and presenting various pianistic problems. "Rondo-March," the most difficult of the four, is written in sixths and thirds in the right hand and uses dotted rhythms; "Rondo-Dance" is a gracious Allegretto requiring a light, elegant touch; "Rondo-Song" requires a singing tone and much expression; "Rondo-Toccata" is the show piece of the group employing various forms of staccato—it is a driving, virile, exciting solo. This collection is an absolute teaching delight. Intermediate to upper intermediate levels.

Muczynski, Robert   Diversions, Op. 23 G. Schirmer/Hal Leonard (1970).

These nine solos are easier than the *Six Preludes*, Op. 6, but they are also written in the same superlative style. Favorites are numbers 5 and 9 which have wonderful, syncopated, jazzy beats. The entire collection is excellent teaching material. Intermediate level.

Nakada, Yoshineo   Japanese Festival MCA/Hal Leonard (1975).

From Japan comes this excellent collection of seventeen varied pieces. Both European and Japanese styles are employed in these engaging pieces. The level of difficulty progresses from about late second year to early intermediate. The sure-fire hit is "Etude Allegro" requiring forearm rotation. For students who can handle the technical requirements, this is a stunning recital solo.

Noona, Walter and Carol   The Contemporary Performer, Level 4 The Heritage Music Press (1975).

This series of four books is designed to introduce students to idioms of twentieth-century style such as polyrhythms, clusters, polytonalities, twelve-tone rows, and ostinato patterns. The information about the compositional devices is concise and informative.

Poulenc, Francis   Villageoises Salabert/Hal Leonard (1933).

In this delightful collection of six pieces even the titles are charming:

Valse Trolienne (reminiscent of Schubert's *Landler*); *Staccato*, a haunting, fast jaunty melody; *Rustique*, a beautiful tune, fast and light-spirited; *Polka*, full of staccatos and accents; *Petite Rondo*, a spirited, rhythmic three-measure melody repeated four times; *Coda*, a reprise incorporating melodies from the other movements. These pieces are a delight to teach. Intermediate level.

Starer, Robert   Sketches in Color, Set 1 MCA/Hal Leonard (1964).

These seven contemporary style pieces are extraordinarily well-written. All are purposely didactic and feature contemporary writing devices linked with their titles: "Purple," polytonality; "Shades of Blue," diatonic melody against a moving bass in parallel fifths; "Black and White" juxtaposes the pentatonic scale of the black keys to the diatonic scale of the white keys; "Bright Orange" employs parallel harmony and jazz syncopation; "Gray" uses a twelve-tone row; "Pink" is tonal but moves away from the tonal center until the last six bars; "Crimson" uses Bartókish divisions of $\frac{7}{8}$ meter. Although contemporary, these pieces are by no means esoteric, and average or better students find them most appealing.

Waxman, Donald   The New Recital Pageants, Books 1, 2, 3, 4 Galaxy (1986).

This four-book series provides excellent study and recital material in a graded sequence from early intermediate to upper intermediate. These pieces were published previously, but are now arranged in this new edition in a slightly different order than before.

Zeitlin, Poldi and **David Goldberger** (eds.) **Russian Music, Book 3** MCA/Hal Leonard (1967).

The best known piece in this book is Kabalevsky's *Sonatina* in A minor. The other compositions are less known and are by a variety of Russian composers. Four duets are included. Early intermediate to intermediate levels.

Jazz & Popular Collections

Most students enjoy studying a variety of popular style music that contains syncopations and intricate rhythms. The following list of books contains a sampling of jazz and popular styles. However, if students request current hit selections, these can be chosen from arrangers such as Dan Coates (Warner Bros. Publications), Pamela and Robert Schultz (Columbia Pictures Publications), and others.

Agay, Denes   The Joy of Boogie and Blues Yorktown/Music Sales (1968).

This book contains an excellent selection of boogie and blues styles, and also includes the following arranged works—"House of the Rising Sun," "Worried Man Blues," "Bill Bailey Rag," "Frankie and Johnny," and others. Intermediate to upper intermediate levels.

Agay, Denes The Joy of Jazz Yorktown/Music Sales (1964).

The arranged works of such well-known jazz buffs as "Fats" Waller, Dizzy Gillespie, Thelonious Monk, plus a good selection of original music by Denes Agay make this an attractive collection for the intermediate pianist. Chord symbols are given for every piece thus providing an impetus for using the music in a combo. Intermediate to upper intermediate levels.

Bastien, Jane Smisor and **James Bastien Pop Piano Styles, Level 4** Neil A. Kjos Music Company (1980).

Boogie, blues, rag, and disco styles are included in this brief book. Early intermediate level.

Caramia, Tony A Guide for Jazz Piano Harmonization Neil A. Kjos Music Company (1983).

This is an excellent book to learn jazz chords; examples are given for many of the concepts introduced. Lists of jazz pianists and recordings, and suggested jazz repertoire are given.

Caramia, Tony Fascinatin' Rhythms Neil A. Kjos Music Company (1985).

The six pieces in this book utilize a variety of jazz styles. Each piece has helpful suggestions to make learning easier. These are fun pieces to play and perform. Upper intermediate level.

Dennis, Matt Introduction to the Blues (1976), **Jazz Piano Styles** (1973), **Ragtime Piano Styles** (1973), **Rock Piano Styles** (1974) Mel Bay Publications.

These books provide students with a clear insight into four different styles. Mr. Dennis is an authority on popular music, and has written songs for Frank Sinatra, Tony Bennett, and many others. Upper intermediate level.

Edison, Roger Jazz Piano Alfred Publishing Company (1978).

For a student who wants to learn jazz styles, this volume is a useful reference. A complete explanation of chord symbols is given to assist the pianist in improvisational experiences. Upper intermediate level.

Gillock, William New Orleans Jazz Styles, More New Orleans Jazz Styles, Still More New Orleans Jazz Styles Willis Music Company (1965, 1966, 1977).

A long-time resident of New Orleans, Mr. Gillock writes with authority in a variety of blues and jazz styles that can still be heard on Bourbon Street in the French Quarter. All three books are well-written and are immediately appealing to students. The rhythms are tricky and require careful attention to the blues and jazz styles. The music in all three books ranges from intermediate to upper intermediate levels.

Gordon, Louis Jazz for Junior Marks/Hal Leonard (1964).

Excellent jazz styles are featured in this little volume. Special favorites are "Deep Roots," "Blues in C Minor," and "Quiet Scene." The others in the collection are more difficult. Intermediate to upper intermediate levels.

Gordon, Louis Junior Jazz Marks/Hal Leonard (1961).

This book was written before *Jazz for Junior*, and the music is slightly easier. Early intermediate to intermediate levels.

Konowitz, Bert The Complete Rock Piano Method Alfred Publishing Company (1972).

For rock devotees, this ninety-six page volume is a must. "Dig on" to rock techniques (accents, rhythm patterns, etc.), improvisational "licks," and direction application in an abundance of Konowitz solos. Some duets are also provided.

Metis, Frank Rock Modes & Moods Marks/Hal Leonard (1970).

The introductory pages explain modality used in rock music and also explain such divergent styles as hard rock, acid rock, psychedelic rock, folk rock, and soul music. Most of the pieces in the collection are on the difficult side (about upper intermediate), but both "Blues Explosion" and "Happy to Be Home" are easier.

O'Hearn, Arletta Love Jazz Neil A. Kjos Music Company (1981).

Seven pieces are included in this book. The first, "Rock with Jazz," is a mostly two-part piece in unison. "Waltz for a Little Ballerina" has a plaintive melody over a moving bass. "Walking Crooked Blues" is an excellent New Orleans style blues piece. "Drifting" is a languid piece. "A Very Gray Day" is quite melancholy. "Nice 'n Easy" is a lively blues style piece. The last, "Downtown Cakewalk," is an attractive duet. Mid to upper intermediate levels.

INTERMEDIATE TECHNIQUE

The intermediate student will be playing music that requires an adequate technical approach to perform convincingly. Intermediate literature contains scale passages in sonatinas; trills and mordents in Bach's *Two-Part Inventions*; and arpeggios, quick-changing chords, and double note passages in many of the pieces assigned. The student must be prepared to meet these challenges. The new areas will probably be trills and arpeggios. Old concepts will be reconsidered in an expanded view, while the student is introduced to new technical studies.

The intermediate student usually spends several years at this level before progressing to the advanced stage. Therefore, the technical suggestions do not apply to any specific year, but are intended as six general guides:

1. scales
2. arpeggios

3. chords
4. parallel note passages
5. trills
6. technique studies

Scales

Most students will have already played scales, both major and minor, for several years. Now, however, scale practice should be expanded to meet the challenges experienced in intermediate music.

This four-measure excerpt from Kuhlau's *Sonatina*, Op. 55 No. 1 is typical of intermediate scale passages.

Example 1 Typical intermediate scale passage.

These scales must be played evenly and smoothly with a good rhythmic pulse, while at the same time shading dynamics accordingly. To prepare for this type of figure, the student should practice scales independent of literature.

Numerous scale patterns may be devised. They may be practiced in one-, two-, three-, or four-octave spans; in parallel or contrary motion; and in various rhythm patterns.

Example 2 Scale patterns.

a. Two octaves, parallel motion.

b. Three octaves, parallel motion.

Pedagogical Techniques

c. Four octaves, parallel and contrary motion.

d. Two octaves, contrary motion with a two-to-one ratio.

e. Two octaves, contrary motion with a one-to-two ratio.

Intermediate Students

184

The two-octave pattern is a basic one that probably will have been learned for some scales within the first few years of lessons. The intermediate student should be able to play all scales, major and minor, two octaves in parallel motion. The three-octave pattern provides an opportunity to play scales in triplets. The four-octave pattern incorporates the symmetry of contrary motion while developing a feeling for a large keyboard span. This pattern is an excellent one and should be learned by serious students for all scales. The two-to-one ratio patterns provide rhythmic variety that aids in developing coordination. These five patterns are only samplings of scale possibilities; the creative teacher should devise others.

Scales should not be practiced in an unimaginative manner. The teacher should suggest several ways of varying scale practice that will aid the student. For example, facility in running passages will be developed by practicing scales at various tempos, from slow to fast. The student will develop a feeling for graded dynamics by practicing scales with crescendos and decrescendos. Likewise, various touches and rhythm patterns incorporated into scale practice will be helpful.

For touch, scales may be practiced all legato, all staccato, one hand legato and the other staccato (Example 3a), or all legato with one hand louder than the other (Example 3b). Rhythmic effects may be produced by displacement of the beat through the use of accents (Example 3c). Also, dotted rhythms (Example 3d) and syncopated rhythms may be used (Example 3e).

Example 3 Scale practice variations.

a. Staccato and legato touch combined.

b. One hand louder than the other.

Pedagogical Techniques

c. Off-beat accents.

d. Dotted rhythms.

e. Syncopated rhythms.

These suggestions, and others offered by the teacher, will make scales more interesting and help relieve the monotony of scale practice.

Arpeggios

The intermediate pianist should practice arpeggios in preparation for literature containing these figures. A good example is found in Beethoven's *Für Elise* (Example 4).

Example 4 Arpeggio passage.

Intermediate Students

Students often have difficulty playing the arpeggio smoothly in this passage. A break in the legato tone often is heard in student performances between fingers 3 and 1 in the right hand. This is the inherent problem in playing arpeggios; the thumb must turn under quickly and smoothly to create the legato effect. Younger students (seven-nine years old) probably will not be able to play arpeggios in this manner, because their fingers are too short and their hands are too small. However, the intermediate student has a bigger reach, and can now begin to practice arpeggios seriously.

Some preparatory arpeggio exercises were suggested in Chapter 8 (Examples 13 and 14). It is helpful for younger students (third year students) to practice these preparatory drills before assigning the full arpeggio.

The intermediate pianist should learn all arpeggios at least two octaves in root position and the other inversions as shown in Example 5. Both major and minor arpeggios should be studied. The fourth finger is circled because students frequently play 3 instead of 4.

Example 5 Two-octave arpeggios.

The four-octave arpeggio (Example 6) should be assigned to serious students. The rhythm is optional; the pattern may be played either as triplets or as four eighth notes.

In addition to the root position given here, inversions may also be learned. Also, contrary motion can be incorporated by using the pattern shown in Example 2c: four octaves up and down, two octaves up and down in parallel motion, then two octaves in contrary motion and two octaves in parallel motion.

Chords

Generally, chord playing is not considered as important as scales and arpeggios. However, chord facility will become increasingly demanding for the intermediate pianist. Intermediate literature such as Kabalevsky's

Example 6 Four-octave arpeggio.

Toccatina, Heller's *Avalanche*, Schumann's *Norse Song*, and Grieg's *Sailor's Song* all contain quick-changing chords. The student will benefit from practicing quick-changing chords as preparation for this and other intermediate literature.

Kabalevsky's *Toccatina* (Example 7a) is a frequently taught early intermediate piece. It is an excellent study in rapidly changing first inversion triads. Grieg's *Sailor Song* (Example 7b) is an upper intermediate piece which contains some awkward chord changes and large reaches. The Kabalevsky and Grieg pieces are representative of intermediate chord pieces, so they are good models for designing chord studies.

The student probably has been introduced to triads and inversions prior to the intermediate grades. However, it is now important to be fluent with *all* positions, both major and minor. It is helpful to learn each inversion as an individual unit, isolated from the pattern of root position, first inversion, second inversion. Learn the first inversion triads ascending by half steps as shown in Example 8. Once these are learned, exercises can be related to this pattern.

Example 7 "Chord pieces" from upper intermediate literature.

a. Kabalevsky's *Toccatina*, Op. 27 No.7.

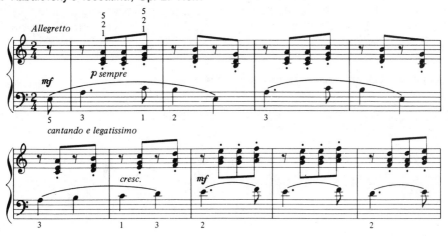

Intermediate Students

b. Grieg's *Sailor's Song*, Op. 68 No. 1.

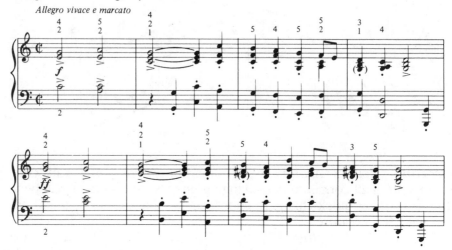

Example 8 Major first inversion triads in ascending half steps.

The inversions should be practiced with *both* hands, first each hand alone, then together. The inversions should be memorized, so that the student can devote full attention to using these chords in exercises without stopping to figure out each chord.

The patterns in Example 9 provide varied rhythmic experiences using the inversions. The hand(s) should move rapidly from one octave to the next, and be in position over the keys ready to play without losing time.

Example 9 First inversion triad rhythm patterns.

Pedagogical Techniques

Once the major first inversion triads have been learned, learn the minor inversions as shown in Example 10. The same exercises in Example 9 can be played in minor.

Example 10   Minor first inversion triads in ascending half steps.

Both major and minor second inversion triads should also be learned. The rhythm exercises may also be applied to these triads.

Example 11   Second inversion triads in ascending half steps.

a. Major

b. Minor

When the triads and inversions were first introduced (probably second year) it was not necessary to play them fast, but merely to learn the correct fingering and become familiar with the pattern. Now, however, an expanded concept may be applied to these chords to increase the student's facility. The student should practice the pattern shown in Example 12 slowly and increase the tempo with each repetition.

Example 12   Triad and inversion patterns.

a.   **b.**

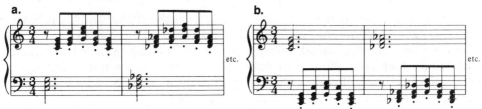

Intermediate Students

Various rhythms may be incorporated in triad and inversion patterns such as those shown in Example 13. They require quick action to get from one chord to another. The student must anticipate each new position so there will be no delay in playing. Minor chords should also be practiced in this manner. Additional rhythm patterns may be suggested.

Example 13   Triad and inversion rhythm patterns.

Diminished seventh chords will become more frequently used in intermediate literature. Therefore, it is helpful to practice all twelve diminished chords shown in Example 14. These chords should be *memorized*.

Example 14   The twelve diminished seventh chords.

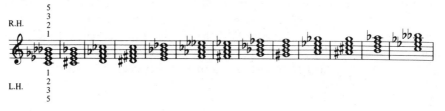

Practice these chords first with one hand, then the other, and then both hands together. A diminished chord is comprised of minor thirds, and as always with spelling chords, they have to be spelled using every other alphabet letter, thus the use of many double flats. Once the diminished sevenths have been learned, use them in patterns shown in Example 15, similar to those suggested for first inversion triads.

Pedagogical Techniques

Example 15 Diminished seventh chord patterns.

When the root position diminished sevenths have been thoroughly learned, practice the inversions as shown in Example 16.

Example 16 Diminished seventh chord inversions.

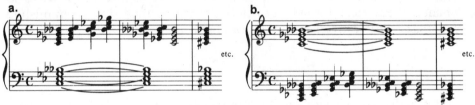

The following series of dominant seventh chord inversions should be memorized in all positions. Note the alternative fingerings given for some of the chords.

Example 17 Dominant seventh chord inversions, ascending by half steps.

Intermediate Students

c.

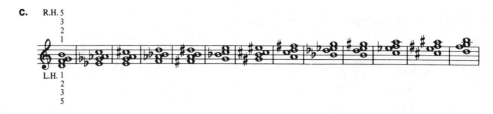

d.

Extensive drill on chords during the intermediate years will provide a solid background. Not only will it improve finger facility, but it will also enhance theoretical knowledge of basic chord inversions, diminished sevenths and their inversions, and dominant sevenths and their inversions.

Parallel Passages

Intermediate music such as Beethoven's *Minuet in G* (Example 18) contains some difficult parallel thirds and sixths.

Example 18   Parallel thirds and sixths in literature.

Parallel thirds probably will have been introduced during the first few years of lessons, but expanded drills are needed at this point. The following exercises can be considered.

Example 19 Parallel third exercises.

Practice these exercises hands separately, then together. On each repetition increase the tempo from slow to fast. Play them with a good firm tone.

Parallel sixths usually fall into the category of advanced technique. However, some drill should be given to the intermediate student. The first exercise presented in Example 20 is based on the sixths in the Beethoven *Minuet in G*. Even students with small hands will be able to play Example 20a because the thumb slides up and down in half steps. The second exercise (Example 20b) should be given only to those students who have big stretches between fingers 2 and 5. These two studies provide a basic introduction to the problem of playing parallel sixths. The teacher may assign others as necessary.

Intermediate Students

Example 20 Parallel sixth exercises.

Trills

Trills are an essential part of piano playing, but often no preparation is given to the student. Bach's *Two-Part Invention* Number 4 (Example 21) contains trills for both hands. They are difficult to play evenly!

A trill may be just a few notes or many notes extending over several measures, as in the Invention No. 4. One of the commonly used short trills found in Bach's works is shown in Example 22. This trill is always started on the upper note and therefore has at least four notes in its "realization."

Example 21 Trills in each hand.

Pedagogical Techniques

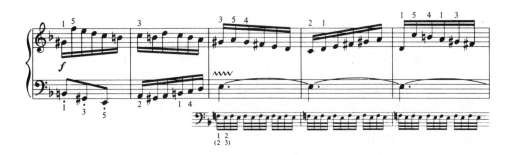

Example 22 Short trill sign often found in Bach's works.

This trill sign is used in the first two measures of the *Two-Part Invention*, Number 1.

Example 23 Trill sign in literature.

The exercise in Example 24 serves as a preparatory drill for Bach's trills. The choice of fingering is determined by the position of the notes before

Example 24 Preparatory trill exercise.

Intermediate Students

196

and after the trill, the tempo, and the particular preference of the student or teacher. The fingerings 3 2, 2 1, or 3 1 are usually used for trills.

The trill with a "termination" (suffix) is commonly used by many composers. Bach either wrote out this figure or used a sign added to the trill symbol: ᴧᴧᵧ The termination consists of two notes added to the trill; these should be played at the same speed as the trill.

Haydn, Mozart, Beethoven, and other composers frequently used a *tr* sign with the termination indicated, instead of the Bach symbol. The following exercise may be practiced as a preparatory drill for this particular trill.

Example 25 Trill with a termination.

Example 26 Exercise for trill with termination.

The trill with a "prefix" from *below* is also commonly found in Baroque music, especially in Bach's works, as well as by other composers later on. Bach used a symbol (⌒ᴧᴧᴧ) for this figure frequently found in both the *Short Preludes* and the *Two-Part Inventions*.

The trill with "prefix" from *above* (⌣ᴧᴧ) is commonly used in Bach's music.

Example 27 Trill with prefix from below.

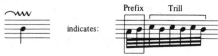

Example 28 Trill with prefix from above.

It is important for the student to *understand* the preceding trill symbols and to play them correctly when indicated in intermediate or advanced literature. As an aid to understanding, the teacher should invent exercises based on these examples. In this manner not only will the problems be solved, but the student will have a better understanding of the trills.

Some additional trill exercises are shown; the teacher may suggest others. In the first exercise (Example 29) the trill should be practiced with the three finger combinations suggested. The second exercise provides trill experience for all fingers, even 4 5 which are seldom used in context. The third exercise follows the chromatic scale fingering: 3 on all the black keys; 1 on the white keys except for adjacent whites—E F and B C, which are played with right hand 1 2 and left hand 2 1.

Example 29   Trills.

a. Using only two fingers.

b. Using all fingers.

c. Chromatic.

Technique Studies

The following list has a variety of intermediate technique books. Some of the books contain exercises, others have etudes, and some include both exercises and etudes.

Exercise Books

Bastien, James and **Jane Smisor Bastien**   Intermediate Technic, Books 1, 2, 3   Neil A. Kjos Music Company (1983).

These three books contain a variety of original exercises by the Bastiens, as well as studies by Czerny, Duvernoy, Köhler, LeCouppey, Schmitt, Pischna, Gurlitt, Concone, Berens, Burgmüller, and Heller.

Intermediate Students

Special emphasis is given to scales, phrasing, notation, repeated notes, wrist staccato, part playing, double note passages, and arpeggios.

Last, Joan Freedom Technique, Books 2, 3 Oxford University Press (1971).

Book 2 provides a number of excellent keyboard experiences at the intermediate level. The exercises stress such items as chords for arm weight, rotation, thirds, scale turns, broken chords, agility studies, repeated note studies, part playing, chromatic and diatonic sequences, expansion studies, and a variety of rhythm patterns. *Book 3* is more difficult, at least upper intermediate level, and provides exercises that can serve to bridge the gap between the upper intermediate and advanced levels. Included are exercises for arm weight, rotation, wide skips, lateral movement for smooth thumb turns in arpeggios, parallel thirds, contractions and expansions, chord sequences, chromatic passages, broken octaves, slurs, rhythmic groupings, repeated notes, trill preparation studies, and octave studies.

Pischna, Johann (Bernard Wolff, ed.) **The Little Pischna** G. Schirmer/Hal Leonard (1908).

The exercises in this volume are similar to the more difficult *60 Progressive Technical Studies* in that they are mostly five-finger drills that are transposed through all the keys. Many exercises require some fingers to "hold" while others move. Also included are various scales, thirds, sixths, and arpeggios.

Pischna, Johann 60 Progressive Technical Studies G. Schirmer/Hal Leonard (1904).

This has been a standard technique collection for many years. The studies feature trills, scales, chords, and arpeggios, and are useful for serious students of better than average ability. The level is at least upper intermediate and beyond.

Schmitt, Alloys (Willard Palmer, ed.) **Preparatory Exercises**, Op. 16 Alfred Publishing Company (1977).

This contains a variety of exercises to develop an even touch. Also included are all major and minor scales, the chromatic scale, and scales in parallel thirds and sixths.

Etude Books
Bastien, James (ed.) **Czerny and Hanon** Neil A. Kjos Music Company (1970).

Included are twenty Czerny studies and the first twenty Hanon exercises. The Czerny studies range from early intermediate to intermediate levels.

Burgmüller, Johann Friedrich 25 Progressive Pieces, Op. 100 Alfred Publishing Company (1973), others.

These etudes serve the dual function of providing easy studies and reading material. The pieces range in difficulty from early intermediate to intermediate levels.

Czerny, Carl The School of Velocity, Op. 299 Alfred Publishing Company (1974), others.

Scales, arpeggios, and various other techniques are incorporated in these well-known studies. Intermediate to upper intermediate levels.

Duvernoy, Jean Baptiste École du Méchanisme, Op. 120 C. F. Peters.

These fifteen etudes include scale passages, arpeggios, etudes for rotation, and one etude using the chromatic scale. Intermediate to upper intermediate levels.

Waxman Donald Fifty Etudes, Books 1, 2, 3, 4 Galaxy (1976).

For the teacher who has become tired of Burgmüller, Czerny, et al, these studies provide welcome relief. The etudes are spread throughout the four books in a progressive order of difficulty. The purpose of each etude is labeled, such as interlocking scales, repeated notes, broken thirds, etc. Some of the etudes have contemporary sounds and effects. The first two books are the intermediate and upper intermediate levels, the remaining two are much more difficult.

INTERMEDIATE THEORY

The purpose of including theory as a basic ingredient in the music program is to make students musically literate. They should be able to analyze the music studied regarding chordal structure, key, interval relationships, modulation, etc. This knowledge will assist students in reading, memorizing, and performing. Basic intervals, key signatures, chords (major, minor, augmented, diminished), scales, inversions of triads and other elements of theory should be continually studied. Keyboard harmony, sight-reading, ear training, dictation, and creative work can be presented in the theory class. Ensemble playing can also be incorporated.

New theoretical concepts to be added during the intermediate years are:

1. recognizing triads of minor scales
2. learning figured bass for triads and inversions
3. recognizing seventh chords
4. learning figured bass for dominant seventh chords

5. learning to modulate
6. learning cadence patterns

Triads of Minor Scales

A triad may be built on each degree of the minor scale as shown in Example 30. The triads are either major, minor, diminished, or augmented. Have the student write these chords in a theory book or on staff paper until they are thoroughly learned.

Example 30 Triads of the minor scale.

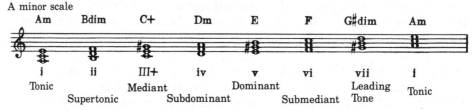

Figured Bass for Triads & Inversions

A figured bass is a method of music shorthand used to indicate the *position* of a chord. Arabic numerals are used to identify the intervals above the bottom note. Give students an example of a triad in root position, first inversion, and second inversion as shown in Example 31.

Example 31 Figured bass indicates intervals above the lowest note.

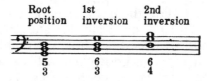

Next, give an example of all the triads in a major scale such as Example 32. Explain that first inversion chords usually are indicated only by the number 6; therefore, the numbers $^6_3$ are abbreviated to 6.

Seventh Chords

Root position seventh chords have four tones: a root, third, fifth, and a seventh. A seventh chord has a triad of some kind plus a note a seventh above the root (Example 33).

Example 32 Figured bass for triads in G major scale.

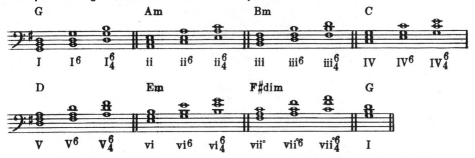

Example 33 Seventh chord in root position.

There are five basic kinds of seventh chords. The triads will be major, minor, half-diminished, diminished; the sevenths may be major, minor, or diminished. See Example 34.

These seventh chords may be practiced in a five-chord sequence as shown in Example 35. This pattern should be practiced in all keys. In addition, they should be written on staff paper.

Figured Bass for Dominant Seventh Chords

It is important for students to learn the correct figured bass for all positions of the dominant seventh chord These same numbers can be applied to any other seventh chord. See Example 36.

Modulation

The transition from one tonality to another is called modulation. This is often done by playing the dominant of the "new" key and resolving to the tonic in the new key. The "new" dominant is called a *secondary dominant*. The chord symbols remain the same for secondary dominants. The Roman numerals, however, are used in relation to the new key: V^7 *of V* (modulating to the key of the dominant); V^7 *of IV* (modulating to the key of the subdominant). Modulations to both the dominant and subdominant are quite common. Students should understand the process and be able to play this type of modulation (Example 37) in all keys.

Intermediate Students

Example 34 Five kinds of seventh chords.

C M7 (chord symbol)

Major Triad — Major seventh

C7 (chord symbol)

Major Triad — minor seventh

C m7 (chord symbol)

minor triad — minor seventh

C ⌀7 (chord symbol)

half-diminished triad — minor seventh

C dim.7 (chord symbol)

diminished triad — diminished seventh

Example 35 Seventh chord patterns in C major scale.

C M7   C7   C m7   C ⌀7   C dim.7   C♯ M7   etc.

Example 36 Figured bass for dominant seventh chord and inversions in the key of C, either Major or minor.

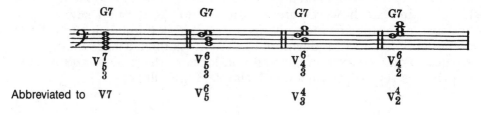

G7   G7   G7   G7

$V^7_5{}_3$ $V^6_5{}_3$ $V^6_4{}_3$ $V^6_4{}_2$

Abbreviated to $V7$ V^6_5 V^4_3 V^4_2

Pedagogical Techniques

Example 37 Modulations.

To the dominant.

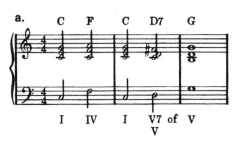

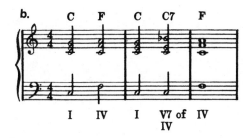

To the subdominant.

Cadence Patterns

A cadence is the close (ending) of a musical phrase. Cadences define sections and are similar to punctuation marks used in literature. The three cadences used most frequently are the *authentic, half,* and *plagal.*

Example 38 Cadence patterns.

a. Authentic cadence: V I or V⁷ I.

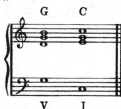

b. Half cadence: I V or IV V or ii V.

c. Plagal cadence: IV I.

Intermediate Students

The teacher should provide students with examples of cadence patterns in the standard music literature, such as those in Example 39.

Example 39 Cadence patterns from standard literature.

a. From Beethoven's *Sonatina in G*.

b. From Pleyel's *Minuet*.

c. From Diabelli's *Bagatelle*.

Only a few theory books provide explanations of modulation and cadence patterns. The intermediate student will benefit from the examples given in *Intermediate Theory, Books 2* and *3* by James Bastien (Neil A. Kjos Music Company, 1983), and *Theory Papers, Book 4* by Robert Pace (Lee Roberts Music Publications, 1985).

FOR DISCUSSION & ASSIGNMENT

1. Would you assign repertoire anthologies or individual composer volumes? Why?

2. How important are editions for intermediate students?
3. Does popular music have a place in the music program?
4. Use an intermediate student(s) to demonstrate the following technical items: a variety of scale patterns, arpeggio patterns, chord drills, parallel note passages, and a variety of trill exercises. Which items do you consider most important? Why? List other technical considerations.
5. In addition to the theory items discussed in this chapter, what others would you include for intermediate students?
6. At a music store or pedagogy library, make a survey of intermediate repertoire books. Present several books other than those listed in this chapter, and tell why they would be useful for intermediate students.
7. From your experience examining intermediate literature, compose an intermediate solo and point out the teaching features.

PART THREE

Special Subjects

The Piano Preparatory Department 10

by E. Gregory Nagode

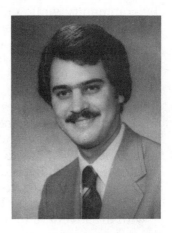

E. Gregory Nagode is Head of Piano Pedagogy, Director of the Piano Preparatory Department, and Associate Professor at the Meadows School of the Arts, Southern Methodist University, Dallas, Texas. Prior to his appointment at SMU, he served on the faculties at Louisiana State University and East Carolina University. He has degrees from Lawrence University, the University of Illinois, and Northwestern University. Mr. Nagode has extensive experience teaching precollege students, the adult beginner, and piano pedagogy. He has been active in the development of piano pedagogy degree programs and teaching practicums. Nagode is a frequent workshop clinician for many local, state, and national convention programs. He has coordinated many piano contests and festivals and is a frequent adjudicator for these events. An active member of MTNA, Mr. Nagode has held many state offices in both the North Carolina Music Teachers Association and the Louisiana Music Teachers Association. He is also the founder and past president of the Greenville, North Carolina Piano Teachers Association.

The piano preparatory department is an ideal setting for instructional opportunities at the precollege level of study. Commonly affiliated with a college, university, or conservatory, a number of fine preparatory departments throughout the country offer quality instruction in piano, voice, and orchestral instruments. As a service to the local community, non-credit instruction can be tailored for students who plan to pursue professional careers in music and for those who want to enrich their lives through a greater understanding of music.

The size and scope of a preparatory department is determined by the available instructional resources including classroom facilities, staff, and the overall function or purpose of the department. Two types of preparatory programs have emerged during the twentieth century. The first type of program has been developed primarily to serve the needs of the community while utilizing the expertise of highly trained university faculty. Additional professional staff members are employed on a full- or part-time basis as these programs grow in size. Students enrolled in such programs generally receive private instruction once a week; group lessons may or may not be available.

A second type of preparatory department is evolving as the traditional college degree undergoes a gradual change in emphasis. More and more university faculties are becoming aware of the need for quality teacher training. Throughout the country, a consensus has emerged that the college degree candidate *must* acquire both performance and pedagogy training. Such training is commonly associated with the field of piano pedagogy, thanks in part to the efforts and enthusiasm generated by the National Conference on Piano Pedagogy.

With the advent of more extensive piano pedagogy course offerings and the proliferation of undergraduate and graduate piano pedagogy degrees, the preparatory department can fulfill an added dimension in its scope and function as a resource center for teacher training. As an integral part of the preparatory department, piano laboratory programs provide an unique model of piano instruction for college students to observe and teach within a well-supervised teaching environment.

In many instances, universities are receptive to pedagogy degree offerings but do not have a well-established preparatory department. In such cases, piano laboratory programs have been developed with a limited precollege student enrollment. The main purpose of these programs is to accommodate the needs of the pedagogy degree program. Within either framework, however, degree candidates specializing in the field of piano pedagogy can effectively serve as teaching interns by observing and assisting the professional staff with various phases of the instruction.

INSTRUCTIONAL OFFERINGS

The piano preparatory department can offer comprehensive piano instructruction for students of all ages and levels from preschool through adult. Early childhood specialists have become increasingly aware of the learning capabilities of the preschool child and endorse music instruction at this level. Music readiness classes for very young children provide an excellent introduction to the world of music. Most programs designed for preschool students consist of one weekly forty-five- or sixty-minute group lesson. The group size is often limited to between six and twelve children.

The preschool curriculum does not consist of piano instruction in the traditional sense. Typically, preschool learning includes a wide variety of activities that emphasize rhythm and movement response, large muscle coordination, ensemble singing, listening skills, visual recognition drills, and preparation for music reading. Many universities are ideally suited to offer specialized instruction at this level because of their involvement in early childhood research. Further, most schools have facilities that are well-suited for large group learning activities. Scheduling is facilitated because classes can be offered during morning or early afternoon hours, when the facilities are more readily available.

A variety of instructional programs are available for the average-age beginner and for continuing students who are enrolled at the elementary level of piano study. With increased studio and classroom space, many preparatory departments are able to offer a unique combination of group and private lessons. One of the more popular program offerings consists of two lessons per week, including ninety minutes of lesson time divided between group and private instruction. The private lesson concentrates on the development of repertoire, technique, and practice habits. In addition, the private lesson reinforces concepts presented in the class lesson and provides for the individual music-learning needs of each child. The group lesson offers musical experiences that further heighten the child's awareness of music and are not readily available in the private lesson. These include weekly student performances, emphasis on ear training and listening skills, music theory, and creative musicianship activities. The group lesson not only enhances the content of the private lesson but also promotes peer motivation.

Instructional formats vary from school to school and are dependent upon many factors. Most teachers prefer that students attend the group and private lesson on different days of the week. If the group lesson is scheduled early in the week, lesson time can be spent presenting new concepts that will be explored later in the week during the private lesson. Organizing such classes by concepts and common learning experiences is an especially effective way to incorporate group lessons in the program offerings of the preparatory program. It is common practice for beginning students to be placed in well-matched groups based on age, grade in school, and ability levels. As students become more proficient, the group may or may not continue to be well-matched and it is imperative that teachers reserve the right to regroup students as necessary. Group size is best between four to ten students.

Piano study for the intermediate level student continues the comprehensive training that was begun at the elementary level. Two instructional

The Piano Preparatory Department

plans are popular. Some programs continue the same combination of weekly group and private lessons that was offered at the elementary level. Another effective plan consists of weekly private lessons for three weeks, followed by a monthly group class in the fourth week. The latter can provide a more flexible format since student learning rates and individual needs become more pronounced and varied at the intermediate level.

As students become older and more proficient with their piano skills, many teachers prefer to increase the duration of the private lesson to forty-five or sixty minutes. The length of the monthly group class may vary from one hour to an hour and a half, depending upon the number of students enrolled. In any case, a comprehensive program of instruction should be offered that includes a balance of repertoire, technique, musicianship skills, and regular performance opportunities.

Older Beginners

Piano study for the older beginner is a growing phenomenon. This segment of the community may include teenagers, adults, and senior citizens. While many traditionally-trained independent teachers prefer teaching the average-age beginner and the more advanced intermediate level student, the preparatory department often employs instructors whose preference and training uniquely qualify them to teach the older beginner. Many adult students are motivated to study piano to satisfy personal enjoyment needs. Adult students are especially enjoyable to teach because of their love of music, and the desire to fulfill both their intellectual curiosity and aesthetic and emotional needs of self-expression.

Adult students may include beginners with no previous piano experience, those who studied piano as a child, and those who have already reached an intermediate or advanced level of ability. Weekly group piano lessons for beginning adult students are especially popular. Most colleges and universities have electronic piano labs that provide excellent facilities for group adult classes. The curriculm emphasizes the development of reading skills, an understanding of basic music fundamentals, and a wide range of keyboard experiences that enhance one's personal enjoyment. The more advanced adult student often benefits more from private lessons.

Music Theory

The preparatory department also provides an ideal setting for the study of music theory. Limited by the length of the private lesson, more and more independent music teachers are seeking opportunities that will enhance their students' understanding and knowledge of music theory. Such classes provide a unique service for teachers and can be conveniently scheduled on Saturday mornings and organized by age and level.

Special Subjects

Recitals

A preparatory department can offer many opportunities for frequent public performances. Because of the large enrollment and use of university facilities, recitals can be regularly scheduled throughout the year. A variety of different recital formats can provide enjoyable performance experiences for students. They include special theme recitals, ensemble recitals, and group demonstration performances. The demonstration program provides an effective means to acquaint parents with the learning activities that their children are experiencing.

PERSONNEL & ADMINISTRATION

The success of a preparatory department is dependent upon diverse course offerings, specialized teaching skills of the faculty, and the overall administration and organization of the department. A well-staffed preparatory department may include faculty specialists whose expertise enables the school to provide varied courses of study. The professional teaching staff consists of the piano pedagogy specialist and full- and part-time adjunct instructors. Specialized instructors are often employed to teach preschool and adult students. In the case of those schools that offer a pedagogy degree and supervised teaching internships, degree candidates are considered part of the preparatory teaching staff. Teaching interns are enrolled in an internship course for credit and therefore should not be given any remuneration.

As preparatory department enrollments increase, the demand for additional faculty can be fulfilled by the employment of outstanding university pedagogy degree graduates. Their unique training and familiarity with the program during their internship is especially beneficial to the overall success of the preparatory department.

The piano preparatory department is usually administered in one of two ways, depending upon university policy. Some schools rely on the services of the Continuing Education Division, while others operate as an extension of the music department. Budgetary considerations can be accomplished in a variety of ways and must be examined carefully. Some preparatory departments are financially independent and self-supporting, while others seek partial funding from the music department. Ideally, the budgetary needs of the preparatory department should be clearly defined from the outset. If there is a profit margin, funds could be budgeted for a well-equipped pedagogy resource center that includes a library of pedagogy materials.

Directing a piano preparatory department is a multi-faceted task which requires organizational skills. One person usually serves as director of the preparatory program. The administrative personnel may also include full- or part-time secretarial assistance. There is ample need in a moderate-to-

The Piano Preparatory Department

large-sized preparatory department for one person to handle lesson inquiries, telephone communications, letters, and the management of instructional and bookkeeping records.

The preparatory department must be as sensitive to the needs of professional studio management as is the independent studio teacher. Policies regarding missed lessons, enrollment and attendance, grouping, the purchase of music, and tuition and fees must be formulated and evaluated annually. Prior to instruction, administrative responsibilities include developing program offerings, studio and instructional policies, establishing a public relations and recruitment plan, conducting placement auditions and parent interviews, and scheduling lessons. The scheduling of lessons must take into account the use of facilities and the coordination of university and public school calendars.

Tuition fees should be based on local economic conditions. Teaching salaries and hourly wages are generally set by the standard of living and the current rates charged by local independent music teachers. No attempt should be made to undercut the local professional music teacher.

CURRICULUM & THE PEDAGOGY INTERNSHIP

Within the parameters of most preparatory departments, the individual teacher is responsible for curricular decisions and weekly assignments. However, as an increasing number of preparatory programs become associated with pedagogy degree internships, curricular decisions become a more complex issue and require continuous supervision. Within this role, the director of the preparatory program is faced with the task of guiding the learning environments of both the pedagogy student intern and the precollege pupil. Thus, the director or supervising teacher must establish specific learning objectives in an effort to unify and maintain a superior instructional program. Protecting the quality of each student's music study must be of primary concern.

Many piano laboratory programs have adopted standardized curriculums to insure a sense of continuity within the preparatory department. Detailed curriculum guides can be designed for each level of study. One quickly discovers that the development of curricular guides is an evolutionary process that requires constant monitoring and refinement. Further, a wide range of ability exists due to the natural differences in the learning needs of both pupils and pedagogy student interns. With these factors in mind, it is more advantageous to utilize a general format that insures curricular flexibility.

An effective curriculum guide can be organized by school grade and/or number of years of study. Specific goals for each level of study can be outlined in a variety of instructional categories including repertoire, technique, theory and musicianship skills, and sight-reading assignments.

To enhance the effectiveness of such instructional formats, the preparatory department can sponsor student achievement tests or "rallies" at the end of each school year. Many MTNA state affiliates sponsor such activities to provide performance goals for students and curricular goals for teachers.

The pedagogy internship creates an experience in which each intern comes face-to-face with questions regarding many aspects of teaching. Having a curriculum guide for each level of instruction minimizes the teaching task for each intern. However, one is still faced with the questions of effective presentational strategies, the development of effective learning activities, motivational techniques, and individual learning needs. If the preparatory department offers a combination of weekly group and private instruction, the pedagogy internship can be ideally structured and supervised. The staff and/or supervising teacher is responsible for teaching the group lesson, planning weekly assignments at each level, and teaching one private lesson from each group. The remaining students from each group can be taught by the pedagogy intern. This arrangement gives student teachers the opportunity to observe and teach at the same level of instruction.

Supervising teachers are responsible for guiding and evaluating the direction of learning for the pedagogy interns and their pupils. This can be accomplished in a variety of ways. A pre-teaching conference conducted by the staff teacher provides weekly or periodic opportunities for the supervising teacher to interact directly with the pedagogy interns. These conferences can be designed to serve many purposes:

1. to assist weekly lesson planning
2. to demonstrate and explore creative teaching strategies that are directly related to an actual assigment
3. to discuss common teaching or learning problems
4. to monitor the progress of the pedagogy interns' teaching skills

Staff teachers should make arrangements to periodically observe the teaching of each pedagogy intern on an individual basis. Videotaping provides an excellent form of observation. After each observation, the staff teacher can meet with the teaching intern and provide constructive feedback.

SUMMARY

Successful preparatory departments are designed to offer comprehensive music instruction for students of all ages. As an instructional center, the preparatory department not only influences the training of young performers but fulfills an added dimension in the training of young teachers. The preparatory department helps to meet today's challenges of teacher

The Piano Preparatory Department

training by creating stimulating learning opportunities for college students as they prepare for their future profession as piano teachers. These unique learning opportunities enhance the music instructional needs of the local community and prove to be worthwhile endeavors for the university music department.

The College Group Piano Program for Music Majors 11

by E. Gregory Nagode

Group piano programs have been established at an increasing number of colleges and universities in the past thirty years as more and more schools require a keyboard proficiency of all undergraduate music majors. A majority of schools currently offer group piano instruction to three types of students: non-keyboard music majors, beginning non-music majors, and keyboard majors. The group setting, rather than private study, is viewed as a practical and effective means for the development of keyboard musicianship skills.

Group piano instruction at the college level is not a new phenomenon. Class piano procedures were well-established by Raymond Burrows, a pioneer in the field during the first half of the twentieth century. As a faculty member at Teachers College, Columbia University, he taught group piano classes, group pedagogy courses, and wrote extensively on group piano instruction. He advocated class piano as an ideal setting for the development of functional keyboard skills. Contemporary group piano techniques have been greatly refined and influenced in part by the significant contributions of Robert Pace, James Lyke, and Lawrence Rast.

The development of functional keyboard skills and basic keyboard facility is the primary instructional focus of the college group piano program. Such courses correlate learning activities from the following categories: theoretical concepts, scales and chords; sight-reading, transposition, and score reading; and harmonization and improvisation. The study of repertoire and technique further enhances the student's pianistic facility at this level of study. Group piano courses are considered part of a core degree requirement within the undergraduate music curriculum and are offered as requirements along with music theory courses in the freshman and sophomore years of study. In many cases, these courses are coordinated with one another and are designed to develop the student's understanding of musical and theoretical concepts.

COURSE OFFERINGS

Specialized course offerings are designed to meet the needs of students with varying pianistic abilities and backgrounds. Keyboard proficiency requirements may vary depending on a student's major course of study. The standard group piano curriculum is arranged in progressive levels of study and is usually offered as a four-semester course sequence for the non-keyboard music major. Classes generally meet for fifty minutes, two or three times per week. Depending upon the particular school, course credit varies from one to two credits per semester.

Class enrollment is determined by room size, the number of available pianos, budgetary considerations, level of study, and teacher preference. Though a large number of students can be enrolled in a given course section, many schools limit class size to between ten and fifteen students for first year classes, and between six and ten students for second year classes. There appears to be a direct correlation between class size and the effectiveness of group piano teaching. Large class enrollments may be more economically efficient, but small class enrollments are usually more effective pedagogically.

Many non-keyboard music majors have never studied piano, or have a limited piano background. In some cases, the non-keyboard music major has already obtained considerable keyboard facility. To accommodate these varying differences in ability, diagnostic exams are administered prior to enrollment and serve as placement auditions. These exams approximate the proficiency level of a given course, and students are subsequently placed in an appropriate level within the group piano sequence according to their pianistic abilities.

An increasing number of schools offer advanced keyboard skills courses for pianists who are enrolled as music education, piano pedagogy, and piano performance majors. These students have attained keyboard proficiency through the study of repertoire and technique prior to college, but have had limited training with musicianship skills. A two-semester course for keyboard majors is offered for such students. Their curriculum focuses on the same concepts as that of the non-pianist. However, the context is much more challenging, and the proficiency level is more advanced.

FACULTY/TEACHER TRAINING

The group piano instructor must be a competent musician who has acquired highly developed solo and ensemble performance skills and functional keyboard skills. Further, the prospective teacher must display organizational skills and demonstrate an understanding of conceptual learning. Such knowledge is invaluable when formulating and implementing a conceptually-based and well-sequenced curriculum of keyboard skills and concepts.

Due to the continued need and interest for quality group piano programs, some colleges have begun to offer piano pedagogy courses that are specifically designed for the prospective group piano instructor. A specialized course in group piano procedures can include the following:

1. an examination of the philosophy of comprehensive musicianship
2. a study of developmental learning theory and the application of psychological principles to group piano study
3. a discussion of the varying learning needs of the older beginnner and adult student
4. a survey and comparison of instructional materials
5. guided experiences with instructional media and the electronic piano laboratory
6. the design of practical learning activities and effective presentation strategies

Of equal importance is the study of group dynamics and an awareness of how students learn within the group environment. Equipped with this knowledge, the prospective group piano instructor is able to develop teaching skills that foster effective patterns of interaction within the group setting. In addition to imparting knowledge and monitoring student progress, the group instructor should become thoroughly familiar with discovery learning as a way to develop student understanding. Highly developed communication skills and listening and questioning techniques are especially useful in this regard, and serve to stimulate and motivate student learning and creativity. The group piano instructor must also provide practical and efficient practice routines for students who are highly motivated musicians, but have minimal time for piano practice.

Most universities assign group piano teaching to both full-time faculty specialists and graduate teaching assistants. Of those schools that currently offer graduate pedagogy degrees, many are also developing unique internships for the training of the group piano teaching assistant. The teaching assistantship can be designed to include opportunities for both pedagogical training and actual teaching. In some cases, teaching assistants can enroll in a practicum course and receive guided faculty supervision concurrent with their teaching responsibilities.

Within this framework, weekly teaching conferences and periodic faculty observations or videotaped observations can be scheduled. Instructional approaches can be explored and discussed as they apply to specific teaching situations. Lesson planning and effective teaching strategies can also be designed with faculty supervision. Some schools advocate a team teaching approach, sharing the instructional duties between the faculty specialist and the teaching assistant. In any case, the teaching/learning experiences of the teaching assistant and those students enrolled in the group piano course must be adequately addressed.

FACILITIES/EQUIPMENT

The group piano classroom consists of multiple pianos and a variety of audio-visual aids. Though acoustic pianos have been used at many schools for a group piano program, educational opportunities were considerably expanded with the emergence of the electronic piano laboratory in the mid-1950s and 1960s. The use of the electronic piano lab is widespread and is ideal for college group piano programs.

The electronic piano lab was designed to enhance instructional approaches, increase communication patterns within the classroom, and expand the range of learning activities conducted simultaneously during a class period. Electronic pianos are not meant to replace the acoustic piano, but rather to serve as a practical vehicle for use in the group learning setting. Because some electronic pianos do not have the touch or the range of an acoustic piano, many piano labs are also equipped with one acoustic piano for the performance of solo repertoire.

Within the electronic piano laboratory setting, a variety of learning modes can be utilized. The piano lab is operated by the instructor at a teacher console, and each piano is equipped with headsets. Instruction can be conducted through either the headset or speaker mode. When utilizing the headset mode, students can work on their own and the instructor can listen, comment, and answer individual questions. The headset mode also provides an opportunity for students to be paired in small groups of two or more. Pairing students increases the opportunities for ensemble practice within the class. When not using headsets, the speaker mode can be employed. Each student plays aloud, and all pianos are heard simultaneously. The speaker mode is especially effective when presenting new concepts and new music examples. Upon completion of a presentation activity in speaker mode, the headset mode can be effectively used for a short period of time so that students can immediately apply or practice the new assignment. Instructors can vary the learning activities by a combination of speaker and headset modes.

Group piano instruction can also be enhanced with the use of instructional media and equipment. In addition to the standard chalkboard, an overhead projector and the Wurlitzer Keynote Visualizer have become popular visual aids. The Visualizer is an electronic visual aid that is connected to the Wurlitzer teacher console. Notes are displayed on the staff and/or the keyboard as the teacher plays from the teacher console.

Transparencies for use with the overhead projector make efficient use of class time when prepared in advance. In addition, transparencies focus one's visual attention, are suitable for graphic presentation of concepts and music examples, and provide an opportunity to isolate portions of more lengthy examples. Teachers must be aware that music editions that are copyrighted cannot be shown on transparencies without the copyright holder's permission.

Some instructors have developed video tapes and filmstrips to present additional visual presentations. The slide projector is especially effective for sight-reading drills because the rate of speed of each slide can be controlled by the instructor.

The most popular audio aid is the cassette tape deck with an adjustable pitch control. This device can be connected to many of the manufactured electronic pianos. Cassette tape decks are attached to individual student pianos or channeled through the teacher console for one or more students. Some group piano textbooks have been enhanced with the preparation of a supplementary cassette tape. Such tapes can be designed for use in either individual practice or for use in the classroom. A variety of musical examples can be recorded on a cassette tape including:

1. accompaniments for the practice of chord and scale patterns
2. accompaniments and progressions for melodic improvisation
3. instrumental and vocal melodies that require a piano accompaniment
4. one part of a duet
5. melodies for harmonization

The use of audio and visual stimuli can enhance and broaden the student's perception of a particular concept. Though the preparation of audio-visual materials is time-consuming, their presence in the classroom contributes to a more varied, meaningful, and effective instructional experience.

One of the by-products of computer technology is the digital keyboard. A variety of manufacturers (including Ensoniq, Yamaha, Roland, and Kawai) offer keyboards with the touch sensitivity of an acoustic piano. Computer technology and synthesizers hold great promise for the future keyboard lab.

COURSE CONTENT

A comprehensive and well-balanced curriculum begins with a list of course objectives designed to provide specific learning competencies for each semester of study. Within the framework, a detailed list of learning tasks and concepts should be sequentially arranged. This outline is especially advantageous when teaching and administering placement exams for beginning and transfer students. Furthermore, many schools employ graduate assistants to teach courses within the group piano program. Their prior knowledge often does not prepare them adequately for planning course content, and instructional continuity can be hampered by their short-term residency on campus. Thus, a well-defined course syllabus provides both curricular unity and consistency.

Some group piano instructors establish course objectives in consultation with music education and music theory faculties. This is especially valuable for students majoring in music education. Their teaching skills are directly related to those functional skills that are developed in the group piano course. Such teaching competencies must be demonstrated during practice teaching or a comprehensive examination administered by the music education faculty. Prior knowledge is helpful in planning a practical course for their future vocational needs. Further, theoretical concepts often overlap in both music theory and group piano courses. Consulting with the music theory faculty is of benefit when group piano and music theory courses are offered as corequisites.

The group piano curriculum has evolved and become standardized over a period of years. Though there can be differences in curricular emphasis from school to school, many group piano instructors strive to offer a comprehensive curriculum of instruction. The following instructional categories are typical:

1. Repertoire (solo and ensemble)
2. Theory (scales and chords)
3. Technique
4. Reading and transposition
5. Harmonization
6. Improvisation

The following course outline lists instructional objectives for a four-semester course sequence for the non-keyboard major. It is presented as a general guide for developing a group piano course curriculum.

First Semester

Repertoire
1. Repertoire selections which illustrate and reinforce reading, technical and theoretical concepts

Theory
1. Major and minor five-note patterns
2. Major and minor scales in tetrachord position and key signatures
3. Major, minor, augmented, and diminished triads in root position
4. Primary triads in root position (tonic, subdominant, dominant)
5. Selected major and minor triads and inversions
6. Progressions using primary harmonies
   a. I IV I V I
7. Major-minor seventh chords in root position

Technique
1. Hand coordination and finger independence
2. Hand-over-hand arpeggios and lateral arm motion
3. Legato pedal
4. Wrist rotation

Special Subjects

5. Two-note slurs
6. Stationary and shifting hand positions
7. Fingering principles: thumb under, crossings, extensions, and contractions
8. Legato/staccato touches

Reading
1. Pre-staff notation, directional reading, and keyboard staff orientation
2. Stationary positions (transpose)
   a. melodic texture
   b. five-note range, hands one octave apart
   c. simple linear texture within a five-note range
   d. melody with simple accompaniment
3. Five-note extended positions
   a. finger crossings (thumb under and second finger over)
   b. finger extensions/contractions (thumb and fifth finger)
   c. five-note and triad hand shifts
4. Homophonic texture (transpose)
   a. RH five-note range accompanied with LH open 5ths-6ths
   b. RH five-note range accompanied with LH root position triads

Harmonization
1. Prepared examples using letter symbols and Roman numerals
2. LH accompaniment patterns
   a. single tones and open 5ths-6ths (I IV V)
   b. root position triads: blocked, broken, chord tone, waltz bass
   c. two-hand accompaniments

Improvisation
1. Free-style examples using black and white keys, half- and whole-steps
2. Free-style melodies within a five-note range
3. Free-style melodies within a tetrachord position

Second Semester

Repertoire
1. Repertoire selections which illustrate and reinforce reading, technical and theoretical concepts
2. Standard works by major composers representing the four major stylistic periods

Theory
1. Major and minor triads and inversions
2. Major and relative and parallel minor scales

The College Group Piano Program for Music Majors

3. Cadential progressions using triads, inversions, and dominant seventh chords
4. Common tone chord building
5. Progressions using secondary harmonies
    a. I IV I V⁷ I
    b. I vi IV V⁷ I
    c. I IV ii⁶ V⁷ I
    d. I iii IV V⁷ I

Technique
1. Major and harmonic minor scales, hands separate, two octaves
2. Major and minor arpeggios, hands separate, two octaves
3. Finger independence and wrist exercises
4. Fingering principles of contraction, extension, crossing over with fingers 2 3 4, and thumb under
5. Sequential patterns using five-note patterns and triad patterns

Reading
1. Stationary positions (transpose)
    a. linear two-voiced textures within a five-note range
2. Homophonic texture (transpose)
    a. melody with LH root position triads and close position triads
3. Changing positions and five-note extended positions (transpose)
    a. scale melodies with hand shifts and finger crossings
    b. five-note and triad hand shifts

Harmonization
1. Prepared examples using letter symbols and Roman numerals for primary chords
2. Sight-reading examples using letter symbols
3. Accompaniment patterns
    a. blocked, broken, arpeggiated, waltz, and Alberti bass
    b. LH root position triads
    c. LH close position (triad inversions)
    d. two-hand accompaniments

Improvisation
1. Motivic patterns based on chord tones over a harmonic progression
2. Free-style melodies within a scale range
3. Melodic improvisation based on a harmonic progression

Third Semester

Repertoire
1. Repertoire selections which illustrate and reinforce reading, technical and theoretical concepts

Special Subjects

2. Standard works by major composers representing the four main stylistic periods

Theory
   1. Major, minor, augmented, and diminished triads and inversions
   2. Major and minor scales
   3. Triads and seventh chords
   4. Common tone chord building
   5. Diatonic triads
   6. Major, dominant, minor, half-diminished, and diminished seventh chords
   7. Secondary dominants
   8. Progressions using secondary harmonies
      a. I IV I V⁷ I (starting in three positions)
      b. I vi IV V⁷ I (review)
      c. I IV ii⁶ V⁷ I (review)
      d. I vi IV ii⁶ I⁶₄ V⁷ I
      e. I V⁷/IV IV V⁷ I
      f. I V⁷/V V⁷ I

Technique
   1. Finger independence and wrist exercises
   2. Major and harmonic minor scales, hands together, two octaves
   3. Major and minor arpeggios, hands together, two octaves

Reading
   1. Sight-reading solos and duets: homophonic, linear, and hymn textures
   2. Transposition
      a. homophonic textures with accompaniment patterns in close position
      b. melodies incorporating finger extensions, contractions, crossing, and hand shifts
   3. Score reading: three-voice open score (choral and instrumental textures)

Harmonization
   1. Examples using letter symbols and Roman numerals
   2. Sight-reading examples using primary chords
   3. Prepared examples using primary and secondary chords
   4. Accompaniment patterns
      a. LH close position
      b. LH extended position
      c. RH chording and LH bass tones

Improvisation
   1. Melodic embellishment with simple accompaniment
   2. Motivic patterns based on chord tones over a harmonic progression

The College Group Piano Program for Music Majors

3. Free-style melodies within a scale range
4. Melodic improvisation based on a harmonic progression

Fourth Semester

Repertoire
1. Repertoire selections which illustrate and reinforce reading, technical, and theoretical concepts
2. Standard works by major composers representing the four main stylistic periods
3. Perform vocal or instrumental accompaniment with soloist

Theory
1. Play and resolve
   a. Dominant and diminished seventh chords
   b. Augmented sixth chords
   c. Neapolitan sixth chords
2. Progressions using secondary and altered harmonies
   a. I IV vii iii vi ii V I
   b. I V⁷/vi vi V⁷/IV IV V⁷/ii ii⁶ I⁶₄ I
   c. modulation to the dominant and subdominant keys

Technique
1. Major and harmonic minor scales, hands together, three—four octaves
2. Major and minor arpeggios, hands together, three—four octaves
3. Dominant and diminished seventh chord arpeggios, hands together, two—four octaves

Reading
1. Sight-reading solos and duets: homophonic, linear, and hymn textures
2. Transposition
   a. homophonic textures with accompaniment patterns in close position
   b. melodies incorporating finger extensions, contractions, crossings, and hand shifts
3. Score reading
   a. three-voice open score (choral and instrumental textures)
   b. four-voice open score (choral and instrumental textures)

Harmonization
1. Examples using letter symbols and Roman numerals
2. Sight-reading examples using primary chords
3. Prepared examples using primary and secondary chords, altered chords, and secondary dominants

Special Subjects

4. Accompaniment patterns
   a. LH close position
   b. LH extended position
   c. RH chording and LH bass tones

Improvisation
1. Melodic embellishment with simple accompaniment
2. Motivic patterns based on chord tones over a harmonic progression
3. Free-style melodies within a scale range
4. Melodic improvisation based on a harmonic progression
5. Homophonic and linear textures in the style of selected composers

LESSON PLANNING

Traditionally, theoretical concepts are presented as isolated factual information. Group piano instruction can effectively illustrate such concepts within musical settings. Often referred to as "concept repertoire," each piece is chosen to exemplify new concepts in a simple, yet musically satisfying context. Additional repertoire should be selected that reinforces technical and musical concepts. College-age students generally find greater satisfaction with sophisticated sounding musical examples that are also not too challenging technically. Many contemporary composers and authors of standard college textbook materials have composed appealing pedagogical music for adult learners. In addition, standard composers such as Kabalevsky and the early classic composers have written elementary materials that are suitable for the beginning college student.

Reading skills develop sequentially with both an intervallic and a gradual multiple-key approach. An increasing number of contemporary piano collections include musical examples based on scale and chordal shapes that reinforce pattern recognition to enhance one's reading skills. As a beginning pianist, the non-keyboard major benefits from reading examples that illustrate standard musical patterns and keyboard figurations.

Technical study leads to one's mastery and control of a specific music example. In addition to assigning standard scale and chord patterns, the group piano instructor should be careful not to lose sight of the fact that teaching technique requires attention to sound, feel, and gesture. Many non-keyboard majors feel technically uncoordinated. Therefore, the group instructor should devise exercises, scales, and chords to help solve this problem.

The development of harmonization and improvisation skills are especially beneficial. Students learn to harmonize familiar folk songs, themes by standard composers, and more contemporary sounding melodies with a wide variety of accompaniment styles. Improvisation skills can be developed through a variety of creative learning activities that

The College Group Piano Program for Music Majors

are based on newly learned theoretical concepts. In addition, learning to play current popular melodies and folk songs by ear is also a valuable skill.

An effective instructional plan is based on three important factors: a varied and balanced approach, the student's readiness for new concepts, and the proper sequencing of concepts. In addition, designing an effective lesson plan is based on an instructor's ability to provide meaningful learning activities that are related to one another conceptually.

Group piano instructors have a wide range of formats to choose from when organizing course content. It is advantageous to list each category of instruction separately at the beginning of the semester. This list can then be subdivided into specific learning tasks and concepts. An outline format can be used that lists specific examples found in the required course textbook. A conceptual format further defines a suggested learning sequence for each instructional category. The following format serves as an example.

Reading
    Concept #1. _____ textbook page:_____
    Concept #2. _____ textbook page:_____
    Concept #3. _____ textbook page:_____
    etc.

Lesson planning is also enhanced with a weekly summary of assignments for each category of instruction. The following format serves as a sample.

Time Frame
    Week Number _____

Area of Instruction	*Assignment*
Repertoire	_____
Theory (scales & chords)	_____
Technique	_____
Reading	_____
Harmonization	_____
Improvisation	_____

This format provides a more varied and balanced lesson plan for the graduate teaching assistant and/or the beginning group piano instructor. This plan may also be helpful for other teachers to use as a guide in lesson planning.

INSTRUCTIONAL MATERIALS

The group piano instructor can choose from a vast number of published textbooks and supplementary materials. The selection of teaching materials is influenced by a variety of factors and includes: the scope and length of the course, the student's previous keyboard experience and current level of proficiency, and the instructor's preference.

Most courses require the use of one textbook or a combination of two supplementary collections. Many of the more recently published textbooks contain a wealth of correlated material that promotes a comprehensive approach for the development of keyboard musicianship skills. Each of these textbooks is highly organized and progresses in a well sequenced manner. Within individual chapters, separate sections are usually arranged by topics to include repertoire, theory, technique, sight-reading, transposition, harmonization, improvisation, and both solo and ensemble repertoire.

The availability of additional supplementary material is also useful for instructional purposes. These materials include collections for ensemble repertoire, sight-reading, harmonization, and score reading. Many group piano programs maintain a library of multiple copies of supplementary books. These collections can be used during class, or can be used for individual practice if the piano lab is open during non-teaching hours. In addition to published materials, many group instructors have developed materials that are not commercially available. The materials listed below are appropriate for both first- and second-year classes.

SUGGESTED GROUP PIANO TEXTBOOKS FOR COLLEGE MUSIC MAJORS

Heerema, Elmer. *Progressive Class Piano*. 2nd ed. Van Nuys: Alfred Publishing Company, Inc., 1984.

Hilley, Martha and Lynn Freeman Olson. *Piano for the Developing Musician, Books I and II*. St. Paul: West Publishing Company, 1985.

Lyke, James, Ron Elliston and Tony Caramia. *Keyboard Musicianship, Books One and Two*. 4th ed. Champaign: Stipes Publishing Company, 1985.

Mach, Elyse. *Contemporary Class Piano*. 3rd ed. New York: Harcourt Brace Jovanovich, Inc., 1988.

Page, Cleveland. *The Laboratory Piano Course, Books 1 and 2*. New York: Harper and Row, 1975, 1976.

Stecher, Melvin, Norman Horowitz, Claire Gordon, R. Fred Kern and E.L. Lancaster. *Keyboard Strategies, Master Texts I and II*. New York: G. Schirmer, Inc., 1984.

A SELECTIVE LIST OF SUPPLEMENTARY MATERIALS

Sight-Reading
Bastien, James. *Sight Reading, Levels 1-4*. San Diego: Neil A. Kjos Music Company, 1976.

George, Jon. *Patterns for Piano*. Van Nuys: Alfred Publishing Company, Inc., 1976.

George, Jon. *Repertoire 1, 2, 3, 4*. Hialeah: Columbia Pictures, 1979.

Havill, Lorina. *You Can Sight Read, Books 1 and 2*. Bryn Mawr: Theodore Presser, 1967.

Lang, C.S. *Score Reading Exercises*. London: Novello & Company, Ltd., 1949.

Melcher, Robert A. and Willard Warch. *Music for Score Reading*. Englewood Cliffs: Prentice-Hall, Inc., 1971.

Wilkinson, Philip G. *100 Score-Reading Exercises*. London: Novello & Company, Ltd., 1947

Harmonization

Caramia, Tony. *A Guide for Jazz Piano Harmonization*. San Diego: Neil A. Kjos Music Company, 1983.

Frackenpohl, Arthur. *Harmonization at the Piano*. 5th ed. Dubuque: Wm. C. Brown Co., 1985.

Kern, Alice. *Harmonization-Transposition at the Keyboard*. Princeton: Birch Tree Group Ltd., 1968.

Mainous, Frank D. *Melodies to Harmonize With*. Englewood Cliffs: Prentice-Hall, Inc., 1978.

Ensembles

Lyke, James. *Ensemble Music for Group Piano, Books One and Two*. 3rd ed. Champaign: Stipes Publishing Company, 1976.

Ogilvy, Susan. *Ogilvy Piano Multiples, Blue-settes; Ogilvy Piano Multiples, Book 1; Ogilvy Piano Multiples, Jazz Vignettes; Pops for Piano Ensemble*. New York: Bradley Publications, 1983.

Page, Cleveland. *Ensemble Music for Group Piano*. Cincinnati: Canyon Press, Inc., 1970.

Sabol, Mary. *Rock and Rhythm Studies for Class Piano*. Cincinnati: Canyon Press, Inc., 1972.

Vandall, Robert D. *The Vandall Piano Ensembles*. San Diego: Neil A. Kjos Music Company, 1977.

Improvisation

Lloyd, Ruth & Norman. *Creative Keyboard Musicianship*. New York: Dodd, Mead & Company, Inc., 1975.

Mack, Glenn. *Adventures in Improvisation at the Keyboard*. Princeton: Birch Tree Group Ltd., 1970.

The College Piano Major 12
by Joseph Banowetz

Joseph Banowetz is a graduate with a First Prize in piano performance from the Vienna Hochschule for Music and Dramatic Arts. Additional piano studies were with Carl Friedberg at the Juilliard School, and with Gyorgy Sandor at the University of Michigan. Mr. Banowetz has concertized extensively as recitalist and orchestral soloist throughout Europe, Russia, Mexico, North America, Asia, and New Zealand, and he is the first foreign artist ever to be invited by the Chinese Ministry of Culture to both record and give world premiere performances of a contemporary Chinese piano concerto. He is editor of many piano music editions, author of the book *The Pianist's Guide to Pedaling* (Indiana University Press), and a Contributing Editor for *The Piano Quarterly*. Recordings by Banowetz appear on both long playing and compact discs for China Records, Hong Kong Records, Orion Master Recordings, and Educo Records. For seven summers Mr. Banowetz taught at the National Music Camp at Interlochen, Michigan. Currently he is Professor of Piano Performance at the School of Music of the University of North Texas, and since 1985 has also been granted the title Permanent Visiting Professor of Piano Performance at the Shenyang Conservatory of Music in the People's Republic of China.

For the pianist, the music profession is a broad one, with many options available to the prospective university graduate. In spite of the increasing competitive aspects of a music career, there are still many opportunities and rewards for the properly trained and dedicated pianist. A university position is difficult to obtain for all but the most skilled performers, so a career as an independent teacher may be the most practical option available to the university graduate.

PRECOLLEGE TRAINING

Good precollege training is vital for the ultimate success of the piano major, for solid habits of musicianship and technique should already have been formed by the time the student enters college. The performing arts cannot be pursued to any high degree of proficiency through a late or badly deficient start. Playing an instrument is similar to excelling professionally in a sport. Muscular reflexes and coordination must be established and developed over time. This is difficult for the late starter to realize, and it is especially tragic to see an individual who is trying to become a performance major struggle with an inadequate background. Without talent or proper early development, such efforts sooner or later become deeply frustrating to one with an insufficient precollege training.

One of the most valuable experiences for the precollege student is the senior high school recital. A typical program might include one or two of the easier preludes and fugues from Bach's *Well-Tempered Clavier*, a Haydn or Mozart sonata, a group of nineteenth-century works such as Chopin waltzes and nocturnes or Schumann's *Fantasy Pieces*, Opus 12, and ending with an impressionistic or twentieth-century group such as Debussy's *Pour le Piano*, Copland's *Cat and the Mouse*, or Bartók's *Allegro Barbaro*.

A common error in the precollege training is the assigning of pieces that are overly difficult both musically and technically. The experienced teacher should develop the student's playing gradually so that proper attention can be given to all areas of musicianship.

The prospective piano major should have acquired a degree of competency in performance, but should also be well-grounded in technique (scales, chords, arpeggios, etc.), have a knowledge of theory, and have some experience in a variety of piano literature styles.

DEGREES FOR THE PIANO MAJOR

There are a number of music programs available to the student desiring a degree with a piano concentration. The list of degree titles includes Bachelor of Music, Bachelor of Music with emphasis in pedagogy, Bachelor of Arts with a music concentration, etc. Carried further to the master's and doctoral levels, there are still more ways to list music degrees such as Master of Music, Doctor of Musical Arts, etc.

Few universities will consider a graduate with a Bachelor of Music degree for a teaching position. A masters degree or doctorate degree is generally mandatory for successfully competing for a university position. Exceptions to this are those individuals who have exhibited extraordinary professional achievements, such as concert performers, recording artists, prize winners, etc.

Those electing to specialize in piano pedagogy can obtain a Bachelor of Music degree in this area. The graduate with an emphasis in piano pedagogy is often chosen to teach in a college preparatory department, or teach non-music majors in a group lab situation.

COURSES FOR THE PIANO MAJOR

In addition to the usual humanities courses, there are various musical areas with which any well-rounded and informed musician must be aquainted. Familiarity with all periods of music history and music literature is vital for a complete musical background as is a knowledge of theory, counterpoint, and composition.

A number of classes specifically designed for the keyboard major can be divided into five general areas:

1. Applied study
2. Keyboard literature and performance practices
3. Piano pedagogy
4. Accompanying and ensemble playing
5. Functional piano

Applied Study

When the piano major enters college equipped with a solid background, further technical development and training should be intensified. The teacher should be able to analyze technical problems, and over an extended period, systematically guide the student toward even greater physical capability at the keyboard. Exercises alone, introduced with scales and arpeggios, will not suffice. The teacher must also be able to explain *how* to produce certain effects, *how* to go about unraveling a technically difficult passage, etc. Unfortunately there is too often the teacher who believes technical development will automatically come simply by going through a set ritual of so many finger drills a day. The results are often discouraging in terms of lost time, sore muscles, and tight, poor playing. Too often this type of training becomes passed on as a firmly entrenched bad habit.

In addition to a detailed technical analysis of piano performance, the student should receive exposure to a broad range of piano literature. Insight into various styles, an understanding of performance traditions, evaluation of editions, and interpretive depth and sensitivity are all areas which should be explored and developed. The repertoire covered should ideally extend from about 1600 to the present. Almost any pianist/teacher will admittedly have certain specialties and preferences; any weak stylistic area eventually will show up in the student's playing, lessening over-all interpretive insight and perspective.

Students should learn to make their own interpretive decisions without always relying on the teacher's suggestions. Matters of fingering, musicianship, tempo, and interpretation should become the student's choice.

Keyboard Literature & Performance Practices

The piano major should study and perform works from a wide range of styles and periods. The college student should have at least a listening acquaintance with the following:

1. Representative seventeenth- and eighteenth-century works by Scarlatti, Couperin, Handel, and J.S. Bach
2. Familiarity with important sonatas, concerti, and other keyboard compositions of Haydn and Mozart
3. A representative sampling from each of the three periods of the Beethoven sonatas, as well as an acquaintance with the concerti and variations
4. A cross section of nineteenth-century composers such as Schubert, Chopin, Schumann, Liszt, Brahms, etc.
5. Familiarity with impressionistic works of Debussy and Ravel
6. A knowledge of twentieth-century composers such as Stravinsky, Bartók, Prokofiev, Copland, Schoenberg, etc.

In addition to the repertory studied, the student should gain familiary with symphonies, chamber music, and choral works to become well-rounded musically. College survey courses can only act as an introduction. If one avoids exposure in these areas, sufficient background will be lacking.

An awareness of stylistic problems and the history and evolution of performance practices are of great importance. From the Baroque and Classical periods the student should have a knowledge of ornamentation, keyboard instruments of that period, and performance practices of the time. This information can be gained from old 78 r.p.m. recordings by the older generation of pianists such as Hofmann, Busoni, Schnabel, Rachmaninoff, Godowsky, Cortot, Fischer, Friedman, Lhevinne, Rosenthal, Sauer, and others. Many of these early recordings are available on long playing records. When compared with current artists in concerts, or on 33⅓ r.p.m. or compact disc recordings, one notes immediately that their interpretations are often different. However, when listening to recordings of Rosenthal or Sauer, for instance, one should remember that these pianists were students of Liszt. If these performances seem overly free and personalized, consideration should be given that these performers represented a very high level of creative individuality often missing today. By careful and thoughtful examination of style and performance practices, the student can develop an ability for artistic judgements.

Along with a sense of historical development of performance style, the student should also develop an acquaintance with the history, literature, and art of the various periods of works studied. Debussy can be more easily understood if one has a knowledge of such French impressionist painters as Monet, Manet, Renoir, and Degas along with literary knowledge of writers such as Verlaine, Rimbaud, Louys, Maeterlinck, and others. Liszt's works become more meaningful through a knowledge of such authors as Goethe, Petrarch, and Dante. The student should not isolate performance study from total cultural development. College courses stimulate and motivate, but alone are not substitutes for continued independent intellectual growth.

Piano Pedagogy

Classes in piano pedagogy take a variety of approaches for teaching the beginner, the intermediate student, and the advanced student. It is virtually impossible to adequately cover all these categories in one semester, so most universities offer pedagogy classes spread out over several semesters to prepare students for various teaching situations.

Generally, most time in the pedagogy class is given to the beginner, with examination of methods and teaching techniques. In addition, group instruction can also be studied. It is at the beginning level that good instructional methodology is most important. Students in the class should experience teaching their own pupils. Audio or video tapings can be used to enable the pedagogy student to gain self-awareness of the teaching skills presented.

The pedagogy class should also provide experiences dealing with intermediate students, both in discussion and observation. Within this group the badly taught beginner may be encountered, and ways to correct the most common faults should be discussed by the class. The transfer student often comes from this age group, and the pedagogy class should provide methods of dealing with this special situation.

Finally, the pedagogy class should examine and discuss teaching the advanced precollege student, the adult beginner, group piano techniques, literature at all levels, technique at all levels, suggestions for practicing, the mechanics of memorization, the recital, the audition and contest, and other topics suggested by the instructor. The pedagogy class should, through discussion, observation and participation, provide meaningful apprenticeship experiences which will form the basis for future teaching.

Accompanying & Ensemble Playing

These two areas should be stressed in any college program for developing familiarity with important repertory outside the solo keyboard literature. Problems of pedaling, rhythm, subtleties of phrasing, and many other musicianship considerations arise in the ensemble situation. Duets, two-piano literature, the large string-keyboard duo literature, or chamber music with larger groups all have distinctive problems that demand great flexibility and constant attentiveness by the performers. The interplay with one or more musicians is a special situation for the normally solitary pianist. Books about accompanying and chamber music are listed in Appendix A.

Functional Piano

Functional piano combines several important areas with which the piano major must be familiar: sight-reading, keyboard harmony, improvisation, and other keyboard skills. This course is generally taught within the first two years of college.

The ability to read proficiently at sight is a valuable asset for any level of piano study. Classes in sight-reading often are little more than supervised reading practice sessions, but when taught properly, can aid the student in transposition and in reading open scores.

The study of keyboard harmony is highly practical for all levels of piano study. Aural acuity will be heightened by functional harmonization. For anyone using the piano, from elementary literature to the performer grappling with the complexities of late Beethoven, an understanding of harmony is essential. Although somewhat outdated with today's "lead sheet" type chord symbolization usage, an advanced keyboard harmony class will probably include work with figured bass realization. Acquaintance with this harmonization technique is useful, if for no other reason than to understand more fully certain basic style characteristics and performance practices of the Baroque period.

The ability to improvise is also important. This is a necessary skill for the student or instructor who will be teaching group piano classes. The instructor should be able to improvise accompaniments to songs, provide chordal harmony for single-note melodies often found in general music books used in the public schools, and be able to play well-known songs by ear. The independent studio teacher can also employ these skills in meaningful ways by offering classes in improvisation, jazz, pop-rock, etc. to students of various ages.

Special Subjects

THE ARTIST-TEACHER

The title "artist-in-residence" is often listed in university catalogues to highlight a prominent pianist on the faculty. The purpose of this special musician is to offer study with a professional performer to students within a university framework. This concept first originated at the University of Wisconsin in the late 1930s, and has been used since by many departments of music.

Depending on whatever understanding has been reached with university officials, the artist-in-residence may be on campus for any period ranging from a few weeks to the complete academic year. If the resident artist is absent for an extended period, an assistant is sometimes used to fill these lesson gaps. The possibility of irregular lessons is a potential difficulty for the pupil who is not advanced enough to work independently.

Study with a professional performer can have great advantages for students. When an artist-teacher has the right insight and personality for inspired teaching, the rewards for students can be of great value.

TEACHING THE APPLIED PIANO MAJOR IN GROUPS

The group system of instruction can have great advantages. It is similar to the masterclass approach which has long been a tradition in European state academies where private lessons are the exception rather than the rule. In this type of instruction the number of students can be about nine, with classes meeting two or three times a week for one hour periods. Classes are divided into less advanced, intermediate, and advanced categories. Competition helps to motivate students, and each can learn from the faults and virtues of the other. An alternative to the "class only" approach is the combination of private lessons coupled with a weekly group session.

For the student who is particularly interested in piano pedagogy, a group learning experience can be invaluable for absorbing teaching methods, in analyzing other's problems, and in being exposed to a wide repertory.

IS A SOLO CONCERT CAREER A REALISTIC GOAL?

The touring performer who can earn a respectable living, after deducting traveling expenses, manager's fees, publicity expenses, and taxes, is a very special musician. Following a handful of names in the Ashkenazy, Brendel, de Larrocha, and Argerich league, there is a rapid drop to the soloist who worries about the next engagement, and who supplements concert fees by teaching.

Assuming that the young pianist is determined to gamble on a performance career, what procedures should one take? Perhaps the most obvious is an international competition such as the Queen Elizabeth in Brussels, the Tchaikovsky in Moscow, the Chopin in Warsaw, the Van Cliburn in Fort Worth, the Bachauer in Salt Lake City, and the University of Maryland in College Park. If one is lucky enough to finish in the top three places, good exposure may be presented with solo and orchestral engagements for one or two seasons. However, even a first prize can ultimately prove a failure for launching an international career. It takes talent, timing, and luck to launch and sustain a career for an extended period of time.

The New York debut recital is another means of giving public exposure to an unknown performer. This involves expenses of at least $7,000 to give the performance in a major concert hall. If a critic is present from *The New York Times*, what usually results is a review listing both faults and praises.

A solo performing career is quite demanding and requires a considerable amount of practice of at least six to eight hours a day to adequately prepare both solo and concerto repertoire. The young performer should realize that a great deal of time and effort is required to launch and sustain a career.

PROFESSIONAL ACCOMPANYING

Another field that offers an avenue for the performing pianist is that of a professional accompanist. The accompanist must be an excellent sight-reader, be able to transpose vocal accompaniments, have a first-class keyboard technique, and must be fully conversant with various musical styles from Bach violin sonatas to Puccini operas.

Preparation for an accompanying career can be gained by as much exposure as possible to all kinds of ensemble and vocal literature. A basic reading and pronunciation knowledge of several languages is helpful, as is an understanding of vocal technique, and the performance capabilities of various instruments. The accompanist must be a well-rounded musician.

If the piano major is studying at a large university, valuable experience can be gained by accompanying lessons in vocal and instrumental studios, playing for opera workshops, accompanying choruses, and performing on recitals. Some universities have special classes or degrees for those students wanting to become professional accompanists, and these provide excellent opportunities for a variety of accompanying experiences.

One further possibility for the accompanist is a position as pianist with a major symphony. This entails playing performances of orchestral works, usually those from the twentieth-century. These parts can be extremely demanding, and often require precise rhythm and a fluent technique;

Stravinsky's *Petrouchka* is a good example of what can be expected. When a position becomes available, an audition is required to fill the vacancy. Advance preparation of major works using piano is advised. Some large symphonies employ a pianist on a full-time basis; however, most smaller symphonies hire the pianist when needed.

REWARDS OF INDEPENDENT TEACHING

The importance of the independent teacher has been minimized for too long. Teachers have the responsibility of training a wide range of students; it is their "products," good or bad, that supply college music departments. Their students frequently become supporters of concert activities through audience participation, and their work in sponsoring contests, festivals, workshops, etc., is of vital importance to the musical well-being of the community.

The graduating piano major may be hesitant to pursue an independent teaching career because of the fear that it will be difficult getting started, or that is will be difficult to make a sufficient income. However, the demand for teachers remains steady. If handled properly the teacher can make a very good living; in some cases, better than the college teacher.

SUMMARY

Entering into the ranks of the professional pianist/teacher requires a number of basic personal traits and inner motivations in order to excel and survive in today's competitive world. Some special musical talent is vital for anyone intending to become a piano major at the university level. Talent is difficult to describe. It generally means an aptitude for learning a particular subject. Talent for the musician requires an ability to learn a new piece in a short period of time, to know it securely from memory, and to be able to play it in a convincing manor.

In many music departments an appraisal is given at the end of the sophomore year to determine the plausibility of continuing as a piano major. Anyone who is advised to change majors after a two-year period should give careful consideration to the evaluation. The door to music may be kept open as a rewarding avocation while pursuing another career.

Once the decision has been made to become a piano major, the student should pursue the chosen field with special determination. Intellectual discipline is a vital personal trait for the piano major, for heavy demands will be made on one's time for music classes, practicing, and other activities that go into the successful pursuit of a university music degree program. However, special opportunities and rewards can be gained upon graduation for the pianist who is willing to share his or her knowledge and work with others in meaningful ways.

The College Piano Major

Is Piano Teacher Training Necessary? 13

by Richard Chronister

Richard Chronister is president and educational director of National Keyboard Arts Associates, an organization active in developing, testing, and publishing new piano education materials for beginning and intermediate students. He is co-founder and executive director of The National Conference on Piano Pedagogy, a foundation whose aim is the promotion of communications amoung those who work in the field of piano teacher training. Mr. Chronister is currently chairman of the piano department of the Los Angeles Community School of Performing Arts. Previously on the faculties of The University of Tulsa, Westminster Choir College, The New School for Music Study, and The University of Southern California, Mr. Chronister has been active in developing piano teacher training programs for more than thirty years. He is known throughout the music world for his frequent lectures and many contributions to the field of piano pedagogy.

The National Conference on Piano Pedagogy is an organization that exists for the purpose of gathering together those whose responsibility is to train piano teachers so they can become more informed, more efficient, and therefore, more successful. The importance of this rests on a very potent question—"Is piano teacher training necessary?" If we believe that teacher education is worthwhile in *any* field, we must also believe that it is possible to create a learning environment for future and/or current teachers to assist them in gaining necessary skills to become good piano teachers.

The best teachers through the years have taught themselves how to solve the problems that confront them. Finding ways to pass on this expertise is what teacher training is all about. When a way is found to accomplish this, through college degree programs or other avenues, we will begin the long road toward changing some of the piano teaching traditions of the past.

When parents come to realize that all children, including those without special talent, are capable of success in piano study, they will begin to look further than next door for a piano teacher, will consider more than just the performing ability of the teacher, will look into the professional status of the teacher, and will start their children's piano study with the expectation of year-to-year progress towards musical competence.

TRADITIONS

Parents have always had the responsibility to choose the piano teacher. After parents ask for recommendations around the neighborhood, talk to the local music store merchant, and look in the yellow pages, they do exactly what they have become accustomed to doing when searching for other services, they look for someone close to home. This is so prevalent that we could safely call it one of the traditions of choosing a piano teacher—"The nearest piano teacher is the best piano teacher."

It is understood that when Beethoven and Chopin taught piano lessons, their roster of piano students certainly included talented players, plus some not-so-gifted students. In those days, some parents could choose a teacher from among the finest composers and performers. This too, has become one of the traditions of choosing a piano teacher—"The finest musician is the finest teacher."

Since the training of fine musicians does not usually include training in how to teach, a third tradition must be added to the first two—"Performance training is sufficient for those who teach piano."

We have no records of the "survival" rate of piano students in the days of the great masters. No doubt, the retention rate was not considered important because teaching was not their main goal. And so, another piano tradition—"Piano teaching is a part-time career."

Only a few students who studied with the great masters became equally famous musicians. We can only speculate about the rest of the students; some of them probably became piano teachers serving the children in their neighborhood. They would not have been important in the large scheme of things because their truly talented students would have eventually moved on to master teachers. This suggests another tradition which is still with us—"Talent will emerge regardless of the teaching at the beginning level, allowing the special student to move on to a more experienced, successful, teacher."

MEASURING SUCCESSFUL TEACHING

It is true that talent often shows itself regardless of the teaching. It is also true that a teacher can be good without maintaining a full-time teaching career, that the ability to perform is a necessary qualification for the piano teacher, and that the best piano teachers will always live near to some students. However, not one of these things, nor all of them together, has much to do with measuring successful teaching.

How, then, should we measure piano teaching success? In a small town where there seems to be an inordinate number of talented piano students, you will invariably find one or more good piano teachers. Does that mean that a good piano teacher heard about that town and moved there instantly in order to take advantage of a good situation? Of course, it is more likely that the good piano teacher was there first, and that good piano teaching allowed all that good talent to emerge. Successful teaching is measured by the total output of a teacher, not by the few special students each teacher seems to have.

BUILDING NEW TRADITIONS

The only way to dispel the effect of all these piano teaching traditions of the past is to place some focus on finding ways for piano teachers to help children develop their musical abilities. Our job is not to discover the talented and separate them from those without talent. That is the easy part! The hard part is to know how to solve the problems for all those occasions when a natural ability is not enough.

Talent and ability are different for both teacher and students. Having the *talent* to teach does not insure the *ability* to teach any more than the talent to play guarantees musical and technical competence. Piano teacher training should provide the opportunity to share the success of teachers who have come before. When we are able to pass on the accumulated knowledge of successful teachers, new traditions will replace the old. The talent of every student will emerge because teachers will be prepared to find each student's particular path to success.

Is Piano Teacher Training Necessary?

When all piano teachers consistently produce students who become musically literate, enjoy making music at the piano, and continue to make music for the rest of their lives, we will have another new tradition—"Piano teaching is a creative, worthwhile, interesting profession."

When it is proved that good teachers can transfer their success, just as good performers can transfer their success, this tradition will take its place among the others that both performance training and teacher training are required to be a successful piano teacher.

PIANO TEACHER TRAINING IS NECESSARY

Piano teacher training is necessary because millions of students are going to the nearest teacher who may or may not be a fine performer, whose training may or may not have included any guidelines for determining what different kinds of students need in order to become successful piano students, whose main interest may likely lie somewhere else, and who may not regard the profession of music teaching as an important part of the educational process for all children. These students deserve to become the best they are capable of becoming. Instead, many drop out of music study each year simply because we continue to live by the traditions of the past.

The National Conference on Piano Pedagogy is a nonprofit organization that exists for the purpose of challenging these old, worn-out traditions and is dedicated to helping develop new traditions. The Conference meets the third weekend of October in even-numbered years in Chicago. For further information, write to The National Conference on Piano Pedagogy, P.O. Box 24C54, Los Angeles, CA 90024.

Memorization Techniques 14

Playing securely from memory is one of the most important aspects of an artistic performance. One must know the music thoroughly, and that comes from careful, systematic practice done over a period of time.

When first learning a piece it is essential to accurately read the notes, rhythm, harmony, and to develop a general feel for the overall concept of the piece being studied. The student should form *correct* first impressions, because mistakes learned early are difficult to eradicate, and may cause problems in a performance. An incorrect initial imprint requires the brain to reprogram the entire event in order to correct the false impression first learned.

Correct memorization procedures include:

1. Slow and careful practice
2. Attention to detail (tempo, phrasing, dynamics, pedal fingering, etc.)
3. Learning the form of the piece
4. Practicing hands separately
5. Developing the correct kinesthetic (muscular) reflex necessary for a secure performance
6. Understanding the harmonic structure of the piece
7. Mental practice
8. Playing one hand and miming the other

When first learning a piece, slow practice is essential so all aspects of the score can be correctly learned. Too often a teacher assigns a new piece and the student returns to the next lesson and plays wrong notes, wrong harmonies, and other inaccuracies. These errors can be avoided by practicing slowly and carefully in the beginning.

The student should pay careful attention to details in the score from the beginning. Correct realizations of all aspects of the music must be learned thoroughly for a convincing performance. These include phrasing, dynamics, fingering, pedaling, tempo, and many other items suggested by the teacher.

It is essential to learn the form of the piece. The teacher can assist the student in finding sequence patterns, repetition phrases, and other aspects of form. The teacher can also help in providing an analysis of a sonatina or sonata form, and point out various themes within the exposition, development, and recapitulation. Most pieces from the Baroque period (other than preludes and fugues) are in binary form. Most pieces from the Romantic period are in ternary form. Pieces from the Contemporary period vary, and the form is apt to be different between various composers.

The teacher can also be helpful in pointing out the advantages of practicing hands separately. Usually the left hand plays music that has no melodic identity, so the bass part is apt to go astray in a performance.

Finger memory and kinesthetic (muscular) reflex are additional memory aids. A student often plays a piece over and over without comprehension and depends on automatic reflexes to learn the piece. This is *not* productive to correct memorization. The student should *think* while practicing, not just play by rote. Once the music is correctly learned, the student can profit by watching exactly where the hands are going on the keyboard.

Harmonic analysis is another element that will aid memorization. The teacher or student can write in the chordal outline of each piece studied to form "guideposts" through the score. This can be done in figured bass fashion: I IV$^6_4$ I V^7-of-V, etc. The Roman numerals can be written below the bass part for easy comprehension while reading the score. Or chord symbols can be written above the treble clef: C G C Am, etc.

Mental practice is an excellent way to learn a piece more securely. This is done away from the piano. Some pianists become so proficient at this that they can learn new music just by looking at the score.

Another aid to memorizing is to play one hand and mime the other. The student can play either the right or left hand, and lightly "play" the other hand without actually pressing the keys down.

Finally, once a piece has been committed to memory, the student should be able to start at various places in the score. One should be able to start from memory at each theme and continue. It is best for the student to learn a piece in phrase groups, rather than trying to learn a new work straight through.

In preparing for a public performance, it is necessary to have performed the piece (or pieces) several times before the recital, competition, or audition. Even young students should seek opportunities to simulate stage conditions by playing for audiences in their own homes or for friends. Some teachers have a special dress rehearsal prior to the recital. Those students who are not thoroughly prepared could wait to play in a later recital. Most professional pianists perform works many times before playing them in a New York recital, or playing a concerto with a major symphony.

The main elements of a secure performance are a thorough knowledge of the work, careful study from the beginning, and the ability to give an artistic rendition of the composer's music in an expressive, convincing manner. It is these qualities that distinguish an outstanding musician from one who is less than convincing!

A Guide to Piano Fingering 15

by Robert Roux

Pianist Robert Roux was a 1984 audition winner of the United States Information Agency Artistic Ambassador Program, under whose auspices he toured Italy, Yugoslavia, Greece, Cyprus, Turkey, and Egypt for six weeks in 1985. The tour included the premiere performance of Morton Gould's *Patterns, Numbers 1-4* for solo piano.

He has frequently performed as soloist with major symphony orchestras as well as in recitals throughout the United States. In the spring of 1986, Dr. Roux performed at a White House reception hosted by Nancy Reagan. Later that year, he played an enthusiastically received debut recital at the John F. Kennedy Center for the Performing Arts in Washington, D.C. In 1987, he received critical acclaim in a tour of Austria and Germany which included concerto appearances and radio broadcasts. He has twice served on the jury of the prestigious Joanna Hodges International Piano Competition in Palm Desert, California.

Dr. Roux was a *cum laude* graduate of Loyola University in New Orleans, and he also studied at the Curtis Institute of Music. He received his masters and doctoral degrees from the University of Texas in Austin. He has coached with a distinguished list of teachers, including James Bastien, John Perry, Lili Kraus, William Race, and Eleanor Sokoloff. Resident pianist for the Lake City Chamber Music Festival in Colorado (1980-84), and currently associate professor of piano at Arizona State University, Robert Roux is following a dual career of teaching and concertizing.

Nearly all pianists agree good fingering is of fundamental importance. William S. Newman writes, "Fingering can make or break a piece."[1] C.P.E. Bach, in his *Essay on the True Art of Playing Keyboard Instruments*, states, "More is lost through poor fingering than can be replaced by all conceivable artistry and good taste."[2] Additionally, there is a manuscript of Chopin containing the words, "everything hangs upon proper fingering."[3]

Fingering is admittedly personal in nature. Heinrich Neuhaus points out, "if we study carefully the playing of great pianists we will see that their fingering differs as much as their pedal, their touch, their phrasing and, in general—their whole performance."[4] Indeed, all aspects of piano playing offer a wide range of options. Discussions of fingering, phrasing, touch, etc., lend themselves more naturally to the spontaneity of the piano lesson where the teacher's demonstrations at the piano can be of invaluable assistance.

Given the divergence of opinion on the subject and the great anatomical differences in pianists' hands, many pedagogues have had an understandable reluctance to apply a systematic methodology to fingering. Even so, the scarcity of adequate printed material on piano fingering implies a lack of courage in this area. Fingering is, generally speaking, less subjective than the other variables of piano playing. For a given passage, the number of viable fingering options is usually smaller than the number of interpretive options. Also, fingering can be notated in a precise fashion, leaving no doubt as to what is intended. This is seldom true of interpretive marks; for example, a staccato mark over a note still leaves some question as to its relative length of duration.

Many editions of piano music published in the past century and edited by notable pianists (Joseffy, Schnabel, Friedheim, etc.) contain an abundance of fingerings. It might be assumed that these fingerings would be of substantial value to the piano student. In my opinion, they do not always prove to be so. First of all, some of these fingerings are not practical for certain hands, and they may not give the underlying philosophy behind the editor's choices. The student should learn and apply general principles of piano fingering, and not blindly follow published fingerings.

The basic issues involved in the selection of fingerings are the following: topography, physical convenience, mental convenience, musical content, and facilitations (redistributions of notes between hands). These categories often relate to each other and cannot be considered independently. For example, accurate musical content permeates all other issues, for no fingering is acceptable if it violates the musical essence of

---

[1]William S. Newman, *The Pianist's Problems* (New York: Harper & Row, 1950), p. 73.
[2]C.P.E. Bach, *Essay on the True Art of Playing Keyboard Instruments*, trans. by William Mitchell (New York: W.W. Norton & Company, Inc.), pp. 41-78.
[3]From an unpublished manuscript of Chopin transcribed by Cortot. Alfred Cortot, *In Search of Chopin* (Westport: Greenwood Press, 1952), pp. 44-45.

Special Subjects

the passage. Also, there is often an interrelationship between hand structure, keyboard topography, and physical convenience.

The following discussion will attempt to clarify the issues listed above. Numerous examples will be given, but the emphasis will be on the reasoning process involved in choosing a correct fingering. The specific fingerings given are not intended as final solutions; variations in individual technique, hand structure, and temperament prevent this. It is often necessary to choose between alternative fingerings, each with its own strengths and weaknesses.

TOPOGRAPHY

Frédéric Chopin was the first teacher to have grasped the significance of the following five-finger position.

Example 1 Five-finger position.

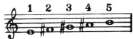

This is the most natural position possible for the hand: long fingers (second, third, and fourth) on the short (black) keys, and short fingers (thumb and fifth) on the long (white) keys. For this reason, the B major scale is probably the easiest to play, and was the first scale Chopin would teach to his students.[5]

For the purpose of this discussion, a fingering will be called topographical if, for the most part, it places long fingers on the black keys and short fingers on the white keys as shown in Example 2.

Example 2 Chopin: *Sonata in B Minor*, Op. 58, 4th movement, mm. 64-66.

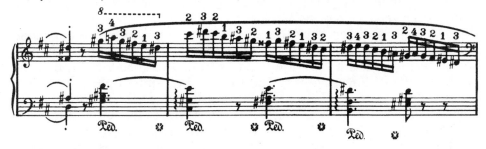

[4]Heinrich Neuhaus, *The Art of Piano Playing*, trans. by K.A. Leibovitch (London: Barrie & Jenkins, 1973), p. 146.

[5]Frederick Niecks cites Madame Dubois (one of Chopin's pupils) as the source of this information. *Frederic Chopin as a Man and Musician*, 3rd ed. (London: 1902; Reprint. New York: Cooper Square, 1973), Vol. II, p. 182.

A Guide to Piano Fingering

This is one of many examples from piano literature that initially appears difficult, but is relatively easy to master due to the keyboard topography involved.

Topographical considerations prompted the earlier teachers to arrive at the rule of avoiding the thumb and fifth finger on the black keys. Nevertheless, beginning with the second half of the eighteenth century, the increasing demands of keyboard virtuosity began to make themselves felt. The new kind of technical passagework demanded more liberal use of the thumb and fifth finger as shown in Examples 3 and 4.

Example 3   Mozart: *Concerto in A Major*, K.488, 1st movement, m. 281.

Example 4   Mozart: *Concerto in E-flat Major*, K.271, 1st movement, mm. 313-314.

Other fingerings for the previous two examples are awkward and clumsy. Paul and Eva Badura-Skoda were prompted to write, "In playing Mozart it is better not to apply the old teaching rule that the thumb and fifth finger are to avoid the black keys."[6]

In 1828, Johann Nepomuk Hummel emphasized, in his treatise on piano playing, the need for a new type of fingering.[7] By the middle of the nineteenth century, piano technique had expanded to such a point that the archaic rules of fingering were laid to rest once and for all. Chopin and Liszt, through their expansion of the possiblities of the instrument, did much to liberate piano fingering from the shackles of the earlier rules. This is shown in Example 5 and in Chopin's *Étude*, Op. 10 No. 5.

In the fingering of scales, topographical considerations may suggest

[6]Eva and Paul Badura-Skoda, *Interpreting Mozart on the Keyboard*, trans. by Leo Black (New York: St. Martin's Press, 1962), p. 150.
[7]Johann Nepomuk Hummel, *Ausführliche theoretische-practische Anweisung zum Piano-Forte-Spiel* (Vienna: Haslinger, [ca. 1828]), pp. 105-389.

Special Subjects

alternatives to the normally taught fingerings. Example 6 gives the traditional fingering taught by the majority of piano teachers today, and found in such exercise books as Hanon's *The Virtuoso Pianist*.

Example 5 Liszt: *Concerto No. 1 in E-flat Major*, 3rd movement, mm. 61-62.

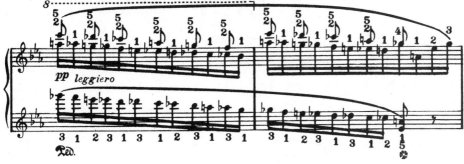

Example 6 G major scale.

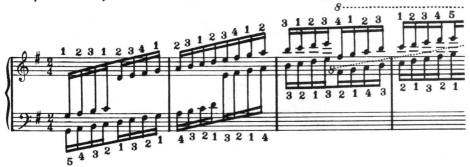

It is easy from a mental standpoint, since the thumbs coincide on G except on the first and last notes of the scale. This coincidence of thumbs also provides a strong sense of tonality, and is convenient in sight-reading and memorization. There is only one drawback with this fingering: topographically, the left hand would be better off with the fourth finger on F-sharp, as shown in Example 7.

This type of topographical fingering has had an increasing amount of interest in recent times. It is based on the principle that, whenever possible, the thumb should cross *under* a longer finger from a black key towards a white key, and a longer finger should cross *over* the thumb from a white key towards a black key. When considering the hands played separately, this fingering is the easiest possible. However, the correlation of the finger patterns to the sense of the tonic G is relatively weak in the left hand, and the coordination of the hands is somewhat more difficult than the fingering in Example 6.

A Guide to Piano Fingering

Example 7 G major scale.

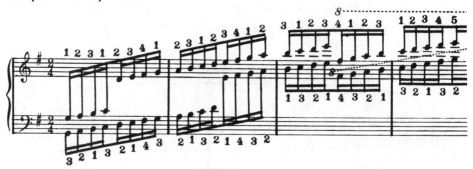

In the concluding scale from Menotti's *Toccata in G Major*, the following topographical fingering prevents unnecessary interference between the hands.

Example 8 Menotti: *Toccata in G Major*, mm. 84-85.

However, in scale passages requiring a strong tonal sense, the traditional fingering is usually the simplest and the best, as shown in Example 9.

Example 9 Beethoven: *Concerto in C Minor*, Op. 37, 1st movement, mm. 111-112.

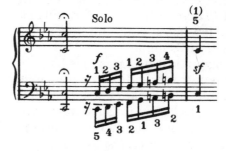

In fingering arpeggios, we generally have a choice between the traditional fingerings, emphasizing mental convenience, and topographical

Special Subjects

fingerings, aimed at minimizing the distance of the crossing. An example of this is:

Example 10 A major arpeggio.

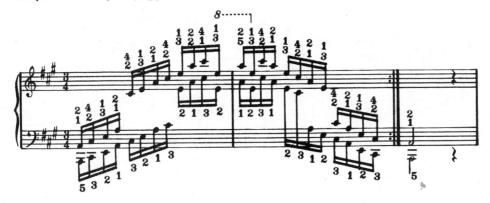

In Example 11, a traditional fingering (thumb on the first triplet of beats one through three) would work well for the first two beats, but would lead to problems on the third beat of the measure.

Example 11 Mozart: *Sonata in D Major*, K.576, 3rd movement, mm. 24-25.

Topographical considerations are weaker in Example 12, however, because of the absence of black notes; the traditional fingering is better here since it is both mentally easier and rhythmically stronger.

Example 12 Mozart: *Sonata in D Major*, K.576, 3rd movement, mm. 93-94.

A Guide to Piano Fingering

At times, topographical considerations may be hidden or latent. Consider the following fingerings:

Example 13 Chopin: *Étude in G-sharp Minor*, Op. 25 No. 6, mm. 29-30.

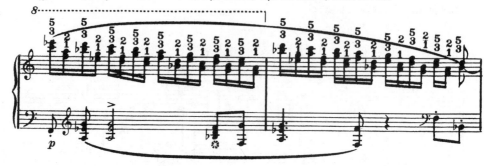

The fingering in Example 13, although mentally easy, requires difficult adjustments of the hand and arm.

Example 14 Chopin: *Étude in G-sharp Minor*, Op. 25 No. 6, mm. 29-30.

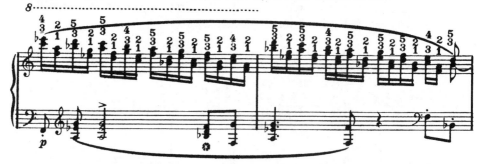

Although this fingering does not immediately suggest itself, it is far preferable to the fingering in Example 13. The fourth finger takes the top black notes when they occur, with good results.

SPECIAL USES OF THE FINGERS

Because of anatomical differences, there are strong and weak fingers. Whenever possible, the thumb, second, and third fingers should take those notes requiring heaviness of tone, while the fourth and fifth fingers should take those notes where a softer sound is needed.

An example of this utilization of the thumb for a desired musical effect is the following fingering, cited by the MCA/Hal Leonard edition and by Neuhaus as the composer's own.[8]

[8]Neuhaus, *op. cit.*, p. 97.

Example 15 Rachmaninoff: *Étude-Tableau in C Minor*, Op. 39 No. 7, m. 22.

Although this fingering is neither physically nor mentally the easiest, it has significant musical advantages: the generous use of the thumb aids in achieving the desired heaviness of the staccato notes; also, the fingering prevents a flippant rendering of the passage. I am nevertheless aware that this unusual fingering will not be acceptable to all.

Another example of Rachmaninoff's fingering given by MCA/Hal Leonard is:[9]

Example 16 Rachmaninoff: *Étude-Tableau in D Minor*, Op. 39 No. 8, mm. 100-102.

The so-called weak fingers can be used to advantage in the following type of passage shown in the lower fingering.[10]

Example 17 Beethoven: *Sonata in B-flat Major*, Op. 106 ("Hammerklavier"), 1st movement, mm. 75-76.

The lower fingering is easier, as it does not involve the crossing over of

[9]Sergei Rachmaninoff, *Études-Tableaux*, Opp. 33/39, ed. by Alfred Mirovitch (Milwaukee: MCA/Hal Leonard, 1950), p. 84.
[10]Neuhaus, *op. cit.*, p. 96.

the thumb, and more naturally conveys the softer dynamics of the notes. The upper fingering is also adequate, and will be more comfortable for some players.

The thinness and weakness of the fifth finger can be used to advantage on the last note of Liszt's *Sonata in B Minor*.

Example 18   Liszt: *Sonata in B Minor*, mm. 755-760.

Conversely, in Example 19, the fifth finger can be used as an extension of the arm to produce a large volume of sound.

Example 19   Rachmaninoff: *Étude-Tableau in E-flat Minor*, Op. 39, mm. 1-2.

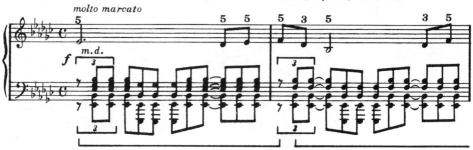

Strong fingers should be used, whenever possible, where clarity of articulation is needed. The lower fingering in Example 20 is recommended. The upper fingering shortens the distance of the leap, but the need for strong articulation outweighs this consideration.

Example 20   Beethoven: *Sonata in A-flat Major*, Op. 101, 4th movement, mm. 5-6.

The third finger also has special uses. In Example 21 the third finger's length and supporting ability makes it ideal for the long jump.

Example 21   Chopin: *Scherzo in B-flat Minor*, Op. 31, m. 780.

In Example 22 a trumpet-like effect is produced when the third finger is braced by the thumb.

Example 22   Debussy: "General Lavine-Eccentric," from *Préludes, Book II*, mm. 1-3.

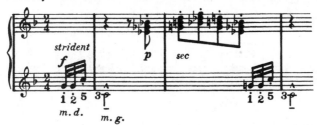

It is sometimes useful to cross a longer finger over a shorter one (third over fourth, or fourth over fifth), or to cross a shorter finger under a longer one (fifth under fourth, or fourth under third). These possibilities are often useful in polyphonic textures requiring legatissimo. The fingering in Example 23 is indicative of the devices necessary in such passages.[11]

PHYSICAL VERSUS MENTAL CONVENIENCE

Topographical fingerings are not always physically convenient, as shown in Example 24. Here, the lower fingering is both mentally and physically easier. The upper fingering, although topographically well conceived, is difficult to execute at a brisk tempo due to the turning under of the thumb.

---

[11]Most of this fingering comes from an example given by Badura-Skoda, p. 286.

A Guide to Piano Fingering

Example 23 Mozart: *Concerto in C Minor*, K.491, 3rd movement, mm. 129-133.

Example 24 Chopin: *Étude in C-sharp Minor*, Op. 10 No. 4, m. 1.

Example 24 is a sequential pattern of four notes in succession. In such situations, both George Kochevitsky[12] and Matthay favor fingerings of mental convenience over topographical fingerings, which are often physically easier. Matthay writes:

> "It is far easier to keep the finger figurations in agreement with the note figuration than to confuse the performer's finger-rhythm sense by altering the fingering of successive groups (of similarly sounding notes) in accordance with the laws of key position."[13]

Chopin also generally adhered to this concept of sequential consistency

[12] *The Art of Piano Playing: A Scientific Approach* (Princeton: Summy-Birchard/Birch Tree Group Ltd., 1967), pp. 48-49.
[13] Tobias Matthay, *Muscular Relaxation Studies* (London: Bosworth, 1912), p. 138.

Special Subjects

in fingering. An example is found in the French first edition of the *Études*, Op. 10.[14]

Example 25   Chopin: *Étude in C Minor*, Op. 10 No. 12, m. 28.

In Example 26, the lower fingering in the left hand is preferable due to the synchronization of hands. The upper fingering would be better if each hand were playing alone.

Example 26   Mendelssohn: *Concerto in G Minor*, Op. 25, 1st movement, m. 218.

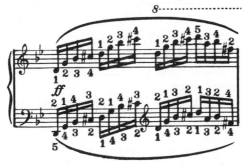

Mental convenience is particularly important in the following passage from Schubert's "Wanderer" *Fantasy*. The lower fingering is far superior since only four hand positions are required for the entire arpeggio as opposed to six in the upper fingering. Also, the synchronization of hands, manifested in the coincidence of thumb and fifth finger, is stronger in the lower fingering.

One may generalize concerning the relative merits of different fingerings based on mental versus physical convenience. These considerations must be balanced when deciding upon the fingering of any specific passage. There is significant interplay between these considerations in that fingerings of mental convenience vary in physical ease, and fingerings of physical convenience vary in mental ease. Fingerings of mental convenience:

1. usually involve fewer changes of position with each position resulting in a greater number of notes played

[14]Frédéric Chopin, *Études pour le piano* (Paris: Schlesinger, 1833), p. 51.

A Guide to Piano Fingering

2. tend toward more open, stretched positions of the hand
3. may involve the rapid repetition of the same fingers due to the emphasis on maintaining a given position as long as possible
4. tend toward a successive use of the fingers, avoiding the crossing over or under of fingers

Example 27 Schubert: *Fantasy in C Major*, D.760 ("Wanderer"), 4th section, m. 118.

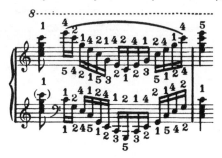

Fingerings of physical convenience:

1. usually involve a closed position of the hand, which is intrinsically more comfortable than a stretched position
2. usually involve more changes of hand position, with each position encompassing fewer notes
3. generally change the fingers on rapid repeated notes

THE RELATIONSHIP OF FINGERING TO MUSICAL CONTENT

A basic premise of this discussion is that an accurate musical rendering is the prime concern in fingering. To quote Heinrich Neuhaus:

"... that fingering is best which allows the most accurate rendering of the music in question and which corresponds most closely to its meaning ... the principle of physical comfort, of convenience of a particular hand is secondary and subordinate to the first, the main principle."[15]

Focus will be given to this issue, specifically dealing with the relationship of fingering to speed, rhythmic grouping, sound, and legato.

Often the composer's original fingering may give us an invaluable clue to the musical effect intended in a given passage. Franz Liszt, for example, shows us a special way to finger a scale when great velocity and brilliance are needed.[16]

[15]Neuhaus, *op. cit.*, p. 141.
[16]*Ibid.*, p. 143.

Special Subjects

Example 28 Liszt: *Spanish Rhapsody*, mm. 29-30.

This innovative fingering flouts traditional scale fingering practice, yet, it is by far the best way to achieve the speed and brilliance necessary.

The following passage calls for much the same musical effect.

Example 29 Rachmaninoff: *Concerto in C Minor*, Op. 18, 3rd movement, mm. 34-35.

This fingering exemplifies mental convenience. The thumb crosses under a minimum of times, and the fingers play consecutively, creating a glissando effect. The proper execution of this fingering requires a supple wrist and loose arm to carry the hand in and out in a series of rapid motions.

Composers' fingerings sometimes give clues to the rhythmic grouping of notes in certain passages. The Henle edition cites the fingering in Example 30 as Beethoven's.[17] Although Beethoven provided finger numbers for the left hand only, it seems obvious that the right hand should use the same numbers in reverse order.

In chromatic scales, there are two possibilities for fingering. Example 31 uses the strong fingers exclusively; it is best for strength, evenness, and a clear articulation.

---

[17]Ludwig van Beethoven, *Klaviersonaten*, ed. by B.A. Wallner (Munich: Henle, 1953), Vol. II, p. 329.

A Guide to Piano Fingering

Example 30 Beethoven: *Sonata in C Minor*, Op. 111, 2nd movement, m. 176.

Example 31 Chromatic scale.

Example 32 emphasizes velocity and a smooth legato.

Example 32 Chromatic scale.

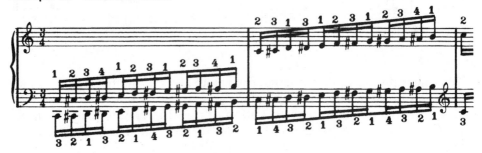

Examples of both types of fingerings are:

Example 33 Beethoven: *Concerto in E-flat Major*, Op. 73, 1st movement, mm. 207-8.

Special Subjects

Example 34 Liszt: *Mephisto Waltz, No. 1*, mm. 593-96.

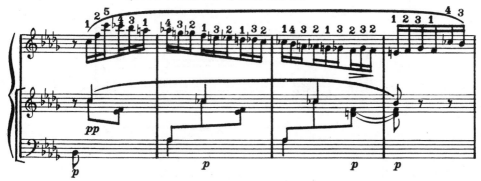

In chromatic runs, the possibility of using the fifth finger can be considered. The lower fingering in Example 35 stresses mental convenience. It is a good fingering for those who have strong third, fourth, and fifth fingers in the right hand. Due to the less frequent crossings of the thumb, great velocity is obtainable. The main disadvantage of this fingering is that it is topographically awkward, using the fifth finger on a black key.

Example 35 Liszt: *Mephisto Waltz, No. 1*, mm. 261-264.

The upper fingering in Example 35 uses strong fingers throughout, resulting in better articulation at the top of the chromatic scale. Also, more crescendo on the ascending part of the run is possible. In terms of obtainable velocity, this fingering is almost as good as the other. The choice between the two ultimately depends upon one's technical equipment and musical concept of the passage.

The fingering in Example 36 is cited in the Henle edition as being Beethoven's.[18] This fingering permits the proper dynamic inflection of the slurs, and helps to clarify the question of whether the repeated notes are to be slurred or tied to each other.

[18]*Ibid.*, p. 300.

A Guide to Piano Fingering

Example 36 Beethoven: *Sonata in A-flat Major*, Op. 110, 3rd movement, m. 5.

Special skill in the art of substituting fingers is often needed in legato playing. Unfortunately, too many pianists rely on the damper pedal for their legato. Observe Chopin's fingering, given in the German first edition of the *Études*, Op. 25, for the following passage.[19]

Example 37 Chopin: *Étude in B Minor*, Op. 25 No. 10, mm. 29-38.

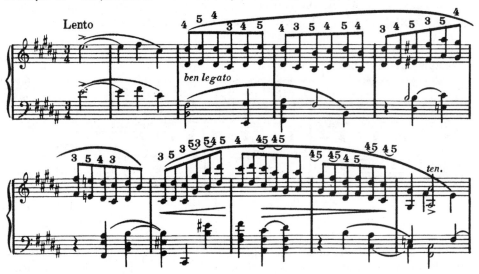

This fingering brings to mind Hipkin's comment that Chopin "changed his fingers upon a key as often as an organ-player."[20] The numerous finger substitutions prevent the excessively fast tempo we often hear in performances of the *Étude*.

[19]Frédéric Chopin, *Douze études pour le piano, Oeuvre 25* (Leipzig: Breitkoff & Härtel, 1837), p. 12.
[20]Edith J. Hipkins, *How Chopin Played* (London: Dent, 1937), p. 5.

FACILITATIONS

A facilitation shall be considered a change in the original distribution of notes between the hands, as written by the composer. It is usually, although not always, clear how the composer intends the notes to be distributed. For example, observe the direction of the note stems in Example 38.

Example 38 Bartók: *Suite*, Op. 14, 3rd movement, mm. 1-2.

In another example, the composer distributes a passage between the hands which could have been taken with the right hand alone.

Example 39 Debussy: "Doctor Gradus ad Parnassum" from *Children's Corner*, m. 7.

A good facilitation, by eliminating technical awkwardness, enables the pianist to better convey the musical essence of the passage in question. In Example 40, the elimination of unnecessary interference between the hands makes a proper musical rendering more likely.

In Example 41, an awkward jump in the left hand is avoided.

Facilitations are frequently necessary for pianists with small hands. The facilitation in Example 42 solves the problem of the large chord in the left hand. The alternative of a rolled chord on the fourth beat is weaker. If the chord is rolled before the beat, the pedaling is problematic; if the chord is rolled on the beat, a certain musical awkwardness results.

One can, however, go too far in the desire for physical ease. It would be difficult to respect the accomplishments of a pianist who would play

A Guide to Piano Fingering

Example 40 Chopin: *Étude in A-flat Major*, Op. 25 No. 1, m. 28.

Example 41 Schubert: *Fantasy in C Major*, D. 760 ("Wanderer"), 1st section, mm. 71-72.

Example 42 Chopin: *Prelude in D-flat Major*, Op. 28 No. 15, m. 9.

the last two measures of Chopin's *Étude*, Op. 10 No. 2 in the following fashion.

Example 43 Chopin: *Étude in A Minor*, Op. 10 No. 2, mm. 47-49.

Special Subjects

This facilitation, of course, defeats the entire meaning and purpose of the *étude*.

In Examples 44 and 45, consider the following two facilitations, given by Musafia.[21] The second rendering is easier to play, divided between the two hands.

Example 44 Liszt: *Mephisto Waltz*, No. 1, m. 813.

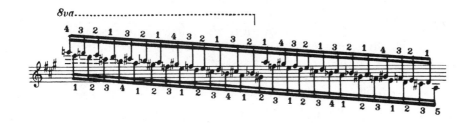

Example 45 Liszt: *Concerto in E-flat Major*, 4th movement, m. 69.

Example 44 is a good facilitation since brilliance of execution is needed here. In Example 45, however, the dynamic is piano, and alternate

[21]Julien Musafia, *The Art of Fingering in Piano Playing* (Milwaukee: MCA/Hal Leonard, 1971), p. 4.

A Guide to Piano Fingering

hammering of the the hands (shown in the second version) more naturally conveys a louder dynamic. This facilitation is inadvisable. Just where the line is drawn between what is acceptable and what is unacceptable will, of course, depend upon the judgement and taste of each individual pianist. This is true of all problems in piano playing.

CONCLUSION

It is recommended that the student be as creative as possible in the area of fingering. All too often, students will tend to simply follow the published fingerings written in the score, which are often not the best, or they will haphazardly go with whatever their hands do upon a first reading. Worse still, students may not be consistent in their fingering habits from playing to playing; this can lead to real problems in public performances. Early in the learning process, the best fingering should be chosen from all the viable alternatives and should then be written in the score. Finally, keep in mind that the best solution is not always the most obvious one; thought and innovation will allow us to discover some of those hidden fingerings which can make the difference between consistent success or failure in a given passage.

Keep in mind also that a passage must be played up to tempo to decide which fingering is most comfortable. Almost any fingering may seem fine at slow practice tempos. If the student cannot play a given passage fast enough in the early stages of learning a piece, the teacher can give fingering suggestions. Nevertheless, the teacher should encourage the student as early as possible to become self-reliant in fingering choices. As in all phases of piano instruction, the final goal is to bring the student to the level where a teacher is no longer necessary.

BIBLIOGRAPHY

Bach, C.P.E. *Essay on the True Art of Playing Keyboard Instruments.* Trans. and ed. by William Mitchell. New York: W.W. Norton & Company, Inc., 1949.

Badura-Skoda, Eva and Paul. *Interpreting Mozart on the Keyboard.* Trans. by Leo Black. New York: St. Martin's Press, 1962.

Beethoven, Ludwig van. *Klaviersonaten.* Vol. II. Ed. by B.A. Wallner. Munich: Henle, 1953.

Chopin, Frédéric. *Études pour le piano*, Op. 10. Paris: Schlesinger, 1833.

_____. *Douze études pour le piano, Oeuvre 25.* Leipzig: Breitkopf & Härtel, 1837.

Cortot, Alfred. *In Search of Chopin.* Westport: Greenwood Press, 1952.

Cowles, Mary Kathryn. "Three Systems of Scale Fingering." *Clavier*, March, 1975, pp. 29-30.

Hipkins, Edith J. *How Chopin Played (Notes of A.J. Hipkins)*. London: Dent, 1937.

Hummel, Johann Nepomuk. *Ausführliche theoretisch-practische Anweisung zum Piano-Forte-Spiel*. Vienna: Haslinger, ca. 1828.

Kochevitsky, George. *The Art of Piano Playing: A Scientific Approach*. Princeton: Summy-Birchard/Birch Tree Group Ltd., 1967.

Matthay, Tobias. *Muscular Relaxation Studies*. London: Bosworth, 1912.

Musafia, Julien. *The Art of Piano Fingering*. Milwaukee: MCA/Hal Leonard, 1971.

Neuhaus, Heinrich. *The Art of Piano Playing*. Trans. by K.A. Leibovitch. London: Barrie & Jenkins, 1973.

Newman, William S. *The Pianist's Problems*. New York: Harper & Row, Publishers, Inc., 1950.

Niecks, Frederick. *Frédéric Chopin as a Man and Musician*. 3rd ed. London: 1902; Reprint. New York: Cooper Square, 1973.

Rachmaninoff, Sergei. *Études-Tableaux*, Opp. 33/39. Ed. by Alfred Mirovitch. Milwaukee: MCA/Hal Leonard, 1950.

Keeping Abreast of New Publications 16

A great deal of new piano music is printed each year by various publishers. New methods and teaching pieces, collections, editions, arrangements, exercises, theory materials, and pop music are released to music stores as "new issues." From this volume of materials, how can teachers become knowledgeable about new publications?

There are several sources available to provide information about new materials:

1. Reviews in music magazines
2. Advertisements in music magazines
3. Workshops
4. New issues in music stores
5. Reference copies available for music teacher organizations
6. Publishers' catalogs or brochures sent via direct mail

A subscription to *Keyboard Companion, Clavier, Piano and Keyboard,* or the *Maxwell Music Evaluation Notebook* will provide valuable information about new teaching music through reviews. In addition to magazine subscriptions, some new music is reviewed in journals sent to members of organizations such as the Music Teachers National Association *(American Music Teacher)* and the National Guild of Piano Teachers *(Piano Guild Notes)*. However, the reviews in these two journals usually are limited.

Of course music must be heard and played; only limited knowledge about a piece can be given in a review. Nevertheless, valuable general information can be obtained through a review. One usually can gain knowledge about grading, style, and price, along with additional remarks. A composer whose music you like will catch your eye from a review, and you will want to try the newly published work. Therefore, reading reviews is a must!

Publishers often send promotional brochures to teachers. Although the product is unseen and unheard, you can rely on composers of merit and feel confident that their new work(s) will have some of the same qualities you liked in previous publications.

Piano workshops provide an excellent opportunity to become familiar with new music. Sometimes workshops are specifically designed to present new music by all publishers, such as the Schmitt Music Center Clinic held in Minneapolis each August.

Numerous music stores sponsor workshops (usually free) to area teachers. These are often given by a composer or publisher introducing new materials. A few hours spent with a composer will acquaint teachers with new music. In addition to learning about this composer's new music, teachers will have an opportunity to ask questions regarding the works being presented. To be informed of area workshops sponsored by music stores, teachers should make sure their names are on store mailing lists. If a teacher moves to a new town, that teacher should give his or her name and address to the new music store, and notify the previous music store to delete the name from its mailing list.

Most music stores subscribe to "new issues" from various publishers. These music stores often have a new issue file for browsing. In addition, some music stores have newsletters or catalogs which feature new music. Unfortunately, many smaller stores are unable to receive new issues, and teachers in these communities are unable to see new music.

Many local teacher organizations purchase new publications for their teachers to survey; the expense can be kept to a minimum by assessing teachers a small annual fee. The publications may be stored in a library, club room, or a teacher's studio. The works can be graded and filed and can serve as a most useful source for becoming acquainted with new music by actual examination. In addition, if a nearby college has a piano pedagogy program, teachers may be able to survey their reference materials.

Most publishers have catalogs. By writing to each publisher you can receive the latest one.

From the foregoing it can be surmised that teachers can keep up with new materials. It is the teachers' responsibility to learn about new issues and to try them. Trying a new method or a new teaching piece or collection will be an added benefit, and will help to prevent teacher burnout!

Special Subjects

How to Prepare Students for Competitions 17

Each year many students participate in contests, rallies, auditions, or festivals. They are judged on the performance rendered, usually in the form of written evaluations by one or more judges. Preparation for these events involves a great deal of work from both students and teachers. There are advantages as well as disadvantages in entering competitions.

PROS

Students generally benefit from preparing one or more pieces for competition. They receive written comments from judges which aid both students and teachers in preparing for future auditions. Also, periodic evaluations provide the following incentives:

Motivation. Students tend to work with increased interest and to practice more when they have to perform in a competition.

Goals. Ratings, certificates, the passing of "grades" or levels, medals, cups, and cash awards, provide tangible goals for students.

Performance experience. Students receive experience in coping with problems of performance under pressure, and they benefit from written evaluations from judges.

Systematic musical growth. The examination system gives standards by which student achievement can be judged.

Teacher improvement. Piano teachers who enter students regularly in competitions are submitting their students for commendation or criticism. Comments on judging sheets can be of great help on how to improve students for future competitions.

CONS

Competitions can be a humiliating experience for both students and teachers if they receive low marks and harsh criticism from judges. Generally, the reason for a poor standard is derived from the following items:

Lack of preparation. To receive top awards in a competition, students *must* be well-prepared. The teacher should make every effort to be sure students are able to play the piece(s) adequately. The students entering a competition should have performed the piece many times. The performance could be a recital, informal gathering, and/or for friends or family.

Choosing a piece too difficult for the student. The teacher should choose music that is not beyond the limits of the student. A poor performance will result if the music chosen is too difficult!

Inadequate technique. Students who have a poor hand position, a general lack of tone balance, phrasing, dynamics, and steady tempo are most certain to receive poor marks from judges.

Memory. The student who struggles through a piece with memory slips will not receive high marks in a competition.

From the preceding items it should be obvious that teachers must strive to have their students well-prepared before entering a competition. In addition, students of below-average ability probably should not be entered. The teacher should strive for high standards!

PREPARATION OF STUDENTS FOR COMPETITIONS

The teacher has the responsibility of preparing students to perform their best under pressure. Some teachers give students ample time to learn a piece adequately, while others try to accomplish the impossible at the last moment. Generally, several months are required to give students sufficient time to learn a work thoroughly.

A superior performance depends on sound teaching techniques. Judges look for good posture at the keyboard, correct hand position, good wrist flexibility (down-up motion used in phrasing), evenness of touch, correct pedal usage, and good facility. These factors cannot be "crammed" at the last moment.

The procedure for a successful performance is to follow the composer's directions explicitly. A steady tempo is desirable; however, for those students unable to meet the requirements of a fast tempo, it is advisable to slightly reduce the tempo so the piece can be played accurately. Also, strict attention to legato-staccato, rests, phrasing, and pedal should be correctly executed. The integration of style, technique, and musicianship should communicate to the listener that this performance is as well-prepared as possible.

One of the principle goals of teaching is to encourage students to listen, not only to themselves, but to others. Recordings and tapes of concert artists help in this regard, and students can gain insights from listening to famous pianists perform the work they are studying.

In addition to hearing their pieces performed by others, students should be encouraged to hear their own performances via a recorder or video tape. Continuity, rhythm, accuracy, etc. is readily apparent. Students often do not realize what is being done incorrectly while they are playing, and hearing the performance will highlight places where improvement is necessary.

After the music is learned, it is helpful to have all the students involved in the competition play their pieces in a recital approximately two weeks before the date of the competition. This performance provides the needed practice of playing under pressure; if mistakes and memory slips occur, these places can be corrected by students before the competition.

SELECTING QUALIFIED JUDGES

The person or persons responsible for hiring judges should try to select those with the highest qualifications. Generally, judges are chosen from university piano faculties; however, independent piano teachers are often excellent judges because they generally have more experience teaching younger children.

The qualifications for good judges include the following:

1. knowledge of the repertoire selected for the audition
2. the ability to recognize and evaluate musical qualities such as voicing of melodic lines, phrasing, pedal, and other items
3. some knowledge of the psychology of students, and experience in communicating with them is also important, especially in making criticism in a positive manner. Students should leave a competition feeling that some benefit was derived from the event to serve as a motivating factor for the next competition!

The following judging procedures should be observed:

1. A welcoming remark helps to calm the student and gives proper time to relax a moment before beginning the audition.
2. The judge should always offer some encouragement to the student on the rating forms, no matter how inadequate the performance.
3. Remarks written on the rating form should be comprehensive and legible.
4. The piano should be placed in a position so the judge can observe both hand position and pedaling of the students playing in the audition.
5. The judge should make an effort to be as quiet and attentive as possible so the student will not be distracted.
6. The judge should follow the time schedule! A slow judge is appreciated by no one—students, teachers, nor officials. Note: those who plan the schedule need to be realistic in allowing enough time for the performance and written evaluations.

How to Prepare Students for Competition

THE ROLE OF THE TEACHER AT COMPETITIONS

The teacher should make every effort to be as unobtrusive as possible at competitions. In private auditions the teacher is generally not allowed to be present. However, in open auditions, the teacher may be in the audience. The teacher should maintain a calm approach; it does not help contestants if the teacher is bustling about in a state of anxiety! The same goes for parents.

Teachers will benefit from listening to open auditions and evaluating the students who performed. Items include hand position, steady tempo, phrasing, dynamics, pedaling, and other musical qualities.

After all ratings have been posted, it is very beneficial to give supportive comments, even though some students did not play as well as expected.

A SONATINA CONTEST

The Music Teachers' Association of California (MTAC), San Diego Branch, has a yearly *Sonatina Contest* in which students compete against others playing a specific required piece at each level. In the early levels students play sonatina movements; in the upper levels sonata movements are required. The repertoire list is changed each year. Below is a sample repertoire list:

1.	Olson	*Sonatina in A minor*, first movement from *Beginning Sonatinas*, p. 13 (This group is open to students who have not reached their ninth birthday.)	Alfred Publishing Company
2.	Bastien	*"Sunrise Sonatina,"* first movement from *Two Sonatinas*	Neil A. Kjos Music Company
3.	Gillock	*Sonatina in C*, first movement from *Accent on Rhythm and Style*, p. 9	Willis Music Company
4.	Kabalevsky	*Sonatina in A minor*, Op. 27 No. 11	
5.	Beethoven	*Sonatina in F*, Anh. 5 No. 2, second movement	
6.	Clementi	*Sonatina*, Op. 36 No. 6, first movement	
7.	Kuhlau	*Sonatina*, Op. 59 No. 1, first movement	

8. Beethoven	*Sonatina in G*, Op. 49 No. 2, first movement	
9. Agay	*Sonatina Hungarica*, first movement	MCA/ Hal Leonard
10. Haydn	*Sonatina in Bb*, first movement	
11. Mozart	*Sonata in F*, K. 332, third movement	

Contest Rules

The following contest rules are sent to all teachers in the MTAC San Diego branch:

Eligibility and fees: Students of MTAC members are eligible to enter the contest for a fee of seven dollars ($7.00). There will be *no* refunds for entrants unable to play. All music must be memorized and performed *without* repeats. A first-place winner from any group must proceed to the next highest group the following year.

Ratings: Superior   These students will be finalists.
        Honorable Mention   Students receiving this rating will not be eligible for the finals, but will receive a Blue Ribbon with the words Honorable Mention.
        Excellent
        Very Good

Awards: Finalists will be selected from the preliminary hearings. First,- second,- and third-place winners will be chosen in each group. The place winners and finalists will all receive awards. All entrants will receive certificates.

Rules for judging: Each entrant will be judged in a private audition by a judge who will give a written evaluation of the performance. This written evaluation shall include commendation for items well-executed as well as constructive criticism. Every student who does not reach the finals shall know the reasons why he or she was not selected to compete in the finals. Judges will be free to choose as many or as few finalists as there are excellent performances. The finalists will be judged in a public audition by a panel of three judges. The judges will vote independently and scores will be tallied by the chairperson and committee. Ties will not be broken.

The following sheet is given to judges in the preliminaries which cover these musicianship areas:

	General Comments
Accuracy	
Rhythm	
Dynamics	
Technique	
Interpretation	
Tone Quality	
Pedal	
Rating	
Judge	

The following judging sheet is given to each of the three judges in the finals who reach their own decision without conferring:

To the Judge: Please consider the following points where applicable. Use plus signs (1-3) for "Good" to "Outstanding;" Leave blank for "Satisfactory;" use minus signs (1-3) for "Less than Satisfactory."

ACCURACY
Tempi   _____
Continuity   _____
Rhythm   _____
Notes & Rests   _____

TECHNIQUE
Tone   _____
Phrasing   _____
Shading   _____
Dynamics   _____
Pedal   _____

MUSICAL CONTENT
Style   _____
Structure   _____
Balance   _____
Voicing   _____

GENERAL COMMENTS_____

_____

Judge's Signature_____

Special Subjects

COMPETITION ORGANIZATIONS

There are numerous local and state organizations that sponsor auditions. The following national organizations are given here for reference:

Music Teachers National Association (MTNA), The Carew Tower, 441 Vine Street, Suite 505, Cincinnati, OH 45202. This organization sponsors the Baldwin Junior Keyboard Achievement Awards, the Young Chang Collegiate Artist Competition, and the Yamaha High School Auditions.

National Guild of Piano Teachers (the Guild), Box 1807, Austin, TX 78767. This organization sponsors auditions on an individual basis, in private, adjudicated by one judge. These auditions are held at the local level throughout the United States.

National Federation of Music Clubs (the Federation), 310 S. Michigan Avenue, Room 1936, Chicago, IL 60604. This organization sponsors national auditions. Repertoire must be chosen from the recommended list which is updated periodically.

The following competitions allow both young students and advanced students an opportunity to compete on a national level:

Young Keyboard Artists Association (YKAA), 30 Goldenbush, Irvine, CA 92714.

Joanna Hodges Piano Conference and Competition, College of the Desert, 43-500 Monterey Avenue, Palm Desert, CA 92260.

Stravinsky Awards International Piano Competition and Festival, 1003 West Church Street, Champaign, IL 61821.

SUMMARY

Preparing students for competitions need not be a traumatic experience. When the event is viewed by teacher and pupils as one factor in the learning sequence, when preparation is orderly and structured, most problems are solved. Further, a competition should be viewed in its proper perspective, and winning or losing should not be the main criteria. Students should realize that the event itself will provide them with constructive evaluations that will aid them and their teacher in future competitions. In many instances students will rise to the occasion and surprise themselves and their teacher!

The Advantages of
the Computer in the Studio 18

by Sharon Lohse Kunitz

Sharon Lohse Kunitz is an independent piano teacher, composer, author, and adjudicator. She holds a Bachelor of Music degree in piano pedagogy from the University of Colorado, Master of Arts degree in music history from the University of Denver, and additional studies at Augsburg College and the University of Washington. She has had varied experiences in education and teaching in colleges and public schools in North Dakota, Colorado, Washington, California, and New Mexico. Mrs. Kunitz is active in the Music Teachers National Association, having served in various positions at the state, division, and national levels. She teaches in her studio in Albuquerque, New Mexico where she also develops and utilizes computer software. Her career is listed in the *International Encyclopaedia of Women Composers, Who's Who in American Music, The International Who's Who in Music,* and the *International Directory of Distinguished Leadership.*

Each year the teacher is expected to teach a variety of repertoire, theory, technique, history, and ensemble to students within the confines of a brief lesson period. The lesson period may range from thirty to sixty minutes one day per week, and occasionally, the teacher may be able to schedule a class for group study. However, with the increasingly busy lives of students and parents, this scheduling problem becomes more acute. What can the teacher do to assist in the teaching environment?

Enter the computer. The computer is one of the technological advancements for which limits have yet to be attained. It can extend teaching and learning time. Both the teacher and student can benefit from this teaching tool.

Many teachers fear that a technological expertise is required to use the computer. While the technology may seem complex, this is contradicted by the widespread acceptance of such technological marvels as the microwave oven and the VCR. Both require minimum operating skills. One needs to read a well-written manual, and in a short period of time, the operator will enjoy the many benefits of the appliance.

COMPUTER SYSTEMS: HARDWARE/SOFTWARE

The computer offers many advantages. There are two components in a computer system: hardware and software. The hardware consists of a monitor (TV screen), disk drive, and C. P. U. (central processing unit). Accessories include synthesizer boards, keyboards, speaker systems, and headsets. Headsets are particularly useful if there is a problem with audio interference with other activities in the room. Many computers provide direct access to the sound going to the internal speaker. Teachers need only a basic system of a monitor, disk drive, and C. P. U. to initiate the use of the computer in the studio.

Now that the hardware is available, the key is having well-designed and easy-to-use software. Many software programs are available. Educators are encouraging programmers to write well-designed programs that fit their needs and offer easy use for students using the computer. Some software programs are exceptional for their "user-friendly" design. If the teacher has to supervise each student at the computer, the purpose of efficient and effective additional education will not have been gained.

It is important that the hardware and software be compatible. Unlike the record player or compact disc player which will play any brand of records or discs, the computer will not accept software written for other operating systems. It will read only the language compatible with its operating system.

Programs for software are commonly available on diskettes. Two types of diskettes are the 5¼ inch floppy diskette, or the 3½ inch mini-diskette. It is very important that the teacher be knowledgeable about the software before purchase of the hardware. The software is the vital component in music education.

CAPABILITIES OF THE COMPUTER

The computer offers innumerable advantages in instruction. The machine provides immediate response to the student. If the answer is incorrect, the correct answer is provided at that time. This immediate feedback leads the student into an active learning process. When properly programmed, this process can develop an extensive interactive relationship between the student and the computer.

The graphics enhance visual concepts taught by the teacher. Often, the student does not listen carefully to the teacher, but if the computer "says" something, then the student believes and understands.

The computer is a nonjudgmental medium. If a response is incorrect, the student is not embarrassed or insulted in front of peers or teacher. This is a very personal learning experience. Only the student and computer know.

So often, ear training is the last designated part of the lesson. Time expires before the lesson is completed, and the teacher postpones ear training to the next week. With the computer, audio reinforces the graphics, and ear training improves with drill. With audio examples accompanying a visual example, the correlation of pitch and location on the staff is reinforced, and the student is exposed to weekly ear training.

Serving as a teaching assistant, the computer can instruct while the teacher works in another capacity. One example is the use of the computer to teach theory while the teacher continues to work at the piano with another student. Prior to the computer, my students used to have only a thirty-minute piano lesson. Now, however, the student has an hour lesson, working thirty minutes at the piano with me and thirty minutes at the computer independently studying theory or related topics. Another teacher may offer computer instruction in conjunction with the monthly group class, while another teacher may only be able to provide fifteen minutes weekly at the computer. Some teachers offer theory instruction as a summer course to students desiring only theory. This can be effective for high school students who may need review before writing a college theory entrance exam. Whatever the situation, each teacher has the flexibility of utilizing the computer according to the studio schedule and students' needs.

EDUCATIONAL SOFTWARE

Two popular types of CAIM (computer-aided instruction in music) are tutorial and drills/games programs. The tutorial program teaches, drills, and reinforces. Tutorial programs that present concepts in a sequential manner similar to a workbook are available.

The drill program presents a concept common in the classroom or group experiences. A game program is similar, featuring drills in a "game-like" format. Both utilize the computer as an electronic flashcard. It is important that the teacher be familiar with the various types, and then schedule the appropriate material for the student. Some students respond more favorably to one type. Variety should be included in the curriculum to provide a comprehensive music program. Similarly, the software should include a mix of programs that fit the needs of the student. For example, a third-grade student would not be suited to work on a program designed for a college student. A game designed for a young beginning music student would have limited appeal to an older student. The same drill cannot be worked each week for months. The student's attention span will cease, and a negative response to the computer will evolve.

A third type of program evolving in software design features simulation. Simulation allows the student to create his or her own selection from a multiple of possible choices. Just as composition allows a student to develop a unique and personal piece, simulation encourages a student to select and choose. Even very young children can create, selecting a second note in relative position to the first note and then hear the audio reinforcement. If the notes are located closely on the staff, the audio interval will also be small. On the next example, the student may elect to move the second note a greater distance from the first note. The audio "feedback" will be a larger interval. Students feel very comfortable with the computer, and will explore many possibilities. Teachers may have apprehensions about the computer, but students will show us how to properly use it.

It is our responsibility to carefully select appropriate software and design a well-paced curriculum for each student. Being sensitive and aware of this development is a new and exciting study in the field of computer pedagogy. By incorporating tutorial, drills/games, and simulation types of software, the student will benefit from the orderly pattern or method used.

ADMINISTRATIVE SOFTWARE

Some software permits the computer to serve as an administrative tool. The computer serves as a typewriter using word processing programs for studio newsletters, invoices, and other business applications. The spread sheet program provides an instant print-out of credits and debits, and eases the burden of tax season. The data base software features a format for inventory of music in the library, and gives an accurate response for a certain piece by a specified composer. To be most useful, these programs need a printer for a print-out of specified material.

Another type of program used by musicians prints out music scores created by the user. It functions in the same way as a word processing program printing musical symbols and notes instead of words. It is very useful for creating worksheets or assignments. Just as a teacher reviews instructional software, so must one carefully review the unique capabilities and features of business software.

ECONOMICS

The purchase of the computer requires a large investment. Its tax status can be determined by an accountant. The purchase of programs for a software library is a second investment. Thus, it is important to review software, and purchase those programs that will give the most student usage segments per dollar.

Since the teacher is providing additional educational instruction with the computer, fees should reflect this benefit. Parents are generally sympathetic to the cost involved in providing this instruction and appreciate the enhanced lesson. As with all fees, local economic conditions should be considered. Some teachers charge a monthly, or annual lab fee. Others charge per lesson. My students are charged for a "music lesson" which consists of thirty minutes at the keyboard, and thirty minutes at the computer. Requiring computer time for each student, rather than offering it as optional, will eliminate many problems of billing and scheduling.

When introducing the use of the computer to the parents, an open house has proved to be very popular and successful. This provides an opportune time to personally visit with parents and students and explain your goals and objectives of the computer programs offered. A carefully-designed curriculum will enhance your music education program, and provide a more comprehensive lesson for each student.

SUGGESTED SOURCES FOR STUDIO COMPUTER-AIDED INSTRUCTION IN MUSIC (CAIM)

Alfred Publishing Company. 16380 Roscoe Boulevard., Suite 200, Van Nuys, CA 91410.

Electronic Courseware Systems. 1210 Lancaster Drive, Champaign, IL 61821.

Maestro Music, Inc. 2403 San Mateo NE, P-12, Albuquerque, NM 87110.

Temporal Acuity Products. 300 - 120th Avenue N.E., Bellevue, WA 98005.

Waterloo Music, Ltd. P.O. Box 366, Lewiston, NY 14092.

Wenger Corporation. 1401 East 79th Street, Bloomington, MN 55420.

Editions of Keyboard Music 19

by Maurice Hinson

Maurice Hinson received his musical training from the University of Florida, The Juilliard School, University of Michigan, and the Conservatoire National in Nancy, France. He is a past president of the Kentucky Music Teachers Association and the Southern Division of the Music Teachers National Association. He has given piano recitals, workshops, master classes, and lectures in many states, Asia, Australia, and Europe and has written articles for some of the leading American musical periodicals. Hinson is the author of *The Pianist's Reference Guide*, published by the Alfred Publishing Company; *Guide to the Pianist's Repertoire*, *Music for Piano and Orchestra*, *Music for More than One Piano*, and *The Piano in Chamber Ensemble* all published by the Indiana University Press. An authority in piano literature and early American keyboard literature, he has been a guest lecturer in piano at the Liszt Academy in Budapest, Hungary, as well as the National Music Camp in Interlochen, Michigan. Dr. Hinson is professor of piano at the Southern Baptist Theological Seminary, School of Church Music, Louisville, Kentucky.

Many editions of the masterworks are available today. A well-informed teacher will try to make authentic and reliable editions available to his or her students. The subject of editions is so broad that this short discussion can serve only as a brief introduction.

It is necessary to choose a good edition because it is highly desirable to follow the composer's intent as closely as possible. We want to be able to interpret correctly what we see on the printed page. Ideally, it would be best if we had access to the composer's manuscript, the autograph. This is mainly useful to the scholar but is not of much value to the average teacher, because many autographs contain markings that can only be deciphered by specialists.

Scholarly and complete editions came into being during the nineteenth century. The *Bach-Gesellschaft*, first complete editions of the works of Mozart, Beethoven and other major composers, became available during this time as the field of musicology became an accepted discipline. Many of these editions are presently being replaced by more up-to-date scholarship and research. The nineteenth century also produced many performer editions, editions that were filled with a famous performer's interpretations. Many of those editions are still with us today, and it is frequently impossible to distinguish the famous interpreter's markings from those of the composer.

The word "urtext" is seen on numerous masterworks printed today. This literally means "unedited" and signifies that the edition is based entirely on the composer's original markings. Few such listed editions can completely justify this claim since some editors have been involved in working with the original manuscript, or first editions, to produce a text that is reliably the composer's intention. The word urtext does not in itself assure authenticity. In fact, it is not possible to cite an urtext edition when the autograph or a first edition reviewed by the composer is available. If it were possible, one would have to restrict oneself to those works supported or documented by autographs that are still in existence. The further one goes back into the past, all the more frequently one becomes confronted with the problem of missing autographs.

The scholar's task is to apply research in the effort to arrive at what may be termed the composer's final wishes. There is no absolute certainty of this being possible. Neither do the autographs themselves always throw light on what the composer eventually intended. Beethoven, for instance, would make numerous corrections without even entering them in the autograph. The same applies to Mozart and Mendelssohn in particular, as well as many others. Haydn, on the other hand, left us with a neatly written fair copy which usually remained unaltered.

So, the reader can understand some of the problems regarding the word "urtext!"

The following criteria should be used in judging a good edition:

1. The editor's markings should be clearly differentiated typographically from those of the composer.
2. Judicious choice of fingering can be helpful to the student and the busy teacher who might have to devote valuable lesson time changing unwise editorial fingerings.
3. Sources the editor has used should be identified, and their location given; the identification should be complete.
4. Comments by the editor about the music, such as the history, style and interpretation, are highly desirable.
5. Reference marks are also helpful. Every fifth or tenth bar, or the first bar of each line should be numbered for easy reference.

GENERAL DISCUSSION OF EDITIONS BY PERIODS

Baroque period. One must be careful in choosing editions from this period because composers generally left the music unedited regarding dynamics, fingering, phrasing, tempo, articulation, and frequently used soprano, alto, and tenor clefs. One problem in music of older periods is the lack of performance directions. As we move closer to the present, composers began adding more editorial directions. The following considerations are offered for music from this period:

1. Some editing is necessary for all but the most thoroughly prepared teacher. However, too much editing is not desirable.
2. If an urtext version is used, the teacher must be prepared to create the edition for the student, which is very time-consuming.
3. Recommended editions for this period are Alfred Publishing Company, Bärenreiter, Henle, Kalmus, Peters, and Vienna Urtext.

Classical period. Clementi, Haydn, Mozart, and Beethoven left more editorial directions in their scores. Recommended editions for this period are Alfred Publishing Company, Henle, and Vienna Urtext (Universal Edition) publications which have clear, easy-to-read print, simple editorial markings (frequently explained in footnotes or extensive prefaces), and often include fingerings.

Romantic period. Composers from this period tended to be more specific in their markings, but pedal indications are frequently lacking and must be added by the editor, teacher and/or student. Pedaling is usually related to the harmonic changes. Ornaments are more frequently written out during this period. Editions by famous pedagogues and performers appeared more during this time.

Twentieth century. Most composers from this period mark their music very carefully; some (Bartók, Crumb) are almost finicky in their effort to indicate even the most minute nuance. Some composers have made special performing editions of their music (Prokofiev, Stravinsky, etc.). New types of notation are used by many contemporary composers such as Boulez, Cage, Crumb, Feldman, etc. This notation must be intelligently understood for an authentic performance.

PRINTED MISTAKES

In spite of all the efforts of a fine editor, mistakes and misreadings sometimes find their way into an edition. On one occasion, Beethoven is recorded to have written his publisher, "Errors, errors, nothing but errors, you yourself are one complete error." Beethoven was not a very good proofreader either! One should therefore always have a certain degree of skepticism concerning the absolute degree of accuracy of any printed page.

Some of the most common printed mistakes are:

1. Omitted accidentals
2. Incorrect accidentals used
3. A note on the wrong line or space (e.g. E instead of D. This is more possible in editions that use more than one color in printing.)
4. Use of incorrect clef
5. Ornament omitted
6. Use of an incorrect ornament
7. Dot of a dotted-note left out
8. A measure or more omitted
9. A measure or more duplicated
10. A measure numbered incorrectly

If, after repeated playings, a measure or passage does not "feel" or "sound" stylistically correct, the performer should make the necessary "corrections," but only after a plausible explanation based on the above or similar criteria has been carefully reached.

RECOMMENDED EDITIONS OF STANDARD COMPOSERS' WORKS

Bach, Johann Sebastian (1685–1750)

The *Two-* and *Three-Part Inventions, Partitas, French and English Suites, Italian Concerto, French Overture, Goldberg Variations, Fourteen Canons, Die Clavierbüchlein für Anna Magdelena Bach* and the one for W.F. Bach are the only keyboard works presently available in the *Neue Bach-Ausgabe* (Bärenreiter); other volumes are forthcoming. Kalmus

(Bischoff) offers the complete works, available in separate copies as well as in collections. Peters (Kroll, Landshoff, Sauer, and Bischoff) also publish the complete works. The editions of the *Well-Tempered Clavier* by Henle (von Irmer and Lampe), Belwin/Columbia Pictures (Tovey and Samuels), and G. Schirmer/Hal Leonard (Bischoff) and Volume I (Alfred Publishing Company) are excellent. Allans (T. Presser) has an edition of the *Well-Tempered Clavier* edited by Warren Thomson that includes an analysis of each prelude and fugue, plus a facsimile of the autograph, and the text is an urtext edition. The *Two-* and *Three-Part Inventions* are available from Henle (Steiglich and Lampe), C.F. Peters (Landshoff), Hansen (E. Fischer), Alfred (W. Palmer), J. Fischer (Friskin), while the *Two-Part Inventions* are available in a facsimile of the autograph along with a reprint of the *Bach-Gesellschaft* edition (Dover).

Bartók, Béla (1881–1945)

Boosey and Hawkes publish most of the works, including the *Mikrokosmos* and *For Children*. Alfred, MCA/Hal Leonard, G. Schirmer/Hal Leonard, and Kalmus have smaller lists. Universal also has a fine catalog including the piano concerti. Dover publishes two large volumes including a broad sampling.

Beethoven, Ludwig van (1770–1827)

The most reliable urtext of the sonatas are available in Henle (Wallner), G. Schirmer/Hal Leonard with preface and notes by Carl Krebs (not von Bülow and Lebert), Universal and Dover (Schenker), and Kalmus. Other excellent editions include Belwin/Columbia Pictures (Tovey-Craxton), especially for the commentary, Belwin/Columbia Pictures (Schnabel), and Peters (Arrau). Vienna Urtext has begun a new edition of the sonatas, bringing them out separately. So far, Opp. 10/2, 13, 14/1, 2, and 49 have appeared. The variations (urtext) are available in Henle (Schmidt-Görg and Georgii) and Vienna Urtext (Brendel). Vienna Urtext and Henle also have the various pieces (Opp. 33 to 129) and Alfred has the *Seven Sonatinas*. Henle publishes all the *Bagatelles* in one volume. Vienna Urtext also has the *Variations on Folksongs*, Opp. 105 and 107.

Brahms, Johannes (1833–97)

Distinguished editions are published by Henle, G. Schirmer/Hal Leonard, Dover (Mandyczewski), International Music Corporation, C.F. Peters (Seeman), and Kalmus (Sauer). *The Fifty-one Exercises* are published separately by Alfred, Kalmus, G. Schirmer/Hal Leonard, and Ricordi. Vienna Urtext has some of the short pieces (Opp. 117, 118, and 119) available, and Alfred has all of them in one volume. The complete *Transcriptions, Cadenzas and Exercises* are available from Dover (Mandyczewski) and C.F. Peters (Seeman). Alfred has the smaller works in one volume.

Chopin, Frédéric François (1810–49)

Highest recommendation goes to Henle, with the Chopin Institute edition (available through Marks/Hal Leonard) coming in a poor second. Well-edited editions, but with many differences, are the C.F. Peters (Scholtz), and Durand (Debussy); Salabert/Hal Leonard (Cortot) has some volumes with English translations of Cortot's notes, but the text is not the most reliable. Vienna Urtext has the *Préludes*, *Ballades*, *Impromptus*, *Nocturnes*, *Scherzos*, and *Études*. Alfred has most of the works (Palmer or Esteban). Special mention should be made of the Norton Critical Score (T. Higgins) of the *Preludes*. Casella has edited most of the works for Edizioni Curci. The Henle volumes are of special merit for containing both the Fontana versions and the original, when great differences occur.

Debussy, Claude (1862–1918)

Most of Debussy's piano music is published by Durand, available through Elkan-Vogal. Alfred, G. Schirmer/Hal Leonard, C. F. Peters, and Dover also have a wide selection. Alfred, Henle, and Vienna Urtext have Volume One of the *Préludes*. Alfred also has a broad selection in the volume *At the Piano with Debussy*.

Handel, George Frideric (1685–1759)

The *Hallische-Handel* edition (Bärenreiter) has five volumes containing the complete solo keyboard works. Volume I contains the eight "Great" suites, Volume II has the Second Set of suites, 1733; Volumes III and IV contain miscellaneous suites and pieces. Durand (Ropartz) has the complete works in four volumes. Peters (Ruthardt) also publishes the sixteen suites in two volumes, and Peters has two other volumes with *Lessons*, *Chaconnes*, *Pieces*, *Fugues and Fughettes*. C.F. Peters also has another complete edition edited by Serouky, in five volumes, more up-to-date than the Ruthardt. The Kalmus edition lists the sixteen suites in two volumes, and in another volume lists *Leçons*, *Pieces*, *Grand Fugues and Fughettes*. Schott, available through European-American, publishes *Seventy-six Pieces* (Fuller-Maitland and Squire). Alfred has an excellent collection of some of the miscellaneous pieces (Lucktenberg).

Haydn, Franz Josef (1732–1809)

Vienna Urtext Edition (Landon, Füssl) and Henle (Feder) publish all sixty-two sonatas (incipits of some lost ones) in three volumes. C.F. Peters has forty-nine of the sonatas in five volumes (Martienssen). Kalmus, available through Belwin/Columbia Pictures, publishes forty-three sonatas in four volumes. Breitkopf and Härtel, available through Associated Music Publishers (Zilcher), publish forty-two sonatas in four volumes reprinted by Dover. Kalmus and Peters publish other solo works and the sets of variations. The Henle and Vienna Urtext volumes of miscellaneous pieces are excellent.

Liszt, Franz (1811–86)

Bärenreiter-Editio Musica Budapest (available through Theodore Presser) has the complete original piano works in eighteen volumes. Henle has a number of volumes. C.F. Peters has a broad selection in twelve volumes (Sauer); since Sauer was a Liszt pupil, this edition takes on added significance. Salabert has a large selection available (Cortot); G. Schirmer/ Hal Leonard has a large amount (Joseffy and other editors); and Kalmus lists a large amount of representative works. Schott publishes *The Liszt Society Publications* (six volumes are available now). Alfred has a volume titled *At the Piano with Liszt* (Hinson) that contains an unusual selection with editorial additions.

MacDowell, Edward (1861–1908)

Hinshaw (Hinson): *Forgotten Fairy Tales*, Op. 4; *Six Fancies*, Op. 7; *Marionettes*, Op. 38; *Fireside Tales*, Op. 61. G. Schirmer/Hal Leonard: *Tragica Sonata*, Op. 45; *Eroica Sonata*, Op. 50; *Idylls*, Op. 28; *Poems*, Op. 31; *Little Poems*, Op. 32. Breitkopf and Härtel: *Modern Suite*, Op. 12; *Tragica and Eroica Sonatas*. Kalmus: *Etudes*, Op. 39; *12 Virtuoso Studies*, Op. 46; *Sonata No. 3*, Op. 57; *Sonata No. 4*, Op. 59; *Witches Dance*; *Woodland Sketches*, Op. 51; *Sea Pieces*, Op. 55. C.F. Peters has a collection with works from Op. 37, 51, 55, 61, and 62. Two volumes are available from Schroeder and Gunther that contain Opp. 51, 55, 61, and 62. Alfred has *Sea Pieces*, Op. 55 and *Woodland Sketches*, Op. 51.

Mendelssohn, Felix (1809–47)

Dover has the complete solo works in two volumes. Durand, available through Elkan-Vogel, offers the complete works in nine volumes edited by Maurice Ravel. Kalmus has the complete works in three volumes. C.F. Peters offers the three sonatas, Opp. 6, 105, and 106, and also some smaller works. G. Schirmer/Hal Leonard publishes a representative list, including the three sets of variations, Opp. 54, 82, and 83 (Hughes) and smaller works. Henle has a *Selected Works* volume that contains Opp. 7, 35, 54, 106, and the *Songs Without Words*. The *Songs Without Words* is also offered by Alfred, Peters, C. Fischer, Lea, G. Schirmer/Hal Leonard (Sternberg), and Presser (analytical edition by Percy Goetschius).

Mozart, Wolfgang Amadeus (1756–91)

Henle (Herttrich) has an outstanding urtext (plus fingering) edition in two volumes of the sonatas. Vienna Urtext also offers a fine urtext in two volumes. Presser has an excellent urtext edition by Broder (unfingered) in one volume. Bärenreiter has two volumes of the sonatas. Alfred, Henle, Vienna Urtext, C.F. Peters, and Kalmus have the variations and miscellaneous pieces.

Prokofiev, Serge (1891–1953)

MCA/Hal Leonard publishes almost everything. Boosey & Hawkes has a few items including *Visions Fugitives*, Op. 22; *Music for Children*, Op. 65; *Two Sonatinas,* Op. 54; and *Tales of Old Grandmother*. Kalmus offers a wide selection. Alfred, Marks/Hal Leonard, Associated Music Publishers, and International offer smaller lists.

Scarlatti, Domenico (1685–1757)

The only reliable complete edition (550 sonatas in eleven volumes) is edited by Kenneth Gilbert, published by Heugel (through Presser). G. Schirmer offers sixty sonatas in two volumes excellently edited by Ralph Kirkpatrick, as well as one hundred sonatas in three volumes edited by Hashimoto. Editio Musica Budapest (Ballo) has two hundred sonatas in four volumes, urtext with fingering. C.F. Peters lists many of the sonatas in three volumes. Other collections are also offered by J. Fischer (Frisken), Mercury (Loesser), Boston, Ricordi, and Kalmus (all of the sonatas edited by Longo). Also see the Alfred collection with an outstanding discussion of style, ornaments, etc.

Schubert, Franz (1797–1828)

Henle has the sonatas in three volumes including the incomplete sonatas, completed by editor Paul Badura-Skoda for practical use. The complete works in five volumes, including fifteen sonatas, is published by Lea Pocket Scores. Breitkopf and Härtel publish the sonatas in three volumes edited by Pauer. The Associated Board of the Royal School of Music (T. Presser) has the sonatas in three volumes. Editions of eleven sonatas, dances, impromptus (Opp. 90 and 142), various pieces and the *Moments Musicaux*, Op. 94 are offered by C.F. Peters and Kalmus. Henle has a fine edition of the *Impromptus and Moments Musicaux* edited by Walter Gieseking. Vienna Urtext has two volumes of *Complete Dances* and the *Wanderer Fantasy* (Badura-Skoda). Bärenreiter has the *Grazer Fantasie* (Durr). Dover reprints all the solo piano music in Volume 5 of the reprint of the Breitkopf and Härtel 1884–97 edition.

Schumann, Robert (1810–56)

Henle has most of the works in four volumes. This edition is based on Schumann's autographs and is highly recommended. Henle also has numerous works available separately. Breitkopf and Härtel and Kalmus publish the complete piano works in the Clara Schumann edition. Editions by C.F. Peters (Koehler) and Salabert/Hal Leonard (Cortot) are almost complete. Hansen, available through MMB (Magnamusic-Baton), has some of the Bischoff edition, one of the earliest and best. Dover has a broad spectrum of the piano works in two volumes. Vienna Urtext has Opp. 2, 12, 15, 18, 19, 68, and 82.

MORE COMPOSERS

Albéniz, Isaac (1860–1909)
Union Musical Española/Hal Leonard, E.B. Marks/Hal Leonard, Kalmus
Bach, Carl Philipp Emanuel (1714–88)
Brietkopf and Härtel, C.F. Peters, International, Universal
Bach, Johann Christian (1735–82)
Oxford, C.F. Peters
Barber, Samuel (1910–81)
G. Schirmer/Hal Leonard
Berg, Alban (1885–1935)
Universal Edition
Bloch, Ernest (1880–1959)
G. Schirmer/Hal Leonard
Chabrier, Emmanuel (1841–94)
Enoch, International, C.F. Peters
Clementi, Muzio (1752–1832)
C.F. Peters, G. Schirmer/Hal Leonard, Alfred, Hinshaw
Copland, Aaron (1900–)
Boosey & Hawkes, Durand, Senart, C. Fischer
Couperin, François (1668–1733)
Durand, Heugel, G. Schirmer/Hal Leonard, Kalmus, Alfred
De Falla, Manuel (1876–1946)
Durand, J. & W. Chester
Dello Joio, Norman (1913–)
G. Schirmer/Hal Leonard, C. Fischer, E. B. Marks/Hal Leonard
Dohnányi, Ernst von (1877–1960)
Doblinger, Universal, E. B. Marks/Hal Leonard, Kalmus
Dvořák, Antonin (1841–1904)
Artia, C.F. Peters
Fauré, Gabriel (1845–1924)
Hamelle, Durand, Heugel, International, Kalmus, Leduc
Field, John (1782–1837)
G. Schirmer/Hal Leonard, C.F. Peters, Ricordi/Hal Leonard, Kalmus
Finney, Ross Lee (1906–)
C.F. Peters, Boosey & Hawkes, Mercury, Hinshaw
Frank, César (1822–90)
C.F. Peters, Durand, T. Presser, Curci, Kalmus, Schott
Gershwin, George (1898–1937)
New World Music (Warner Bros. Publications), Chappell

Ginastera, Alberto (1916–83)
Durand, Ricordi/Hal Leonard, C. Fischer, Boosey & Hawkes, Barry

Gottschalk, Louis Moreau (1829–69)
T. Presser, C. Fischer, Kalmus, C.F. Peters, Chappell

Granados, Enrique (1867–1916)
G. Schirmer/Hal Leonard, Kalmus, E.B. Marks/Hal Leonard,
International

Gretchaninoff, Alexander (1864–1956)
Schott, Max Eschig/Hal Leonard, Belwin/Columbia Pictures

Grieg, Edvard (1843–1907)
C.F. Peters, C. Fischer, G. Schirmer/Hal Leonard, Kalmus, Alfred

Griffes, Charles Tomlinson (1884–1920)
G. Schirmer/Hal Leonard

Hindemith, Paul (1895–1963)
Schott

Honegger, Arthur (1892–1955)
Editions Salabert/Hal Leonard

Hovhaness, Alan (1911–)
C.F. Peters, Peer International, Fujihara

Ibert, Jacques (1890–1962)
Alphonse Leduc, Foetisch

Kabalevsky, Dmitri (1904–87)
MCA/Hal Leonard, C.F. Peters, International, Kalmus, Alfred,
G. Schirmer/Hal Leonard, Boosey & Hawkes

Khachaturian, Aram (1903–78)
MCA/Hal Leonard, Kalmus, C.F. Peters, Alfred

Lully, Jean–Baptiste (1632-87)
Durand

Martinu, Bohuslav (1890–1959)
Boosey & Hawkes, Max Eschig/Hal Leonard

Moszkowski, Moritz (1854–1925)
C.F. Peters, G. Schirmer/Hal Leonard, Ricordi/Hal Leonard, Musica
Obscura

Muczynski, Robert (1929–)
G. Schirmer/Hal Leonard

Mussorgsky, Modest (1839–81)
International, C. F. Peters, Kalmus, Vienna Urtext, Schott, Breitkopf
and Härtel

Persichetti, Vincent (1915–87)
Elkan-Vogel

Poulenc, Francis (1899–1963)
J. & W. Chester, Salabert/Hal Leonard, Durand, Heugel, Eschig/Hal
Leonard

Rachmaninoff, Sergei (1873–1943)
G. Schirmer/Hal Leonard, International, Boosey & Hawkes, Belwin/

Columbia Pictures, Kalmus, Alfred Publishing Company, Marks/Hal Leonard, Hinshaw, C.F. Peters

Rameau, Jean–Philippe (1683–1764)
Bärenreiter, Durand, Belwin/Columbia Pictures, International, Kalmus

Ravel, Maurice (1875–1937)
Durand, G. Schirmer/Hal Leonard, Kalmus, Alfred Publishing Company

Reinagle, Alexander (1756–1809)
Hinshaw, Belwin/Columbia Pictures, A-R Editions

Saint-Saëns, Camille (1835–1921)
Durand, C.F. Peters

Satie, Eric (1866–1925)
Salabert/Hal Leonard, Eschig/Hal Leonard, Associated/Hal Leonard, Kalmus

Schoenberg, Arnold (1874–1951)
Universal, Wilhelm Hansen, Belmont

Schuman, William (1910–)
Howard Music Co. (G. Schirmer/Hal Leonard), G. Schirmer/Hal Leonard, Presser

Scriabin, Alexander (1892–1915)
C.F. Peters, MCA/Hal Leonard, Alfred, International, Kalmus, Dover Publishing Company

Stravinsky, Igor (1882–1971)
Boosey & Hawkes, Associated/Hal Leonard, Faber, J.W. Chester, Schott

Tansman, Alexandre (1897–)
Eschig/Hal Leonard, Editions Salabert/Hal Leonard

Tchaikovsky, Peter Ilyich (1840–93)
C.F. Peters, G. Schirmer/Hal Leonard, Alfred, Kalmus, Marks/Hal Leonard

Tcherepnin, Alexander (1899–1977)
G. Schirmer/Hal Leonard, C. F. Peters, Schott, Durand, Marks/Hal Leonard, Heugel

Toch, Ernst (1887–1964)
Schott, Belwin/Columbia Pictures, MCA/Hal Leonard

Turina, Joaquin (1882–1949)
Editions Salabert/Hal Leonard, Eschig/Hal Leonard, Associated/Hal Leonard

Villa–Lobos, Heitor (1887-1959)
Consolidated, Marks/Hal Leonard, Peer International, Mercury, C. Fischer

Weber, Carl Maria von (1786–1826)
C.F. Peters, Salabert/Hal Leonard, G. Schirmer/Hal Leonard

Webern, Anton (1883–1945)
Universal, C. Fischer

SUMMARY

One must make a continuous and conscious effort to know what editions are available. The most important question to keep in mind when selecting an edition is—"Can I distinguish between the composer's markings and those of the editor?" If the answer is no, you should continue to search for such an edition. It may not exist, but you should be unsatisfied with that answer until you have exhausted all possibilities.

Teachers should make sure their students know what edition to purchase when they need to buy music. Price may be a factor, especially in foreign publications, but an excellent edition is most valuable.

Build your own library with editions of documented authority by outstanding performers such as those by Arrau, Schnabel, Kirkpatrick, etc.

FOR FURTHER READING

Andrews, Ruth P. "Preferred Editions." *American Music Teacher*, 21 (November–December, 1971): 30.

Benton, Rita. "Some Problems of Piano Music Editions." *American Music Teacher*, 6 (November–December, 1956): 6–7, 21.

Dexter, Benning, and George Loomis. "Choosing the Best Edition," *Clavier*, 8 (September, 1969): 50–2.

Dexter, Benning, and Charles Timbrell. "Another Look at Editions—The Piano Works of Twelve Important Composers." *The Piano Quarterly*, 116 (Winter, 1981): 39–41.

Emery, Walter. *Editions and Musicians*. London: Novello, 1957.

Ferguson, Howard. *Keyboard Interpretation*. New York and London: Oxford University Press, 1975.

Goodman, Roger. "Choosing Editions of Baroque Keyboard Music." *Clavier*, 25/5 (May–June, 1985): 20–25.

"Guide for Selecting Editions," *The Piano Quarterly*, 56 (Summer, 1966): 14–36. Compiled by the editors.

Halford, Margery. "Editing: Some Problems, Puzzles and Solutions." *The Piano Quarterly*, 114 (Summer, 1981): 32–34.

Hinson, Maurice. *Guide to the Pianist's Repertoire*. Bloomington: Indiana University Press, 1973. 2nd ed. revised and enlarged, 1987.

Oberdoerffer, Fritz. "Urtext Editions," *American Music Teacher*, 10 (July–August, 1961): 2, 15–18.

Serkin, Rudolf. "Some Thoughts on Editions for the Artist Student." *Comprehensive Guide for Piano Teachers*. New York: The Music Education League, 1963, 94–5.

Ornaments & Embellishments in Eighteenth-Century Keyboard Music 20

by George Lucktenberg

George Lucktenberg is recognized as one of America's most distinguished early-keyboard performers, appearing widely as a soloist and chamber player. His versatility with historical keyboards, including harpsichord, clavichord, and fortepiano, complement his mastery of the traditional literature as a teacher and performer on the modern concert grand. Dr. Lucktenberg is a veteran faculty member at Converse College in Spartanburg, South Carolina and the National Music Camp in Interlochen, Michigan. At both institutions he established innovative curricula integrating historical-keyboard study into standard keyboard training. He founded the Southeastern Historical Keyboard Society in 1980, which led to the creation of a major harpsichord performance competition for young players, attracting international participation and attention. His leadership of the Alienor Harpsichord Composition Awards keeps him at the forefront of efforts to promote new solos for the harpsichord through commissions and contests. His world premieres of such works in New York City and Washington D.C., and many other activities have made a significant contribution to the body of recent contemporary music for the Baroque harpsichord. Dr. Lucktenberg has been awarded Fellowships by the Ford Foundation and the Fulbright Commission; his publications include numerous articles and editions of music for both pedagogical and student use. He was the initial president of the South Carolina Music Teachers Association in 1960; he has also held two vice-presidencies and the presidency of the Music Teachers National Association's Southern Division.

INTRODUCTION & BACKGROUND

"No one disputes the need for embellishments. This is evident from the great numbers of them everywhere to be found. They are, in fact, indispensable. Consider their many uses: They connect and enliven tones and impart stress and accent; they make music pleasing and awaken our close attention. Expression is heightened by them; let a piece be sad, joyful, or otherwise, and they will lend a fitting assistance. Embellishments provide opportunities for fine performance as well as much of its subject matter. They improve mediocre compositions. Without them the best melody is empty and ineffective, the clearest content clouded."[1]

Carl Philipp Emanuel Bach

Why does the topic of ornaments and embellishments cause discomfort among teachers? Why do so many consider it vexing or mystifying? Because more and more teachers are aware of its importance to the satisfactory performance of literature from various periods.

Historical perspective is very helpful. Mankind's urge to decorate music with "extra" notes goes back as far as anyone can trace in any culture. By 1700 in Europe it was already a well-developed but still evolving essential of the Baroque style. During the next one hundred years it became a flexible, diversified art of the utmost refinement which was commented upon extensively by writers and critics of the time.

Our fascination with the eighteenth century began in the late nineteenth, accelerating rapidly after World War II. The majority Romantic view was that eighteenth-century music was a bit insipid for the most part, and needed "modernizing" before it was fit to be heard; they tried to make it sound something like Romantic music. These excesses brought about a sharp counter-reaction early in our century: a "purist" approach resulting in insistence, by the leaders of the movement, upon playing in a bare-bones, "urtext" way.

The warnings and outcries of the purists generated many fine urtext editions (the composer's original score, with nothing added or subtracted). However, sometimes the composer's score was mainly an outline to be filled in at the discretion of the performer. Urtext-playing was therefore criticized for being dull and uninteresting. A player from the Baroque or Classical period would also have shared that opinion.

ORNAMENTS & EMBELLISHMENTS

"Embellishments may be divided into two groups: in the first are those which are indicated by conventional signs or a few small notes; in the second

[1]From Carl Philipp Emanuel's *Essay on the True Art of Playing Keyboard Instruments*. Translated and edited by William J. Mitchell (W.W. Norton & Company, Inc., 1949).

are those which lack signs and consist of many short notes."[2]

Carl Philipp Emanuel Bach

To expand upon C.P.E. Bach's statement, in arriving at some system of classification one finds two categories:

1. Those which are indicated by the composer in original manuscripts or first printings done under his supervision (urtexts). These may be:
   a. standardized formulas indicated by shorthand "signs;" or
   b. non-standard, passagework either in normal-size or small notes
2. Those which are added later by someone else and may be:
   a. added by an editor, whether or not they are clearly identified as not being original; or
   b. improvised (with or without some prior planning and practice) on the impulse of the player, without appearing anywhere in the score

There is, unfortunately, no clear universally accepted terminology to help us distinguish between types 1a and 1b. It has been proposed that we do away with the confusion of the words "ornament" and embellishment" by calling 1a "ornaments" and 1b "embellishments." One further pairing should be noted: ornaments with shorthand signs are primarily identified with the French, particularly with their harpsichord composers; and small-note free embellishment, with the Italians, particularly their stringed-instrument and vocal writing.

The French, who inherited an ornament tradition from the early Baroque lute school, developed it to the highest state of refinement and taste. As early as 1670 (Chambonnières' *Pièces de Clavecin*) printed tables systematically showed how ornaments should be played. At its peak, ca. 1700–1740, the French practice was widely copied elsewhere in Europe. The famous table of ornaments that J.S. Bach wrote at the beginning of Wilhelm Friedemann's *Little Clavier Book* is essentially that of d'Anglebert (*Pièces de Clavecin*, 1689), one of the many great French keyboardists. This little table (Example 1) appears in Bach's own hand as he wrote it for his son, and for that reason is an extremely valuable reference source. Since it contains most of the essential French Baroque ornaments it is well worth memorizing. Bach's own treatment of keyboard ornaments is typically, and almost totally, French. He, of course, knew and was a consummate master of the Italian embellishment style as well. Like other Germans of his time, he probably saw himself as a synthesizer of the two styles, together with his great native northern counterpoint, into a grander art. That he succeeded so well indeed is not necessarily because he was German, however, but because he was Bach.

---

[2]Carl Phillipp Emanuel Bach, *op. cit.*

Ornaments & Embellishments in Eighteenth-Century Keyboard Music

Example 1 Bach's table of ornaments from the *Clavier-Büchlein of 1720*.

The following discussion of ornamentation is based primarily on Bach's table shown in Example 1.

The Trill: *t*, *tr*, ∿, ∿∿

The trill is a rapid alternation of the printed note with the half- or whole-step above. It has no set speed or length; it may be short or long. Realizations of the trill sign include:

It may have a prefix from below:

Special Subjects

It may have a prefix from above:

It may also have a suffix:

When no suffix is indicated, the trill can stop on the printed note—*point d'arrêt*, as the French called it:

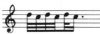

Or it can take up the whole length of the printed note:

It may also have both a prefix and suffix:

Prefix from below and Suffix

Prefix from above and Suffix

There are two general rules:

1. Trills, like ninety percent of all eighteenth-century ornaments, begin **on the beat**—that is, they start on the printed note, not *before* it.
2. Trills start from *above*—not on the printed note. This goes for Haydn, Mozart, and early Beethoven (including most of his "teaching-pieces") as well as for the Baroque period. Only one exception can be made: when the note preceding the written trill is in effect an upper appoggiatura, that note can be tied over into the trill. This trill was specifically identified as a *Pralltriller* by C.P.E. Bach. The French had a convention for this—a slur from the preceding note to the trilled note; J.S. Bach and others often used a "prepared trill" sign:

Ornaments & Embellishments in Eighteenth-Century Keyboard Music

A pedagogical exception may occur in the execution of the trill because the player is not facile enough or not mature enough to handle even the minimum four notes in the basic trill. In the Baroque period especially, a quick, single appoggiatura or acciaccatura from above is usually a better choice than the three-note or short *Schneller* or snap (C.P.E.'s term).

The Mordent: ᴧᴧ, ↑, ‖; ᴧᴧᴧ (long); ꜱ (after, not over, the note)

The mordent is a very quick alternation of the printed note with the half- or whole-step below. It starts on the beat as usual, but unlike the trill, the printed note comes first. Normally it consists of only three notes, but occasionally sounds well if prolonged to five, seven, or even more:

This ornament largely disappeared in the Classic era, although Haydn used a variant of it which was more like a very fast turn:

The Turn: ∾ (or ϩ, rare)

The turn, played at varying speeds, starts with the half- or whole-step above the printed note, goes to the printed one next, then a half- or whole-step below, and ends on the printed one:

In the Baroque and Classic eras this simple four-note device, at varying speeds, was the sole on-the-beat kind. As far as we can tell, the five-note turn beginning *on* the printed note comes from a later time:

A relative of the unaccented trill described in the exception (Pralltriller) noted earlier under "Trill," the unaccented turn occurs when the turn sign is *between* the notes rather than over them; in this case it is rather like a group of passing notes, and is unaccented.

The Appoggiatura: ♪, ♪, ⌐, and ⁀ (with a trill)

The appoggiatura is an accented note of variable duration a half- or whole-step on either side of the printed note. The appoggiatura (from the Italian verb *appoggiare*, to lean) is a dissonant tone usually occurring on the beat, and normally takes up at least half (sometimes more than half) of the time occupied by the printed note, to which it resolves. Realizations include:

Ascending Appoggiatura

Descending Appoggiatura

It can preface a trill:

Ornaments & Embellishments in Eighteenth-Century Keyboard Music

It can also preface a mordent when coming from below:

A much less common variant is the double appoggiatura:

Yet another variant is the passing appoggiatura, an unaccented small note occurring between two notes of a melodic third, usually descending:

The following additional ornaments are not in J.S. Bach's table, but are used in his and other composers' music frequently.

The Slide: (,) , / , \ , ⩘

The slide is another very short note (which, confusingly, the Italians also call acciaccatura), occurring between two notes of a harmonic third (occasionally between a fourth or more):

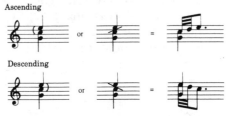

In the previous examples the slide was added to chords. Another commonly used slide, the melodic slide (or German, *Schleifer*), is added to single-line melody:

Special Subjects

The notes are released instantly, except perhaps in Scarlatti where the dissonant effect may be prolonged in the "tone-clusters" of which he was fond. In his case, however, they tend to be written out in full with normal-sized notes. This ornament was freely interpolated by Baroque performers, especially in accompaniments, and was probably used far more often than we are now apt to acknowledge in our own playing. Although the practice seems to have died out in the Classic era, it may be added, occasionally, in music up to ca. 1775.

The Arpeggio: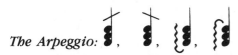

The arpeggio is the practice of playing the notes of a chord with a very slight upward or downward roll, rather than playing them simultaneously:

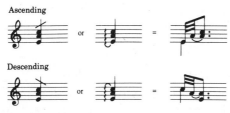

The roll can also be done at a slower pace, particularly on the last chord of a final cadence, which is often arpeggiated very elaborately, both up and down, with a ritard. All the chord tones are sustained, and are held by the fingers, rather than released, as became the custom later on the pianoforte with its sustaining pedal.

The Acciaccatura:

The acciaccatura is a very short appoggiatura, usually from below. Its name is derived from the Italian, *acciaccare*, to crush. The two notes are struck almost together, with the acciaccatura being released immediately as if it were marked staccato:

It is used more often in the Classic period than in the Baroque.

There is insufficient consistency in the manuscripts of any major composer to give us a precise indication of the length of acciaccaturas or appoggiaturas. The notion that ♪ *always* meant appoggiatura (long), and

Ornaments & Embellishments in Eighteenth-Century Keyboard Music

that ♪ *always* meant acciaccatura (short), is absolutely without foundation and must be discarded. Secondly, in determining whether a half- or whole-step is to be used in any of these figures, the ruling principle is that the prevailing tonality must be supported, not negated, by the accidentals used; stay within the key of the moment.

ADDING IMPROVISED ORNAMENTATION & EMBELLISHMENT

"...It is supposed by many that a real good Taste cannot possibly be acquired by any Rules of Art; it being a peculiar Gift of Nature, indulged only to those who have naturally a good Ear: And as most flatter themselves to have this Perfection, hence it happens that he who sings or plays, thinks of nothing so much as to make continually some favourite Passages or Graces, believing that by this Means he shall be thought to be a good Performer, not perceiving that playing in good Taste doth not consist of frequent Passages, but in expressing with Strength and Delicacy the Intention of the Composer."[3]

Francesco Geminiani

The basic procedure in improvised embellishment is to replace long note values in melodies with groups of shorter ones, referred to as "diminution" in scholarly terms. In the period from 1600–1700 they tended to be written out in long, involved passagework: see the *Fitzwilliam Virginal Book* and works of Frescobaldi for elegant examples. Later, the practice became improvisatory rather than specified in notation, and during much of the eighteenth century, especially the late Baroque and the Rococo, it was expected of all performers beyond the most elementary level. To what extent it is called for, and indeed, allowable in the Classic works of the mature Haydn, Mozart, or early Beethoven is much less apparent; but it is clear that its use after 1760–1770 is far more restricted than during the first two-thirds of the century.

The Italian violin and vocal school provided the leadership for this kind of embellishment. The slow movements of instrumental sonatas from this period—those of Corelli's (Opus V, 1700) or Handel's (Opus 1, 1722) for violin, flute, etc. are excellent examples. They are usually mere outlines upon which the performer must add tasteful flourishes and passagework of all kinds. Tasteful is the key word. It is necessary for the performer to have both a thorough grounding in eighteenth-century counterpoint, and an affinity for the personal idiom of the composer's piece that is being played. One can find reliable guidance from eighteenth-century masters who left ample amounts of written-out embellishments that serve as models for us, and they also left some very helpful treatises.

---

[3]From Geminiani's *Treatise of Good Taste in the Art of Musick*. Edited by Donington (Da Capo Press, 1969).

Special Subjects

Of special interest are the varied reprises and "doubles;" these were popular in two-part dance movements and other repeating forms. One plays the first time through as written; on the repeat, extemporized embellishments are added. Some of the finest examples occur in the works of J.S. Bach. Many of his sarabandes have doubles, in which he shows an infinite variety of inspired figuration. The sarabande in the third English Suite is a magnificent demonstration of this art. That he would occasionally embellish even fast movements is evident in the second courante of the first English Suite. Both of these movements are well worth careful study. For contrast, see the ingenuous, simple sarabande of the fourth English Suite. Just because Bach provided none, are we to assume that no embellishing of its repeats were intended? It would seem to be very doubtful.

There are two kinds of performer-added ornaments which can be inserted:

1. The cadential trill. At major cadences, such as a final one in a movement, or the first half of a movement, especially when the melody is:

A trill on the first of the notes shown is not only invited, it is virtually mandatory even though not indicated.
2. When a composer has given ornaments for certain notes in the opening statement of a theme (a fugue subject, for example), one may freely repeat these ornaments any time the identical theme is repeated, even though the ornament signs may be lacking. Again, one is referring here mainly to music of the Baroque; the more explicit notation of the Classicists suggests caution in all such matters.

In the more difficult "free" embellishment of the Italian kind, one can hardly do better than to look to J.S. Bach for yet another example: this time the second movement of his *Italian Concerto*. This is a fully realized sample of an ornate slow movement, typifying the best of that sort of improvising. For a superb specimen from the Classic period, see Mozart's A-minor *Rondo*, K. 511. Each time the main thematic elements recur they are subtly and ingeniously varied.

Sources for detailed study are listed at the end of the chapter. A few general guidelines are that one can embellish by adding:

1. Formula ornaments of the sort usually expressed by conventional signs
2. Short "filler" notes between skips of various kinds:
   a. "slides" between notes of chords, particularly when arpeggiating

    b. filling in the steps between melodic skips with fast notes, usually stepwise (diatonically; rarely chromatically)—sometimes even skipwise, usually in thirds, if the interval to be spanned is quite large

    c. imitation: that is, figures which closely or exactly duplicate other material that the composer has previously introduced, when a good opportunity occurs

In each of these things, the normal procedure is to move from the simple to the complex by gradual stages. Above all, one must strive to preserve a feeling of spontaneity and improvisation, to constantly vary the figuration and not get in a rut with one or another formula. Without taking unnecessary chances, it is useful to make very minor changes from time to time in live performances to provide variety in one's playing.

THE TECHNIQUE OF ORNAMENTATION

"Besides the Graces in general use, such as trills, mordents, appoggiaturas, etc., I have always given my pupils little finger-exercises to play; either passages, or strings of trills or tremolos of various intervals, beginning with the simplest, and on the most natural intervals, and gradually leading them to the quickest and to those most transposed. These little exercises, which cannot be too varied or too multiplied, are, at the same time, material all ready to be put in place, and may prove serviceable on many occasions."[4]

François Couperin

"When practicing trills or shakes, only those fingers which are in use should be raised as high as possible. However, as the movement becomes familiar, these fingers are raised less and less and the considerable movement employed at the outset is finally replaced by a movement which is light and brisk."[5]

Jean-Philippe Rameau

"An ornament badly played is like a smile in a toothless mouth."[6]

Wanda Landowska

The first cardinal principle to be observed is that almost all embellishment consists of numerous quick notes. Particularly on the pianoforte, these should be "little" in loudness as well as in length. Both the speed and the lightness of the notes comprising embellishments invite finger action alone, unaided by hand or forearm activity.

[4]From Couperin's *Art of Playing the Harpsichord* (Breitkopf and Härtel, 1933).
[5]From the essay in Rameau's *Pièces de Clavecin* (Bärenreiter, 1958).
[6]From an article Landowska wrote on interpreting ornaments which is now in the book, *Landowska on Music*, collected, edited, and translated by Denise Restout (Stein and Day, Publishers, 1964).

Second, most ornaments and embellishments sound best if they are played just a little off-center, or non-symmetrically, in time. The Baroque ornament tables showed the small notes in even, regular sixteenths, thirty-seconds, or sixty-fourths; and the miniature notes of Classic embellishments, which took the place of many older signs, seem equally even and regular. All the best authorities from the eighteenth century, however, agree that they were not intended to be played in a mechanical way. Playing trills, turns, and other figures in such a way robs them of charm and freedom. Trills in particular rarely need to be measured. It is generally best to allow them to accelerate gradually and consistently until their end. Sometimes they can also start slowly, accelerate, and slow down again toward the end. Short trills, of course, are generally played quite fast, with no attempt to make them conform to any particular time unit or pattern; the same goes for mordents, unless a particularly expressive effect is sought.

Third, ornaments should be a natural and integral part of the melodic line they decorate. Every effort must be made to keep them smoothly flowing within the context of the phrase. The technique of a fast trill is virtually an involuntary reflex, while improvised embellishments require more intellectual discipline.

Finally, a few specific hints may be useful.

1. It is rarely advisable to "force" an ornament with power and tension. A relaxed hand and arm will almost invariably yield better results.
2. When the same ornament occurs over and over again, to avoid monotony it is best to slightly alter the way of playing by using varied timing and dynamics.
3. When playing very rapid trills on the piano one can hold both keys very slightly "below surface" owning to its sophisticated double-escapement action, thus reducing the time between repercussions of each key.
4. If a pupil complains of clumsiness in trills and other figures, try some less common fingerings using non–adjacent pairs: 1–3, 2–4, and 3–5. Forearm rotation and changing fingers are also helpful in improving articulation. Changing fingers is also helpful in a four-note trill: 3 1 3 2; and in longer trills: 3 1 3 2 3 1 3 2, etc.
5. One must be careful that the very last note of an embellishment group should be played solidly so that it is clearly heard as the final, or resting-point, of the figure.

SUMMARY

Musical tastes change quite a lot in the course of one hundred years. It is well to remember that the eighteenth century encompassed three distinctly separate, although overlapping styles: the late Baroque (ca. 1700–1740), the Rococo or "Galant" (ca. 1730–1770), and the Viennese Classic (ca. 1760–1800), each with its own subtle differences and preferences as to embellishment. In this brief discussion it is impossible to cover the gamut of ornamentaion with any real depth; the purpose here has been to provide an overview and a guide to basic usages of the times. For a greater insight into periods and styles examine the music of various composers, listen to leading artists specializing in Early Music (especially harpsichodists and fortepianists), and refer to the following suggested readings.

In closing, it must be said that most eighteenth-century ornaments could be improved by keeping just three basic "A B C's" in mind:

Always Be Careful to:
Start from **above** on trills and turns; start on the **beat**, *not* before; and **cling** to accented appoggiaturas, holding them long enough and resolving them legatissimo.

FOR FURTHER READING

A look at entries in well-known, reputable music dictionaries is useful, such as *The New Grove Dictionary of Music and Musicians* (1980) and *The New Harvard Dictionary of Music* (1987). Also, there are numerous articles to be found in back issues of magazines such as *Clavier, American Music Teacher, The Piano Quarterly*, and others. Chapters in the following books give specific and more detailed information, as well as general information.

Bach, Carl Philipp Emanuel. *Essay on the True Art of Playing Keyboard Instruments.* Translated and edited by William J. Mitchell. New York: W.W. Norton & Company, Inc., 1949. A comprehensive, authentic, highly detailed treatise for musicians concerned with fingering, technique and ornamentation of the time.

Badura-Skoda, Eva and Paul. *Interpreting Mozart on the Keyboard.* London: Barrie and Rockliff, 1962. Included are valuable discussions of phrasing, articulation and ornamentation.

Couperin, François. *The Art of Playing the Harpsichord.* Wiesbaden: Breitkopf and Härtel, 1933. The text of this reprint is in French, German, and English. First published in 1717, this volume is a definitive reference source on ornamentation and style. This book is now available in an edition edited by Margery Halford (Van Nuys, CA: Alfred Publishing Company, Inc., 1975).

Donington, Robert. *The Interpretation of Early Music.* London: Faber and Faber, 1974. This and the following book are authoritative reference sources.

Donington, Robert. *A Performer's Guide to Baroque Music*. London: Faber and Faber, 1973.

Ferguson, Howard, ed. *Style and Interpretation (An Anthology of 16th-19th Century Keyboard Music)*. 4 vols. London: Oxford University Press, 1964–1966. Each volume contains an invaluable preface with a precise discussion of ornamentation.

Harich-Schneider, Eta. *The Harpsichord: An Introduction to Technique, Style, and the Historical Sources*. St. Louis: Concordia Publishing House, 1954. Contains a witty and thought-provoking chapter on ornamentation.

Newman, Anthony. *Bach and the Baroque: A Performer's View*. New York: Pendragon, 1985. Contains an excellent summary of embellishment practices, and much additional useful information.

Newman, William S. *Performance Practices in Beethoven's Piano Sonatas*. New York: W.W. Norton & Company, Inc., 1971.

Rameau, Jean-Philippe. *Pièces de Clavecin*, edited by Jacobi. Kassel: Bärenreiter, 1958. Contains Rameau's essay on technique and styles.

Soderlund, Sandra. *Organ Technique: An Historical Approach*. Chapel Hill: Hinshaw, 1980.

Tartini, Giuseppe. *Treatise on Ornaments in Music*. Edited by Jacobi, translated by Girdlestone. Celle: Moeck, 1961. Offers specific advice on eighteenth-century embellishment practices in the Italian manner.

Troeger, Richard. *Technique and Interpretation on the Harpsichord and Clavichord*. Bloomington: Indiana University Press, 1986. Has a complete chapter on ornamentation.

PART FOUR

Interviews

An Interview with Nelita True 21

During recent years, pianist Nelita True has emerged as a leading example of that rare individual who is able to combine successfully the demanding careers of concert artist and teacher. Formerly Distinguished Professor of Piano at the University of Maryland, and now Chairman of the Piano Department at the Eastman School of Music, Miss True has achieved a national reputation as one of this country's most productive teachers. Her master classes and workshops for piano teachers have drawn praise throughout the United States and in Europe. At the same time she has maintained a full schedule of recital performances and appearances as soloist with symphony orchestras.

Miss True first attracted attention as a performer when, at age seventeen, she appeared as a soloist with the Chicago Symphony. Her student years brought a growing list of honors. At Juilliard she won the Concerto Competition and was a featured soloist with the Juilliard Orchestra at Avery Fisher Hall at Lincoln Center. Studies at the University of Michigan resulted in her receiving the Stanley Medal as the most distinguished graduate in music in her class. Also at Michigan, she was elected to Phi Beta Kappa and was named the nation's most outstanding member of Mu Phi Epsilon. Following graduation, she continued her studies as a Fulbright scholar in Paris where she worked with the legendary Nadia Boulanger and appeared in recital on French National Television. Returning to the United States, she completed her doctorate in performance as a student of Leon Fleisher at the Peabody Conservatory of Music.

Nelita True has drawn praise whenever she has performed. Noted for her broad and varied repertoire that includes many works by American composers, she has recorded more than seventy works, ranging from Scarlatti to Schoenberg. With her husband, Fernando Laires, Miss True premiered the *Concerto for Two Pianos*, written for them by Pulitzer prize-winner Leslie Bassett. They have given many performances of this work, including a concert at the Inter-American Festival at the Kennedy Center in Washington, D. C. Since 1980, Miss True has presented over 600 recitals and master classes in forty-seven states, Mexico, and Europe.

Nelita True is a remarkable pianist and teacher, and I know that her personal views will be most valuable to all teachers. In this interview she discusses important teaching and performing areas that are of interest to both students and teachers of all levels. This interview took place via telephone in February, 1988.

When you accept a student for study, what do you expect in the way of progress over a period of time?

In the first two years at Eastman, I would hope that the student would learn how to use practice time effectively, solidify technique, and develop aural sensitivity. In addition, the student should learn what questions to ask of the music to increase awareness, thus becoming conscious of not only what is on the page, but what is implied in the score. Naturally, the time this takes can vary from student to student.

What do you often find missing in a student's precollege training?

Two primary areas—sound projection and technique, which of course are related. No matter how gifted and imaginative the student, without a palette of beautiful sound and good facility, he or she does not have the means with which to communicate musical values.

What do you find lacking in students when you give master classes?

Often students do not convey the character of the music. Even something so simple as understanding the title would help vitalize the performance. Also, students frequently do not listen well for such things as balance among voices or clarity in the rhythm. In choosing a tempo, too often they will subdivide beats. If the piece is written in three-four they feel it in six; if it is in compound meter such as six-eight, they feel it in six instead of in two, which robs them of a fundamental element in experiencing large gestures and any kind of motion in the music. Pedaling is another problem—again, related to listening. Sometimes the harmonic structure of a piece is not clearly understood so that one does not have a feeling for the larger paragraphs within the score. I don't mean for this to sound negative, for I have heard many wonderful performances in master classes. These are merely some of the teaching challenges we all encounter.

In accepting a student for study, how much importance do you give to talent?

A great deal. It is one of the few qualities one can assess at an audition. This does not mean that I think it is the only consideration, because intelligence is, in some ways, more important. Fortunately, a gifted student usually has both musical and intellectual talent. Dedication is another important consideration that is not easy to determine with just one hearing. It is also helpful to talk with the student, as I am interested in his or her personal qualities and attitudes toward music and work.

What practice suggestions do you give when a student is learning a piece?

Before beginning practice, the student must be excited about the music. I don't see how this will happen unless the sound of the piece is in the ears. So, if the student is unfamiliar with the work, I'll read through it. Then I suggest studying the score away from the keyboard, first to get an overview of how the whole piece is put together and then to sort out the details. In this way the pianist is more likely to learn patterns and hear relationships rather than focusing on just the notes. After all, one would not learn a poem letter by letter.

Do you suggest hands separate practice?

Rarely. I think that compounds the problem of developing good sight-reading skills. If we give students this crutch for reading hands separately, they don't confront the reading of two clefs simultaneously. (This is with the clear understanding that they are practicing hands together slowly enough so that they can manage the two clefs.) Of course there are exceptions to this. In more complex music, such as a two-part invention, there are advantages to practicing hands separately. First of all it is easier to learn the patterns and, more important, it aids the ear in listening to independent lines.

Do you have students do a harmonic analysis of the piece?

Yes, but that is only one part of the analysis. One has to find out what is happening in terms of dynamic shapes, texture, articulation, register of the piano used for different sections, melodic, harmonic, and rhythmic patterns—and then what is their implication for performance.

Once a piece is learned, what advice would you give for memorizing?

Memory should begin immediately after the piece is in the student's fingers, even though it may not yet be up to tempo. Security in memory is strengthened if the piece is memorized for a good period of time before it is performed. I have a procedure for memorizing that my students have found helpful, and that is to memorize backwards. I don't mean note-for-note backwards, but phrase-by-phrase. Sometimes it is helpful to have the starting places at unpredictable spots in the music, like mid-phrase.

What suggestions do you give to your students for fingering, or do you let them choose their own?

With an understanding that they have a firm grounding in scales, arpeggios, broken chords, so that they have finger patterns on which to draw, I ask them to do this on their own. However, I would not do this with a young, inexperienced student. I feel that it is very important for some guidance there. But for more advanced students, if they are encouraged to use common sense and remember that a singing legato is an important consideration, then these two elements will lead them to good fingering choices. Of course I give isolated suggestions when problems arise such as the wrong sound or awkwardness.

An Interview with Nelita True

Do you believe in mental practice away from the piano, just thinking about the score?

Yes, for two basic reasons. One is to check on memory to see if the student can reproduce the piece in his or her mind without having the aid of tactile memory. Also, mental practice is exceedingly helpful in freeing the imagination—one is not bound up by concern for which lever to press next. I think one can often feel movement in the phrase by singing it or just thinking it through. When one gets back to the keyboard, that kind of freedom is translated into performance.

Do you assign sight-reading for your students?

Yes, I do, and very specifically. We have this wonderful challenge of becoming familiar with a huge, rich repertoire—a rather daunting prospect. I look for ways to reduce this challenge to manageable units. So, for example, if a student is studying a Chopin nocturne, I advise that he or she read the other nocturnes in the collection. This serves to hone sight-reading skills and, at the same time, acquaints the student with a segment of the repertoire. If a student is learning a Beethoven sonata, I would not expect all thirty-two sonatas to be read, but rather four or five sonatas surrounding the one being studied. This gives some historical perspective as well.

What suggestions do you give for projection in performances?

Projection in performance is the end goal of our teaching—the essence of teaching—because we want more than anything to communicate with the listener. This involves concentration, which is a word I don't use very often, because I feel that if a pianist is listening, he or she is concentrating. To my mind, projection is virtually impossible without listening. Our raw materials for projection are sound and time, the two basic elements of music. I suppose this is self-evident. Yet, even though that is rudimentary, I don't believe students spend enough time experimenting with different kinds of sound in order to project the musical ideas inherent in the score, nor do they experiment with flexibility in time. Some students are surprised to learn that not every eighth note in a piece is going to be the same length. When comparisons are made between an artist playing a piece accurately and a student who is also playing it "accurately," the artist is distinguished by what is done with sound variety and time flexibility. Those are the two areas that I focus on the most in musical projection.

Do you give students assignments in repertoire from all periods?

Absolutely, because one style of music enhances the understanding of another. For example, the fact that one must listen polyphonically in Baroque music can only help in listening polyphonically in all types of music. One could argue that there are polyphonic implications in homophonic writing, which can be heard both as linear and as harmonic progressions.

Do your students have a choice in repertoire selections?

Yes, I welcome ideas from students concerning repertoire choices, especially if they are excited about a certain piece. This often motivates them to accomplish more.

What advice would you give for technique?

Of course I urge students to practice for technical proficiency. Every time a key is depressed we are involved with technique. The more control we have at the keyboard, the more musical options we have available to us. As I suggested earlier, if we cannot produce it technically, it is not going to happen musically.

Do you divide technique into categories such as scales, arpeggios, etudes, and exercises?

Absolutely. In addition I assign octaves, double notes, chords, etc. with an emphasis given to listening. I do not think technique can improve without listening, regardless of what you do with your hands, arms, and body.

Do you require your students to accompany, or play chamber music?

At Eastman, students are required to do both—accompany and play chamber music. For students not enrolled in these classes, I suggest participation in these two activities, for these experiences tend to refine their listening and enhance their control of tempo and rhythm. Working with singers gives students exposure to a kind of natural expressivity in music-making which stems from breathing and which I think translates to the keyboard.

Do you sometimes get involved as a coach?

Yes, I enjoy doing that a lot.

How do you feel about entering students in competitions?

I think it is all right for some students; it can be a good stimulant for them to work harder. I do make a point of telling my students that they will receive no pressure from me to enter competitions. I have two reservations about their entering: first, if it is going to limit their repertoire. Students sometimes don't wish to start new pieces because old ones served them well in the last competition. I believe that that can be extremely limiting. Second, I object to a student's assessing his or her level of playing on the basis of the results of a competition, whether or not it was won or lost. We must develop our own criteria for judging our performance. Piano competitions, after all, are attempts at putting art into a scientific mold—an impossible contradiction. A piano performance can't very well be "measured" like the distance a skier can jump.

Do you think it is realistic for students to want to become concert artists?

We know that concertizing, by definition, is an elitist profession. The number of pianists who earn their living as concert artists is very small. However, I believe that a young student should not be discouraged from

An Interview with Nelita True

aspiring to become a concert pianist. This kind of idealism is wonderful and a stimulant for students to work hard and to develop discipline. With maturity they become aware of other options that might be open to them. They could become prominent pianists or teachers in their communities. I suggest that high school age students read Harold Schonberg's book, *Great Pianists from Mozart to the Present*, because it then becomes quite clear to them that what they think is the phenomenon of the child prodigy is actually the norm for those who are going to become concert artists. When they read about a pianist at the age of thirteen or fifteen who is concertizing and playing the major repertoire, it makes them a little bit more realisitic in gauging their own place in the musical hierarchy.

How personally involved do you think a teacher should become in the relationship with students?

When you are dealing primarily one-to-one with students, it is very hard not to have some kind of personal relationship. I work at not prying into my students' personal lives. Sometimes they choose to discuss their problems with me, and I think it is important to listen and give advice, if they wish it. But I also want to maintain a professional environment in the studio. I would like to establish an atmosphere that is unthreatening. This is important to me, because I do not want to do anything that would cause a student to lose his or her sense of dignity.

What do you feel are the most important qualities of a successful teacher?

Two of the most important things are imagination and a discriminating ear. Also, a musical open-mindedness—an alertness to all the different possibilities in a work. A sense of humor helps, too.

What would you suggest for teachers who have been teaching for many years to upgrade their teaching skills?

If possible, return to piano study. It makes us much more aware of how we relate to students if we ourselves become students once again. If that is not possible, then one could play for other teachers. Attending master classes and workshops can be helpful in terms of learning teaching techniques. Also, there are many books available on piano teaching and literature that contain invaluable information for teachers. Most important, hearing artistic performances in concert or on recordings keeps us aware of the standards to which we must aspire.

What suggestions would you give to new graduates to help them in their teaching?

From their first lesson, I give what I hope are useful tools for their future teaching, for my goal is their eventual independence. If they can, by themselves, make sense of a piece of music and can solve its technical challenges, then, with practice, they should be able to pass these skills on to their own students.

An Interview with Rosina Lhevinne 22

Rosina Lhevinne—born in Kiev, Russia in 1880—was a legendary figure in the world of music and ranks as one of the great piano teachers of all time. During her remarkable teaching career she guided to stardom such talents as Van Cliburn, John Browning, Daniel Pollack, Mischa Dichter, and a host of others.

Madame Lhevinne's own career began when she graduated from the Moscow Imperial Conservatory in 1898, winning a gold medal. She married Josef Lhevinne, the famous concert pianist, in 1898. She made her debut with the Moscow Symphony Orchestra in 1895, and subsequently toured widely in Europe and the United States. She frequently appeared in two-piano recitals with her husband.

Rosina Lhevinne joined the faculty of The Juilliard School of Music in 1925 and also joined the summer faculty of the Aspen Music Festival in 1956. During her teaching career at The Juilliard School, which spanned five decades, Rosina Lhevinne had a spectacular career and produced some of the world's greatest pianists. Madame Lhevinne died on November 9, 1976, in Glendale, California. Thus a great tradition came to an end, but her influence will live on in the many talented students who were fortunate to have received her inspiration and guidance.

No book on piano teaching would be complete without the personal views of one of the world's great teachers, Rosina Lhevinne. She was a personable, pleasant grande dame whom I found most gracious. She made an appointment for the interview through her secretary, and when I arrived she had just been out for a daily walk and was resting in the living room of her summer home. Her secretary offered us tea, and we had a lovely chat during the better part of two hours in the late afternoon. Before the actual interview began, we had an informal discussion of her childhood training in Russia. Her sense of humor was quite keen. In her reminiscences she jokingly told that when she grew up in Russia it was very unusual for girls to pursue a concert career; she said that after her marriage everyone told her she would be ruined and divorced in a year! She also said that at that time in Russia two-piano teams were quite rare. She discussed the beginnings of her concert career and the first tour she and her husband made in this country in 1906.

An excellent book on Josef and Rosina Lhevinne is *A Century of Music-Making* by Robert K. Wallace published by the Indiana University Press, 1976.

Madame Lhevinne was eighty-eight at the time of the interview; she was spry, witty, and offered astute, brief answers to the general teaching questions I asked her. Similar questions were asked of Adele Marcus; it is interesting to compare answers.

What qualities do you find necessary in a student before acceptance for study?

The qualities that I am most concerned about are musicality and sensitivity—they cannot be taught. Technique can be taught, and the Russian school stresses technique, but only as a means to the end; but beyond that there must be an inner feeling for music that transcends the purely mechanical.

What do students generally lack in their playing and background upon entering college?

You know, we get some fantastic talents at The Juilliard School; sometimes their auditions are really quite amazing. But the thing I notice very often is fingers, fingers, fingers, when I would rather hear music, music, music. However, concern with musical qualities rather than with the mechanical often grows as the student matures and is surrounded with good music day and night.

How would you define a talented student?

Talent to me means a special inner creative ability that is difficult to define. A genuine love for music and the determination to work hard to achieve one's goals also implies talent.

Do you feel that perfect pitch is a must for a pianist?

No. Sometimes it is a detriment because a person may be thrown by the varying pitches of different pianos. However, it is a desirable quality to have.

It has been said that a student's beginning training is so important that it can either "make or break the student." How important do you think correct teaching is in the beginning?

I think beginning training is of great importance—this is an excellent question. The first teacher, or teachers, is so important because that teacher must instill love, understanding, and interest in music.

How personally involved do you think a teacher should become in the relationship with his or her students?

To understand the pupil and his needs thoroughly, I must feel very close to him. I can only teach him if I know him personally. You cannot have one formula which will work for all students; what is right for one is not right for another.

Very often a student will work very hard to please the teacher, especially if one has great respect for the teacher; this must certainly be true in your case. What pleases you most in lesson-to-lesson work with a student?

I am pleased most by individual understanding. Also, I want week-to-week improvement.

I often hear students practicing in university practice rooms. It seems to me that they repeat and repeat, often aimlessly, the same passage over and over again without really much thought and direction. How can you teach a student to practice correctly?

Well, first practice does mean repetition, but it should be meaningful, not haphazard. One must practice with one hundred percent concentration and must stop when thoughts wander. If concentration begins to go, don't continue, only resume practice when you are fresh. I usually tell my students to listen carefully to what you are doing; be your own critic, if it does not sound right to you, find out why and fix it, that is what practice is for.

How do you feel about mental practice away from the keyboard?

I am very much for it! Actually, it should be taught from the beginning; one must first hear the sound, then practice. Reading a score without the piano develops a better understanding of the music; one will be able to think slower in the fast passages. I like to think of the whole page when I am playing, the phrasing, the dynamics, pedal, etc. These details should be worked out mentally away from the piano. In this way, a meaningful performance will be given.

An Interview with Rosina Lhevinne

Can a student be taught to project in performances, or is this an inborn quality?

A musical student can improve greatly, but if he does not have it, I don't think he can be taught how to project, because then it would be imitation. In the beginning the student may imitate the teacher in learning how to shape the phrase, how to pedal, etc., but projection of the music for the artist-student must transcend imitation and come from inner feelings that the performer wants to communicate to the audience.

What importance do you give to sight-reading?

I consider it so important that I insist from very early study that students practice a minimum of fifteen minutes a day on sight-reading. By doing some reading each day they will know the repertoire better; then when it comes time to discuss a program, they will have a knowledge of the literature and will already have an idea what interests them most. I teach students to read the melody and bass line; the reading of the top and bottom is so important, and the inner parts can be filled in as much as possible. Learning to read in this manner will devolop a reading skill and help students to read faster over a period of time. Practice time should be divided into repertoire, technique, and reading; reading should not be neglected.

You have had so many excellent students in your teaching career, and, of course, not all these students became concert artists. Many of them have become important teachers. What do you feel are the most important qualities to become a successful, inspiring teacher?

In my long career at Juilliard—forty-three years—I have had a great number of talented students, but talent alone is not enough to become a great success. Personality is the determining factor in the make-up of a great teacher, as well as being a fine performer. This is a quality that is quite indescribable. To develop and grow musically as an individual one must be constantly reading; not just on music, but one must develop an acquaintance with the other arts, go to museums, lectures, one must travel. All these are a great help to continue the growth and development of the personality. Also, the teacher must be willing to give special assistance to help the students being taught. The teacher really must be interested in teaching to produce well-trained students.

Do you think it is a realistic approach for all students studying with you to want to become concert artists?

Definitely not, and this is a great mistake which is made by young pianists. Out of one hundred students, when you ask them what they want to do, nearly all say they want to be concert pianists. Only a few are destined to become great pianists. A much nobler occupation than concertizing is teaching. By teaching you can pass on the art of piano playing from generation to generation and continue this art forever.

An Interview with Adele Marcus 23

Adele Marcus, distinguished faculty member of The Juilliard School, is one of the most outstanding piano teachers in the world. Her fantastic teaching capabilities have produced such famous pianists as Byron Janis, Augustin Anievas, Thomas Schumacher, Horacio Gutierrez (who won second prize in the 1970 Tchaikovsky Competition in Moscow), and Santiago Rodriguez (who won second prize in the 1981 Van Cliburn Competition). Miss Marcus studied with Josef Lhevinne and Artur Schnabel and was Josef Lhevinne's assistant for seven years.

She has given numerous master classes and demonstration lectures in this country and abroad. Miss Marcus was on the faculty at the Aspen Music Festival for many summers, and has also been on the summer faculty at the Temple University Festival at Ambler, Pennsylvania. She has represented the United States by serving on international piano juries for such contests as the Marguerite Long in Paris and the Munich International Piano Contest in Germany. Adele Marcus is a unique musician with a meteoric career in three fields as a performer, teacher, and lecturer and is unparalleled in these capacities.

After seeing Adele Marcus work with students in master classes and seeing her present several demonstration lectures, I realized that because of her remarkable capabilities as a teacher and performer, her personal views would be most valuable. She is an energetic, pleasant, spontaneous woman who inspires her students to amazing achievement. In observing her master classes one realizes that the work there reveals only a small portion of the teaching potential of which she is capable; but even this brief encounter with students often brings remarkable improvement. Of special interest to teachers and students is her presentation of technique that is quite special. Fortunately, her views were printed in *Clavier* magazine (Vol. XI No. 6, September, 1972) as related by Dean Elder. Also of special interest is her book of interviews titled *Great Pianists Speak* published by Paganiniana Publications, Inc., 1979.

In the following interview Adele Marcus discusses important teaching items that are of special interest to teachers of all levels. Similar questions were asked of Madame Lhevinne, and it is interesting to compare answers. The interview took place at Miss Marcus' summer home in Aspen, Colorado in 1968.

What qualities do you find necessary in a student before acceptance for study?

In my estimation the most essential quality for a student who is about to embark upon serious study, would be for that person to have a genuine emotional response to music. This person must also have the capability to penetrate a piece of music and get an appropriate response. Also, the physical equipment is important in that one has to handle the instrument adequately in order to convey the musical message to other people. There must be some degree of proficiency at the piano, and there must be a desire to become technically equipped—this is of utmost importance.

What do students generally lack in their playing and background upon entering college?

Often the communicative quality is not present; there is too much moving of the fingers, too much practicing and not enough studying. There is not enough emphasis on the character and mood of the composition. The students are working primarily with externals.

How would you define a talented student?

A talented student is one who is thoroughly dedicated and able to enjoy discipline, which means to me, the *love* of work. Also, talent means the desire to improve one's standard, not to compete with others, but rather to compete with his or her own standard.

Do you feel that perfect pitch is a must for a pianist?

No, I don't think perfect pitch is a must; it's one of those physical phenomena. However, good relative pitch is very important. It probably is necessary for a string player, a conductor, and only in rare cases for a singer. But I don't think it is necessarily an indication of a great talent. I know many great pianists who do not have perfect pitch.

It has been said that a student's beginning training is so important that it can either "make or break the student." How important do you think correct teaching is in the beginning?

Elementary training is of paramount importance. It does not necessarily make or break a student, but any experienced teacher on the advanced level knows immediately when the elementary training has been excellent. It is like the foundation of a house; if the foundation is really solid from the standpoint of musicianship and basic principles of study and practice, then it is much easier to work on an advanced level and the whole structure will not fall apart so easily.

How personally involved to you think a teacher should become in the relationship with his or her students?

The personal involvement should direct itself primarily toward evaluating the student's potential. The teacher should try to create for the pupil an exact image of himself relating to potential and any lacking ingredients. Also, one should take a long-range view of what possibilities might lie ahead—either as a performing career, or as a teaching-performing career. The teacher can also counsel and guide the student when advice is needed concerning auditions, the much dreaded competitions, or other aspects of the professional world. However, I do not think it is advisable for the teacher to become too involved with the personal matters of the student.

A student will often work very hard to please the teacher, especially if he has great respect for the teacher. This must certainly be true in your case. What pleases you most in lesson-to-lesson work with a student?

The main thing that pleases me most is progress. This is my basic and initial interest and my ultimate one. I usually tell a student I will work with you as hard as I know how, with all of my integrity and knowledge, and I expect you to do the same.

I often hear students practicing in university practice studios. It seems to me that they repeat and repeat, often aimlessly, the same passage over and over again without really much thought and direction. If this is so, how can you teach a student to practice correctly?

This is one of my pet subjects! I think music is the only profession in the world where people practice first and study afterwards. A lawyer would first study, then practice—in medicine the same order would follow. The student often practices too much. While practicing there should be a constant questioning, because to be of benefit, one must develop a creative approach. Practice must be creative; teaching must be creative; and performing must be creative. One must learn to study a score first and find out where the problems are. One cannot successfully solve a problem until one first knows what the problem is. After it has been

An Interview with Adele Marcus

solved, then one should practice the solution. Regarding repetition, too much repetition of a passage can very easily stifle the imagination. One should only repeat by constantly questioning: "Why am I repeating? Is it for a different fingering, a different nuance, a different phrase, a different pedaling, a different tonal effect?" If one repeats aimlessly, the constant repetition can lull one into a stupor.

How do you feel about mental practice away from the keyboard?

I think it should go on all the time. In visualizing a score, I think a big talent usually lives with a great work by thinking of it constantly. Study away from the piano enhances a certain security, not only in the interpretive concept, but also in the ability to memorize more securely. I believe in it one hundred percent!

Do you think even a young student can be taught this type of practice?

Definitely. I always say that a student should learn to "hear" through his eyes and "see" through his ears. In other words when he hears a score, he should be able to visualize how it might look on the printed page, and when he sees the printed page, he should hear what it might sound like looking at it.

Do you think that when a student plays a composition he should somehow visualize how it appears on the page?

This is, of course, having a photographic memory, and I think it is one of the four facets of knowing how to memorize. My feeling is that the other three are also very important. I happen to have a photographic memory, most people don't, and many people are afraid of it because they feel that it is exhausting and nerve-racking, particularly before a performance. In addition to visual memory, one must know the basic harmonic structure of a work. Also, one must be able to hear it to some appreciable extent—if without perfect pitch. Finally, the tactile sense is very important in memorization—being able to anticipate and "feel" patterns on the keyboard. So, the visual or the photographic memory very often goes with an important talent, but other memorization items are also necessary. I firmly believe in visual memory!

Can a student be taught to project in performances, or is this an inborn quality?

Many students project naturally, but projection goes with wanting to communicate. You cannot project projection, you have to project something, and if you have something vital you want to say, you usually want someone to hear it. The art of projection has to do of course with *how* you study, how you are able to listen, not only to what you feel about the music, but what you actually hear coming out of the piano. You feel it subjectively and you hear it objectively as a listener does—then, you are actually projecting.

Would you consider stage deportment one aspect of projection?

Very definitely. The moment you leave the wings and are faced with the public, you are already being evaluated as a person who either belongs to the task, or someone who is totally detached. There is nothing divorced from the making of music when you are involved with it on stage. There is sometimes more meaning in a gesture than all the notes in the world.

Usually, teachers are concerned with the perfection of a piece or the perfection of a number of compositions. This effort directed exclusively to one area of musicianship often leads to neglect of another—sight-reading. How do you feel about this?

I think sight-reading is of paramount importance. I like to feel that students can read fluently, not necessarily as fast as possible, but easily, and preferably in depth. I think a certain portion of every day should be devoted to sight-reading. When I find that a student is lacking in this particular ingredient of the whole musical output, I insist that between a half hour to forty-five minutes a day be devoted to reading something. The reading selected does not have to be difficult. Music from various style periods can be selected, so that over a period of time, the student can become acquainted with a variety of composer's works. I believe that reading at sight is a phenomenon with some students; they read inordinately fast, and they get over a tremendous amount of material. While reading, however, it is extremely important to play with *meaning*, not just play fast!

Would your approach to teaching beginners be channeled through sight-reading or playing scales and exercises?

I believe that after fundamentals of hand position and finger coordination have been established, it is important to read music from the earliest stage possible. Young children should learn to enjoy their music and not be made to practice scales and exercises; this drudgery will either produce unmusical results or discouragement with music. I was singularly fortunate in having taught children exclusively for ten years. That experience served as a most valuable apprentice period, and I feel that teaching children was the greatest factor in developing me as a teacher.

Would you include some sight-reading work as part of your teaching program, and would you hear sight-reading during the course of your lessons?

Very often if a student has only been able to prepare half of the lesson assignment, I will say, "Let's read through this particular work and let me see what you read into it, and what ideas you will bring forth." I think that one should read, but not just ramble through a lot of material—the reading should be serious. One should really penetrate the score and at the same time one should not only just see one or two things, but many things: primarily the character, the mood, and the tempo of the work.

An Interview with Adele Marcus

You have had so many excellent students in your teaching career, and of course not all these students became concert artists. Many of them have become important teachers. What do you feel are the most important qualities to become a successful, inspiring teacher?

A good teacher does not teach by stereotyped formulas. The teacher should direct his or her creative prowess toward handling the potential of each student. I do not have any methods; I try to evaluate the total personality of each student. The primary factor in teaching is to take a long-range view of what the student might accomplish and determine what the various goals might be. The teacher should discuss with the student how the two of them go toward building and developing rewarding progress.

Do you think it is a realistic approach for all students studying with you to want to become concert artists?

I am probably renowned for being singularly discouraging about reaching for *only* the performing career. Fortunately we are living in an age where the performer-teacher has come into his own. The demands of becoming a concert artist are severe. I think it is rare indeed to find a person who at a very early age manifests an almost spectacular talent, can carry through with proper training, build a large repertoire, develop excellent nerves, be blessed with an attractive appearance, find a manager, launch a career, and sustain it! These special musicians are very, very far and few between. As we know, these are the peaks, but the peaks are easy to slide down from. Sometimes the musician who is able to achieve a more modest goal, a little less than the highest peaks, usually, and very often, will have a happier life in music. I do not encourage students to become exclusively concert artists. I believe that the teaching field is tremendously rewarding, creative, and fulfilling personally.

Do you personally take as much interest in a student that you know will not make a concert career, even if the student is very gifted and proficient?

I definitely do. If the student is serious and is willing to work hard, I take an interest, because to me, it means that I am confronted with an individual whose life and livelihood is really important. I usually try to outline a four-year course of study to bring the student to a competent level, so upon graduation at The Juilliard School, that person will feel well-equipped to face the professional world.

What do you think teachers who have already been teaching for a number of years can do to upgrade their own work?

I think they should reach out for the understanding of all the new trends in music, even if it is music which does not particularly appeal to them, like avant-garde music, electronic music, etc. We must all be conversant with what is going on in the world around us, and we all need to broaden our horizons. Also, I think that the various periodicals are very helpful, such as *Clavier, The Piano Quarterly*, and various books written on music. I also feel that personal contact with workshops, with master classes, and with participation in local, state, and national organizations have a very broadening effect. Also, teachers should not be afraid to expose their students to competitions, auditions, and master classes. Certainly, none of us can know all the answers. I think it is very rewarding when students find that their own teachers' ideas have been upheld by other people. Finally, I advocate that teachers get back to the piano and try to practice some each day. We all need self-improvement, and teachers must strive for personal attainment for a rewarding and full life!

An Interview with James Dick 24

James Dick is an outstanding pianist in various musical idioms. Whether playing a concerto or a newly commissioned work, he is a musician of the highest caliber. The list of conductors he has performed with include Eugene Ormandy, Lorin Maazel, Kiril Kondrashin, Sixten Ehrling, Lawrence Foster, Alain Lombard, and the late Arthur Fiedler. As a chamber artist, Mr. Dick has performed with the world-renowned Tokyo, Cleveland, and Colorado Quartets, the Dorian Woodwind Quintet and with some of today's most prominent string players, such as Yo-Yo Ma, Young Uck Kim, Raphael Hillyer, and Donald Weilerstein. Mr. Dick founded the Round Top Festival in Texas in 1971. In the summer of 1984, the *Today Show* broadcast a feature story on Round Top as one of the cultural highlights of Texas, including an interview with James Dick.

Within an eight-month period during the 1966 season, Mr. Dick was a top prize winner in the Tchaikovsky, Busoni, and Leventritt International Competitions. He studied in the United States with the noted pianist Dalies Frantz at the University of Texas, from which he graduated with Special Honors in Piano in 1963. Subsequently, Mr. Dick was the recipient of two Fulbright Fellowships to the Royal Academy of Music in London where he studied with the renowned British pianist Sir Clifford Curzon. While at the Academy, he was awarded the Beethoven Prize, Tobias Matthay Fellowship and Recital Medal for performance, and was elected an Honorary Associate of the Royal Academy by its Board of Directors in 1968. In the summer of 1979, he was awarded the prestigious Presidential Citation, the top honor given by the National Federation of Music Clubs.

Mr. Dick has represented the United States on the juries of major international competitions, including the Tchaikovsky in Moscow and the Van Cliburn in Fort Worth. As a performer with a distinguished career, James Dick is an ambassador for the arts who continues to make a significant contribution to the musical life of this country.

James Dick is an exciting pianist whose views are of special interest because of his long association as a student of the brilliant teacher, Dalies Frantz. Frantz, himself a noted concert pianist, studied with Vladimir Horowitz in Switzerland and Artur Schnabel in Berlin. Thus, he had a rich background to bring to his students and was one of the most outstanding teachers of his time. James Dick discusses highlights of his association with Frantz, along with highlights of his personal career. This interview took place in Shreveport, Louisiana during the fall of 1972.

How long did you study with Dalies Frantz at the University of Texas?
Five years.

Was there anything seriously lacking in your precollege training—would you have liked to come to the university with a more complete background?
Rather than single out what I wish I might have had more of, I believe it should be pointed out that I had remarkably fine teaching on a local level. It began well and continued up to the time I left for the university. I had three teachers; the first evidently started me out very well because I made good progress. My mother assisted in my practice for the first four years, which was of great benefit to me as a young boy. It demonstrated her interest in what I was doing and made it a pleasure rather than a task. Parental interest and participation is essential for any family contemplating a musical career for their child.

At what age did you start lessons?
One month before I was six. For about the first four years my mother would sit down with me to see that I was reading the notes correctly and would pay particular attention to the rhythm. She would also play duets with me which interested me enormously. I felt that both my parents were completely behind my work, and there was nothing whatever they would do to interfere with my practice. My father would often come in from work very exhausted, as he worked both on a farm and as an auto mechanic. Even so, he encouraged my practice and took genuine pleasure in it. The importance of that kind of interest and help is very clear to me now.

How much interest in piano did you have at a young age? Did you ever think you wanted to become a concert pianist?
No. I never thought about that. The main thing was study with my teachers, expanding my repertoire, and practicing at the piano. That seemed to be the main goal at the time. My parents took me to all the concerts that came to Hutchinson, Kansas, and I was always thrilled by the artists. They made a tremendous impact on me. And, as my experience grew, my interest heightened.

Did your interest ever wane at any time—when you were a teenager, or when you had more activities in high school?

I became very interested in school politics and I thought then that it was an important thing that I must do. I was president of the class in my junior year and student body president in my senior year. But of course it was only a phase. However, much of that experience in working with committees and organizing activities gave me contact with others who had interests quite different from my own and has proven invaluable in my career.

How much were you able to practice during your high school years?

What I feel about practicing is not how long, but how much one concentrates during the practice period. This is true for concert artists and students alike. Fortunately, I had the ability to concentrate very well and thoroughly, and I was able to practice less in actual hours than one might think would have been required.

What was the actual time you spent at the piano per day?

As I recall, two hours at the most. I was not always able to have that much time, but I did manage to practice at least an hour and a half because I worked early in the morning. I would have one practice session before school and another forty-five minute session or so afterwards.

How was your repertoire when you came to the university?

Well, my repertoire was good in that I had learned many pieces that I feel increased my musicality, particularly in the romantic works. In other ways I had much work to do when I arrived at the university, in learning new concerto repertoire. Astonishingly, I had learned only one movement of one concerto when I entered the University of Texas! It has been a blessing in that the so-called "old war horses" are unburdened by any preconceived ideas and are fresh for me.

Were you encouraged to enter competitions while in high school?

During my precollege years I did have the opportunity to enter a number of competitions and auditions, and this did much to strengthen my repertoire. One in particular was the National Guild of Piano Teachers, which I entered from a very early age. It was an event to which I looked forward, and it brought all the work I had done during the year to a polish—there was focus and culmination to the year's work. The Guild, as you know, is not a competition but an audition in which we knew there would be a competent judge, and thus it was a learning experience. I also entered other competitions and auditions such as the Naftzger Young Artists Award in Wichita, the Kansas Federation of Women's Clubs, the Federation of Music Clubs, and so forth. I believe in competitions and auditions from a very early age, as performance experience is crucial to both musicality and technique. Performance experience is the only effective way to prepare a student for the realities of a career.

An Interview with James Dick

In your university work with Dalies Frantz, can you describe some of his teaching techniques? Did he play for you, or did he insist you do things a certain way?

Dalies had a remarkable ability to teach music with clarity and to keenly focus on each student's interpretative problems. He was careful to let students have freedom, but in order for them not to become chaotic or erratic musicians without any idea of what makes music breathe and communicate; he gave strict guidelines as well. I feel that students must first imitate someone who has had professional experience. It is an important and necessary part of learning, especially in the beginning. However, a brilliant teacher, as was Dalies Frantz, shows students that imitation eventually ends and that individual styles and qualities must be asserted. It was a great part of Dalies' teaching to show students that they can find something in music that is their own because of their personal discovery, and that they can work toward the realization of that discovery, not as self-expression or subjective gratification only, but as the realization of a well-thought intelligent conviction.

He would direct students' attention to rhythm and phrasing, what the music itself said, not pedantically trying to interpret only the printed page, but beginning the arduous task of realizing the composer's intent and meaning. From hearing students at master classes, and judging competitions and tapes, I think that rhythm and the structure of a piece are most often overlooked in performances. This, in addition to musical sensitivity, was one of the basic things upon which Dalies insisted.

Did he discuss pure technique with you, hand motions, etc?

Dalies was concerned with letting students discover their own solutions to technical problems. However, he would always advise if things were out of place, unnecessary, or needed correcting. Technique without musical sensitivity or poetic instinct does not support the concept of an artist. I believe that technique has built some careers, but has never sustained an artist. Although Dalies was concerned mainly with musical considerations, he still had very disciplined ideas and approaches to technique. He did stress the importance of flexibility over the entire keyboard. One area he certainly stressed was clearness of articulation in passages.

Did Frantz assign etudes or special pieces for work in clarity?

Yes. There is an E-flat Major Czerny study which he would give to most students for developing clarity. He would frequently assign students the Schumann *Toccata* or the *C minor Variations* of Beethoven as a basis for discussing technical ideas. I found the Schumann very difficult when I first came to Dalies.

Were there any exercises per se prescribed?

He was very interested in stretching exercises for fingers at the keyboard; he felt this developed clarity and strength. Dalies was also particular about being "over a note" before it was played. We would do many jump chords in which I would get to the chord before it was actually struck. This was done at great distances from one end of the keyboard to another. Any exercises that can be devised in that way, getting from one place to the next at a lightning speed, is extremely beneficial. It gives command and ease over the whole keyboard, which a performer must develop.

Did Frantz give any special advice on practicing—to practice a phrase hands alone, or to play with one hand and conduct with the other— anything of that sort?

He felt that rather than arbitrary practice measure-by-measure, it was better to practice to the end of the phrase, or to the beginning of a new phrase. His intention was for his students to always practice within a music sphere rather than a contrived or arbitrary line.

Regarding practice, did he consider mental practice as important as physical practice?

Definitely, in many ways more so. He emphasized that if something was not clearly conceived in mental practice, it would be performed unclearly. Concept precedes the reality in a performance. I believe this is true in all the arts. That is why in practice the standard for a serious musician must never be how long in time, but rather a disciplined concentration.

How did you develop facility in mental practice?

It is similar to developing physical technique at the piano, by working slowly and painstakingly, one phrase at a time.

Can you actually visualize the notes and fingering on the page?

Yes. To begin with you must visualize it almost basically, and then suddenly it becomes a part of you. You must be able to visualize the notes and actually hear the performance within your mind's ear. The final step in mental practice is to sit away from the keyboard and be able to visualize and experience the same performance that you would actually give in a concert. It is difficult to achieve, yet very necessary. Mental practice demands that a performer be completely honest and look deeply within his understanding of a work. I believe that endless rote practice sessions are like a narcotic. Technique can be approached through such practice, but never musical understanding.

Do you know the music so well that you could actually write it out note for note?

If one wished to use his time in that way, it could be done, yes. However, it would be a situation of not seeing the forest for the trees. I would not advise a student to use mental practice for that purpose, because it could then be harmful for a performance. The performer should be interpreting all the elements together in one entity. How well a performer knows the music mentally plays a vital role in a convincing interpretation of the musical content. However, mental practice is beneficial for the total

An Interview with James Dick

concept, not notes for notes' sake. It provides an indelible blueprint of the entire structure and interpretation of a work.

Did Frantz play portions or complete works for you at a lesson?

Sometimes Dalies would play parts for emphasis to demonstrate certain points. When I came to the University of Texas he was no longer giving concerts, although he had already attained a fantastically acclaimed concert career before coming to Austin. His health was at the point where he could not afford to travel and support the rigors of concert life. It was beyond what his health would allow him to do. It was a great loss for concert audiences. As a teacher, Dalies was a magnificent musician. I remember him coming to class about a month before he died and giving a rare performance of several Beethoven movements—one of the most moving experiences I have ever witnessed.

In his teaching did Frantz sing phrases for you to demonstrate melodic contours?

I cannot remember that he would sing a specific phrase, but there was always a strong insistence on lyricism in our work, and the intelligent student would be caught up by that.

In your university work were you influenced by what other students were doing?

Happily, there were some magnificent talents at the university when I attended. I was certainly inspired by competition and the general activity of others engaged in music.

Do you think Frantz took a very personal interest in you and in other of his students?

Definitely. Dalies would never be content to hear the lesson and then go home. He would telephone additional suggestions that he had been thinking about, or he would say "Let's have another session tomorrow, because I want to see something else in this piece." When I first studied in Austin the music building was closed on Sunday morning, and Dalies would come and personally open the building, lock me in, and then come back to let me out when the time was up. I can fully attest to his inspiring personal interest in all his students.

How much encouragement do you think a teacher should give a student who aspires to concert performance, but lacks the ability?

Frankly, I think there is too much emphasis placed on whether or not a student is capable of developing into a concert artist; this judgment is often premature, and more concerns the student's teaching or lack of it rather than his or her ability. Some teachers equate a concert career with stardom; that is instant commercial success, and they feel it is their duty to discourage all but those who blossom first. Several summers ago a young girl came to me after a concert and asked where she could go to become a concert pianist. That told me much about her outlook and to some extent how she had been trained. One should not dwell on the potential for a performance career.

Rather than focusing on a career as a performer, don't you think that while students are in college an important aspect of their training would be to study how to teach, since most graduates will be teaching in some capacity or another?

Certainly. Pedagogy classes can be of great help in this direction. It is difficult to discover just what one has learned from simply attending such a class. I feel that all students should have some practical experience in teaching before they graduate. Of course a great insight into teaching comes from what one's own teacher assigns regarding repertoire, technique, and other information, to give the student proper guidelines.

Regarding Frantz's personality as a teacher, what was it that influenced you? Was he enthusiastic, energetic, outgoing, etc.?

To know him and the qualities of his character and personality could not help but inspire anyone. When I came to the university his health was in such a state that some would have discounted his ability to teach, but he had magnificent qualities to offer. His concern, passion and enthusiasm for the music itself overcame his physical problems.

Was he able to maintain a cheery attitude with his students even though he was in very poor health?

Not only cheery, but he created a great intellectual excitement. Dalies was a brilliant mind in many areas. He was a great reader and thinker, and I feel this transferred to his music and to his students. They knew that his interest was not limited to music alone, but extended to literature, philosophy, drama and so many facets which make the total musician and human being, and this inspired everyone who came into contact with him.

When you completed your studies with Frantz, was it his idea for you to continue your studies in Europe, or was it your idea?

Dalies felt that after five years of study with him I should have another teacher. Even though I could not disagree with him, I felt that it would be difficult to find a greater musician with whom to study. However, his suggestion to study with Clifford Curzon, the great British pianist, was a marvelous choice. When you reach the level of both my teachers, Mr. Frantz and Mr. Curzon, you really cannot compare them, because they are in another strata of existence. There are simply no comparisons of great artists, they are all singular.

I know that you must have gained much from your work with Mr. Curzon in London. Were there special things that you would care to relate?

I learned many things from Mr. Curzon. Firstly, I was inspired onward. He was a wonderful musician. I believe that some of the greatest performances I have ever attended were those given by him while I was studying at the Royal Academy. He gave me many new insights regarding some of

An Interview with James Dick

the same ideas that Dalies had given me. They were two different artists approaching the same ends in music, but in different ways. Regarding my experiences in London, I would advise all young persons to study abroad at some time in their lives. It is important to live outside of one's own culture in order to fully appreciate it and that of others.

When you first began your career I know you were given impetus by the competitions you entered. What did you find to be of most value in the two major competitions you entered, the Tchaikovsky International in the Soviet Union and the Edgar M. Leventritt in New York?

The opportunity to go to the Soviet Union was obviously an exciting one. Unfortunately, I was ill during most of the time, having two Russian doctors giving me penicillin shots each day. In many ways this was a unique experience, certainly no other contestant was in a position like that! Many times I thought that I must give it up and return home because I saw no chance of achieving what I had hoped and worked for. Nevertheless, I saw it through. As I was confined to bed with fever, I could not practice as much as I would have liked; however, I was greatly benefited by my long association with mental practice. With the limited ability to practice I was indeed fortunate to go on to the finals and then to receive one of the top prizes—fifth place in the 1966 competition. It was terribly exciting to be there to begin with and it was especially inspiring to be able to perform the Tchaikovsky First with Maestro Kondrashin. I think that this was the high point of the Moscow experience.

Regarding the Leventritt, I think that it is, along with the Van Cliburn Competition, one of the most important competitions in the world. It offers finalists an opportunity to perform under Leventritt auspices for as long as three years, throughout the United States and Canada. This opportunity provides the necessary experience for a young artist to perform in a variety of situations—with orchestra, at universities, and on various concert series. This is essential and vital to anyone who aspires to a concert career. Artists must continually grow musically, and no management or recording contract can provide that development for them. Only a constant succession of live performances and study and restudy of the repertoire can do that.

True, there is so little room for the young performer to gain experience before going on to bigger and better things, and I am sure that the Leventritt was of tremendous value for you.

Where else can a young performer gain this experience? Most competitions do not provide it sufficiently. A young artist cannot possibly know what he must still discover and learn about the technique of performance unless he has an opportunity to develop this skill over an extended period. I have been named to represent the United States as a member of the jury at the Fourth International Van Cliburn Piano Competition in 1973. I had several meetings with the Competition Board to discuss this same matter. The 1973 Competition will follow the example of the Leventritt and stress concerts for top prize winners. Already over forty performances are promised for the first prize winner. I am happy to have had a part in that decision, for I could certainly speak from my own experience with the Leventritt.

Didn't you perform an incredible number of concerts this past season under a variety of circumstances?

Yes. Under the Leventritt sponsorship I performed over a hundred concerts during the 1967–68 season alone. In the past five seasons I have given over three hundred concerts. In addition, I give free performances in public schools in cities where I am engaged for concerts, which I feel to be of the greatest importance. I have performed in prisons, for senior citizens, in state schools and institutions as a public service as well. When my schedule permits, I also give concerts for several charities of particular interest to me, such as the Institution of International Education (IIE), which administers all Fulbright Awards for the U.S. Department of State. It was the IIE that sponsored my Fulbright Fellowship to the Royal Academy and made it possible for me to represent the United States at the Tchaikovsky Competition and the Busoni Competition in Italy. I feel very close to the IIE and their magnificent work.

In addition to concertizing, would you like to teach someday?

Well, you know it is not "someday." I have been teaching since I was fifteen. When my teacher went on vacation I would sometimes have charge of her class, and I taught several students at home during high school. I have often been asked to take students privately and there are offers from several universities each season. Perhaps that might happen someday. I do not feel that I would be able to fairly devote time to both my career and students under an ordinary conservatory or university arrangement. For that reason I established the Festival-Institute at Round Top, Texas in 1971.

Why is it that you decided to establish a Festival at Round Top? Why not in a larger city?

Round Top is a unique and historic area dating back to the 1830s, settled by German and Czech families. The major part of the old village has been restored. Festival Hill was inaugurated in 1976, and the Festival now has its own eighty acre campus. There are ten restored buildings that serve as concert and living facilities, and there is also a large concert hall for student and faculty performances.

Do you offer any unusual performances or performance opportunities for those students attending?

Yes, we try to offer as much variety as possible. During the 1971 Festival I gave the American premiere of Soviet composer Arno Babajanian's *Six Pictures for Piano*, and the students performed two concerts. This past June and July I invited the American composer, Benjamin Lees, to be composer-in-residence. I intend to include a guest composer and an

An Interview with James Dick

American or world premiere each year. The 1973 Festival will feature the premier of a new *Nocturne* for piano by Ulysses Kay, and the 1972 Festival commissioned a new work for piano and orchestra from Mr. Lees entitled *Five Etudes for Piano and Orchestra*.

The Festival also includes chamber music as part of the summer concerts. The Festival is built around the students, who are selected on their advancement and major musical potential. They need experience, as we have discussed, and that is what the Festival is really about. I have combined intensive study with myself and others, with performance opportunities. It is a program designed to assist young artists in accomplishing the difficult transition from student life to professional careers.

When you perform in the United States and abroad and during your annual Festival, you give master classes and listen to many student performances every season. Are there any special deficiencies that you notice?

I would not say deficiencies as such, but rather something that cannot be discovered and realized by students all at once, that is solid rhythmic projection in music. Rhythmic pulsation is a dominant factor in every performance; one notices if it is captivating, and one notices if it is less than so. I also believe that the ability to express musical ideas imaginatively, without being mechanical, is absolutely necessary. Dalies stressed this to me as a student, and I stress it today. Mr. Curzon once told me that evey performer must have the courage to take chances, even in a performance.

To conclude, do you think that American audiences are gaining or losing as far as participation at concerts?

Definitely gaining. I see this happening on university campuses and in organized concerts in general. As long as people are willing to concentrate on the optimistic aspects of attending concerts, enthusiasm will gain. Music will continue to communicate and speak, whether it is from four hundred years ago or contemporary music of today. Music and its influence will become more and more a part of everyone's life. This will be accomplished, in part, through the selfless contributions of concert performers, young artists, and students giving of themselves where the Arts are not always available or recognized. It is through the Arts that civilizations are remembered. It is within the Arts that we must strive to be responsible and significant to future generations.

An Interview with Irl Allison 25

Dr. Irl Allison (1896–1979) was an outstanding figure in the field of music education. He was the founder and organizer of the National Guild of Piano Teachers
which has an annual participation of approximately 80,000 students. Dr. Allison
received a BA degree in 1915 and an MA degree in 1922 from Baylor University.
His piano teachers were Ernest Hutcheson in New York and Percy Grainger in
Chicago. Upon graduation from Baylor, his teaching career began with a private
studio in Dallas.

His college teaching career included positions as Dean of Music at Rusk Junior
College, Rusk, Texas; Dean of Music at Montezuma Baptist College in New Mexico;
and Dean of Music at Hardin-Simmons University in Abilene, Texas. Because of
his outstanding work in the field of music education, Dr. Allison received honorary doctorates from Southwestern Conservatory, Dallas (1947), Hardin-Simmons
University (1949), and from the Houston Conservatory (1953).

Dr. Allison composed numerous compositions including *Through the Years*,
and he was the editor-author of a thirty-three volume library titled *The Irl Allison
Piano Library*. Through the founding and building of the Guild to national pro-
minence, Dr. Allison's contribution to the field of music was unique and commendable.

Because of the magnitude and scope of the Guild organization which includes 663 chapters, 10,000 teachers, and approximately 80,000 piano students who play upwards of 850,000 memorized pieces annually, I thought that Dr. Allison's personal views on the vision and organization of the Guild would be of special interest to piano teachers. Dr. Allison was a deeply religious man whose devotion to the formation and promulgation of the Guild was carried on with great fervor and personal zeal. The Guild offers an opportunity for students of all levels and abilities to play for an impartial judge in which each student receives a rating.

In 1950 Dr. Allison expanded the auditions to include the National Piano Recording Competition which is an important annual event that offers cash awards and founder's medals to all entrants. In 1958 he carried the Guild concept another step forward by working with Grace Ward Langford in Fort Worth to plan and develop the now world-famous Van Cliburn International Quadrennial Piano Competition which has helped launch the careers of many young artists.

From its meager beginning at Hardin-Simmons University in 1929, Dr. Allison's personal hand has guided the Guild to the fantastic success which it now has reached. It is this story that I wanted to record. The interview took place in Dr. Allison's lovely home in Austin, in the spring of 1970.

I want to ask you particularly about the formation of the National Guild of Piano Teachers. I noted that the first auditions were held in Abilene, Texas in 1929. How did the idea come to you for the beginning of this tremendous organization?

If you remember the financial situation of the country at that time, we were facing a depression. It had not yet struck West Texas, but everyone was frightened. Due to the panic of the stock market crash, many college piano students simply stopped studying. I had had one of the largest departments in the state at Hardin-Simmons University prior to that time, and it was growing tremendously. However, beginning in the fall of 1929 we felt an abrupt decrease in enrollment. In order to meet this situation I felt that we should try to interest more students from the city to attend the university. So I started what we called the Junior Piano School at the university in which we combined class work with private teaching. I had a number of advanced students who aided me as teaching assistants.

In this preparatory department that you started, what type of work was done in classes?

I began organizing the piano curriculum so that various elements of technique could be taught in class, such as scales, chords, and arpeggios. I prevailed upon the school board to purchase ten Howard (Baldwin) uprights. We converted our small recital hall into a class piano studio. We had two grands on the stage. Each student had a piano, two on stage, and one at each piano. Besides myself, we always had an assistant in the room to help the children when necessary. We advertised in the paper, and enrolled a class of fifty students. To schedule these students in sections we needed five hours which filled a week of class lessons.

Did you present programs of any kind to interest other teachers and students?

Yes. We rehearsed materials for our twenty-piano concert at the end of the year. We had students playing duets, trios, etc., with some twelve to twenty pianos going at the same time. This was one of the first piano ensemble presentations in the United States. In preparing for this event we outlined a step-by-step progam carefully that first year. Throughout the year my purpose was to have about eight or ten numbers that my groups would work up for this concert. Because we had a unique situation, and in order to create enthusiasm for piano playing, we invited students from the area to participate in an all Southwestern Piano Tournament.

Was that the first Guild tournament?

Actually, that first event was the beginning of the national piano playing auditions. At that time I set up goals for our students so that every one had a complete program in repertoire and technique to play for an important examiner. As a point of interest, the first examiner was John Thompson. He was giving a workshop there for teachers, and afterwards he stayed over three days for the auditions. That first event had only forty-six entrants; thirty-three of them were from my own class from the Junior Piano School. Several children came from far away. When Mr. Thompson came out of the room that first day, he said "Irl, is this your idea?" When I answered "yes," he said, "This ought to be everywhere, it has all the advantages of a contest but without the disadvantages." This was my purpose; each student was winning some kind of award, and in a sense they were all winners, none were losers. If Thompson thought the student performed the pieces well, with a grade of 90 or above, the student was awarded a blue ribbon for each piece that was played. The minimum requirement at this first audition was four pieces, the maximum was ten. Even at that time we set up district, state, and national honors. Students would get national honors and receive blue ribbons if they made a grade above 90 on all four pieces; state honors and red ribbons went to those whose grade was from 80 to 90; district honors and white ribbons went to those whose grade was from 70 to 80. In any case, every child came out with a handful of ribbons.

How did you promote this idea to other areas, out of the state of Texas?

At first it was one teacher telling another. However, when I conceived of having auditions outside of Abilene, I sent out a little booklet stating the rules and regulations. I sent this booklet to various music stores and asked them to send me a list of teachers in their area. The first year I sent out about five hundred booklets. The entries were very small that first year. To build interest and numbers of entrants, I tried some unusual methods. To start the Dallas center, for example, I sent twenty-four of my own

An Interview with Irl Allison

students to play for the judge there. For a period of about eight years I worked very hard at building interest and enthusiasm for these auditions. I visited about one hundred and fifty cities during that time. We moved to Los Angeles for one year from which I traveled to other cities in the area.

Did you organize and set up the centers alone?

Yes. I organized the centers myself. During the early years my wife acted as the national secretary helping me greatly in this project.

Did you move to other cities for a period of time other than Los Angeles?

Yes. I went to New York and organized the center there in 1935, and I stayed there for a period of time. I had a great deal of help from Edwin L. Gunther, the owner of the publishing company Schroeder and Gunther. Mr. Gunther knew many teachers there, and his help in soliciting their support was invaluable. We also had excellent support from the various newspapers in New York.

What kind of support did the New York papers give you?

Well, it was really fantastic. We held the first audition in Aeolian Hall which was a very beautiful recital hall on Fifth Avenue. This audition was well received, and the New York papers gave us good coverage of this event. Our largest direct support came about through a coincidence. The president of Hardin-Simmons University was Dr. J.D. Sanford, and his son-in-law was none other than Stanley Walker who was the editor of the *Times Herald* in New York. When Mr. Walker found out that this project was taking place, he sent reporters to cover the story. The stories featured the auditions, and also featured some unusual children who performed. One young prodigy who was only five at the time played the Mozart C Major Sonata, among other pieces. The prodigies were featured on the front pages of some of the leading New York papers; in fact, we got 329 articles in the papers that first year!

At that time, 1935, how many students auditioned nationally?

We had about 1,700 students from coast to coast in twenty-nine cities.

Were there any other unusual events that led up to this first national audition?

One person who was very helpful was Charles L. Kliner who lived in Cisco, Texas. He had just struck oil on his land and it turned out to be something really fabulous. He soon had seventeen wells which produced an income of $600 per day! He called me for an appointment, and on Sunday afternoon I drove out to see him. I explained to him what I wanted and he listened very respectfully, but he did not commit himself. I told him that I would like to set up centers in 100 cities. It was not possible for me to visit all of these cities myself, and I was not sure how this could be accomplished. When I went home I told Mrs. Allison that I thought we had wasted our time, I thought Mr. Kliner was not interested in giving support to this project. However, the next day Mr. Kliner called and said he liked the idea and wondered how much money I would need. I suggested an amount of $4,000. He said "You will get your check," and I did have it just a few days later. With that money I was able to find three people to help me. These three people covered three parts of the United States, and I took the fourth myself. On that meager budget of $4,000 we got this program started in twenty-nine cities that included Boston, Portland, Seattle, New York, Dallas, and many other centers.

Was that the only backing you received?

Yes, and it turned out to be just as well. After the first year when we had 1,700 students audition, I decided that since this project was for the students and for the students' teachers, there should be some way for them to support this program themselves. So the next year we had the first membership dues which were five dollars. We had about 1,000 teachers to start. With these dues I was able to reach 150 cities over the next eight years.

You mentioned the benefits for teachers belonging to the Guild; what are they?

First, the audition provides incentives. The teacher can hold up goals to work toward. The program can be planned in advance so that the material will be learned in time for the examiner. The student knows that judgment day is coming. Every scale learned, every piece, will have an opportunity to be heard and appraised objectively by an impartial party. It helps increase the student's repertoire and technique. The goal is to learn from four to ten pieces by memory. Also, the literature to be performed is specified in that certain selections such as a Bach piece, a sonatina, etc., are required. This not only helps the student in providing a guide to repertoire selections, but it also helps the teacher to choose materials from four periods.

Have you noticed improvements in teaching standards over the years after the Guild came into being?

Very definitely. Actually at that time many teachers had no idea of piano repertoire. One music dealer told me that a revolution had been made with the suggested repertoire the Guild required. He said almost no teacher at that time was assigning Bach Inventions, and very few were assigning sonatinas. As you know, the Guild requires a structured program of selections from the Baroque, Classical, Romantic, and Contemporary periods.

Where did you get the idea to require a structured program covering four eras of music?

That idea evolved in my work with Ernest Hutcheson with whom I studied after I graduated from Baylor. Hutcheson asked me to play a Two-Part Invention, and I didn't know one. So he started me on these polyphonic pieces, and until that time I had never played anything polyphonic. Likewise I had not played a Mozart sonata, and he introduced

An Interview with Irl Allison

me to these. My background was limited to certain areas of music, and I saw the need for an expanded, comprehensive survey of four-period literature.

Did you find that classical repertoire was gaining in popularity at that time?

Yes. G. Schirmer made a survey of the sales of the Edwin Hughes *Master Series for the Young*, and discovered that in one year alone sales had increased twenty percent. On the basis of these results, Schirmer gave me ads in our Syllabus for their publications, that was before we had our *Piano Guild Notes* magazine.

When you judged in different centers I'm sure you heard some outstanding students who had been well-prepared by their teachers. In this regard, what do you think are the qualities of fine teachers?

Mainly, they must be enthusiastic. They should assign music for each student that is not too difficult to be performed in the audition. Also, teachers must generate the feeling that everything that is taught and practiced is really worthwhile. Teachers should also include theory and technique in each lesson to help build the student's knowledge of these two important areas. These are the main items for consideration.

What would you like to see happen to the continuation of the Guild, and what would you hope for its future?

I would like most of all to see an organized plan for providing concert engagements for our young artists who have been produced through the Guild auditions.

Would this be your main hope for a new direction for the Guild?

Yes. I would like to give deserving young performers an opportunity to play for appreciative audiences throughout the country sponsored by teachers and students in the Guild organization. I wish I were young enough to begin this project, I think I could make it a success!

PART FIVE

Appendices

Music Reference Books A

DICTIONARIES & ENCYCLOPEDIAS

Ammer, Christine. *Musician's Handbook of Foreign Terms*. New York: G. Schirmer/Hal Leonard, 1971.

Arnold, Denis, ed. *The New Oxford Companion to Music*. 2 vols. New York: Oxford University Press, 1983.

Claghorn, Charles. *Biographical Dictionary of American Music*. West Nyack: Parker Publishing Company, Inc., 1973.

Gilder, Eric, and June B. Port. *The Dictionary of Composers and Their Music*. New York: Facts on File, Inc., 1978.

Griffiths, Paul. *The Thames and Hudson Encyclopedia of 20th-Century Music*. New York: Thames and Hudson, Inc., 1986.

Grove, Sir George, ed. *Grove's Dictionary of Music and Musicians*. 6th ed. Edited by Eric Bloom. 20 vols. New York: Macmillan Publishing Company, 1980.

Hindley, Geoffrey, ed. *The Larousse Encyclopedia of Music*. New York: The World Publishing Company, 1971.

Kennedy, Michael. *The Concise Oxford Dictionary of Music*. Oxford: Oxford University Press, 1985.

Lyle, Wilson. *A Dictionary of Pianists*. London: Robert Hale, Ltd., 1985 (distributed in the U.S. by Schirmer Books/Macmillan).

Slonimsky, Nicolas, ed. *Baker's Biographical Dictionary of Musicians*. 6th ed. New York: Schirmer Books/Macmillan, 1978.

Randel, Don Michael, ed. *The New Harvard Dictionary of Music*. Cambridge: Harvard University Press, 1986.

_____ , ed. *Harvard Concise Dictionary of Music*. Cambridge: Harvard University Press, 1978. Paper.

Thompson, Kenneth. *St. Martin's Dictionary of Twentieth-Century Composers 1911–1971*. New York: St. Martin's Press, Inc., 1973.

Thompson, Oscar, ed. *The International Cyclopedia of Music and Musicians*, 9th ed. Edited by Robert Savin. New York: Dodd, Mead & Company, 1964.

Westrup, J.A., and F.L. Harrison. *The New College Encyclopedia of Music*. Rev. New York: W.W. Norton & Company, 1976.

HISTORY

Baroque Period

Bodky, Erwin. *The Interpretation of Bach's Keyboard Works*. Cambridge: Harvard University Press, 1960.

Borroff, Edith. *The Music of the Baroque*. Dubuque: William C. Brown Company, 1970. Paper.

Bukofzer, Manfred. *Music in the Baroque Era*. New York: W.W. Norton & Company, Inc., 1947.

Newman, Anthony. *Bach and the Baroque: A Performer's View*. New York: Pendragon, 1985.

Newman, William S. *The Sonata in the Baroque Era*. 3rd ed. New York: W.W. Norton & Company, Inc., 1972.

Palisca, Claude V. *Baroque Music*. Englewood Cliffs: Prentice-Hall, Inc., 1968. Paper.

Classical Period

Landon, Howard Chandler Robbins. *Essays on the Viennese Classical Style: Gluck, Haydn, Mozart, Beethoven*. New York: Macmillan Company, 1970.

_____ . ed. *Studies in Eighteenth-Century Music*. New York: Oxford University Press, 1970.

Newman, William S. *The Sonata in the Classic Era*. 2nd ed. New York: W.W. Norton & Company, Inc., 1972. Paper.

Pauly, Reinhard G. *Music in the Classic Period*. 2nd ed. Englewood Cliffs: Prentice-Hall, Inc., 1973. Paper.

Rosen, Charles. *The Classical Style*. New York: W.W. Norton & Company, Inc., 1972. Paper.

Rushton, Julia. *Classical Music*. London: Thames and Hudson, Ltd., 1986. Paper.

Contemporary Period

Austin, William W. *Music in the 20th Century*. New York: W.W. Norton & Company, Inc., 1966.

Cope, David H. *New Directions in Music*. 4th ed. Dubuque: Wm. C. Brown Publishers, 1984. Paper.

Hansen, Peter S. *An Introduction to Twentieth-Century Music*. 3rd ed. Boston: Allyn and Bacon, Inc., 1971.

Holmes, Thomas B. *Electronic and Experimental Music*. New York: Charles Scribner's Sons, 1985. Paper.

Machlis, Joseph. *Introduction to Contemporary Music*. New York: W.W. Norton & Company, Inc., 1961.

Appendices

Myers, Rollo, ed. *Twentieth-Century Music: A Symposium*. New York: Orion Press, 1968.

Peyser, Joan. *Twentieth-Century Music: The Sense Behind the Sound*. New York: Schirmer Books/Macmillan, 1980. Paper.

Salzman, Eric. *Twentieth-Century Music: an Introduction*. 2nd ed. Englewood Cliffs: Prentice-Hall, Inc., 1974. Paper.

Yates, Peter. *Twentieth-Century Music: Its Evolution from the End of the Harmonic Era into the Present Era of Sound*. New York: Minerva Press, 1968. Paper.

General

Grout, Donald J. *A History of Western Music*. 3rd ed. New York: W.W. Norton & Company, Inc., 1980.

Machlis, Joseph. *The Enjoyment of Music*. 5th ed./Regular. New York: W.W. Norton & Company, Inc., 1980.

Medieval Period

Bukofzer, Manfred. *Studies in Medieval and Renaissance Music*. New York: W.W. Norton & Company, Inc., 1950. Paper.

Parrish, Carl, and John F. Ohl. *Masterpieces of Music Before 1750*. New York: W.W. Norton & Company, Inc., 1951.

Reese, Gustave. *Music in the Middle Ages*. New York: W.W. Norton & Company, Inc., 1940.

Seay, Albert. *Music in the Medieval World*. Englewood Cliffs: Prentice Hall, 1965. Paper.

Romantic Period

Gillespie, John and Anna. *A Bibliography of Nineteenth-Century American Piano Music*. Westport: Greenwood Press, 1985.

Klaus, Kenneth B. *The Romantic Period in Music*. Boston: Allyn and Bacon, Inc., 1970.

Longyear, Rey M. *Nineteenth-Century Romanticism in Music*. Englewood Cliffs: Prentice-Hall, Inc., 1969. Paper.

Newman, William S. *The Sonata Since Beethoven*. 2nd ed. New York: W.W. Norton & Company, Inc., 1972. Paper.

Plantinga, Leon. *Romantic Music*. New York: W.W. Norton & Company, Inc., 1984.

INTRODUCTORY/MUSIC APPRECIATION BOOKS

Christ, William, Richard DeLone, and Allen Winold. *Involvement with Music*. New York: Harper & Row, 1975.

Gillespie, John. *The Musical Experience*. 2nd ed. Belmont: Wadsworth Publishing Company, Inc., 1973.

Hickock, Robert. *Music Appreciation*. 2nd ed. Reading: Addison-Wesley Publishing Company, Inc., 1975.

Machlis, Joseph. *The Enjoyment of Music*. 5th ed./Shorter. New York: W.W. Norton & Company, Inc., 1984.

Manoff, Tom. *Music: A Living Language*. New York: W.W. Norton & Company, Inc., 1982.

PIANO

Accompanying

Grill, Joyce. *Accompanying Basics*. San Diego: Neil A. Kjos Music Company, 1987.

Johnson, Katherine D. *Accompanying the Violin*. San Diego: Neil A. Kjos Music Company, 1984.

Lishka, Gerald R. *A Handbook for the Ballet Accompanist*. Bloomington: Indiana University Press, 1979.

Moore, Gerald. *The Unashamed Accompanist*. Reprint. Danbury: F. Watts, 1985.

Spillman, Robert. *The Art of Accompanying*. Bloomington: Indiana University Press, 1985.

Care & Maintenance

Smith, Virgil E. *Your Piano & Your Piano Technician*. San Diego: Neil A. Kjos Music Company, 1981.

Construction & Design

Barthold, Kenneth van, and David Buckton. *The Story of the Piano*. London: British Broadcasting Corporation, Ltd., 1975.

Bie, Oscar. *A History of the Piano and Piano Players*. New York: Da Capo Press, 1966.

Clossen, Ernest. *History of the Piano*. London: Paul Elek, 1947. New ed., 1973.

Colt, C.F., and Antony Miall. *The Early Piano*. New York: Stainer & Bell, 1981.

Appendices

Dolge, Alfred. *Pianos and Their Makers*. New York: Dover Publications, Inc., 1972. Paper.

Gill, Dominic, ed. *The Book of the Piano*. Ithaca: Cornell University Press, 1981.

Grover, David S. *The Piano: Its Story, from Zither to Grand*. London: Robert Hale, Ltd., 1976.

Kentner, Louis. *Piano*. London: Macdonald, 1976.

Hollis, Helen Rice. *The Piano: A Pictorial Account of Its Ancestry and Development*. London: David & Charles, Ltd., 1975.

Oringer, Judith. *Passion for the Piano*. Los Angeles: Jeremy P. Tarcher, Inc., 1983.

Summer, William Leslie. *The Pianoforte*. New York: St. Martin's Press, Inc., 1966.

Duets & Multiple Piano Music

Hinson, Maurice. *Music for More than One Piano*. Bloomington: Indiana University Press, 1983.

Lubin, Ernest. *The Piano Duet*. New York: Ernest Lubin, 1970.

McGraw, Cameron. *Piano Duet Repertoire*. Bloomington: Indiana University Press, 1981.

Literature, History, & Style

Allen, Warren Dwight. *Philosophies of Music History*. New York: Dover Publications, Inc., 1962. Paper.

Apel, Willi. *Masters of the Keyboard*. Cambridge: Harvard University Press, 1947.

———————— . *The History of Keyboard Music to 1700*. Translated and revised by Hans Tischler. Bloomington: Indiana University Press, 1972.

Appleby, David P. *The Music of Brazil*. Austin: University of Texas Press, 1983.

———————— . *Heitor Villa-Lobos, A Bio-Bibliography*. Westport: Greenwood Press, Inc., 1988.

Bach, C.P.E. *Essay on the True Art of Playing Keyboard Instruments*. New York: W.W. Norton & Company, Inc., 1948.

Badura-Skoda, Eva and Paul. *Interpreting Mozart on the Keyboard*. New York: St. Martin's Press, Inc., 1962.

Blom, Eric. *Beethoven's Pianoforte Sonatas Discussed*. London: J.M. Dent, 1938. Reprint. New York: Da Capo Press, 1968.

Bodky, Erwin. *The Interpretation of Bach's Keyboard Works*. Cambridge: Harvard University Press, 1960.

Bonis, Ferenc. *Béla Bartók, His Life in Pictures and Documents*. London: Boosey & Hawkes, Ltd., 1972.

Brown, Maurice J.E. *Chopin, an Index of His Works in Chronological Order*. 2nd ed. London: The Macmillan Press Ltd., 1972.

Caldwell, John. *English Keyboard Music Before the Nineteenth Century*. New York: Praeger Publishers, 1973.

Dolmetsch, Arnold. *Interpreting Music of the 17th and 18th Centuries*. London: Novello & Company, Ltd., 1949.

Drake, Kenneth. *The Sonatas of Beethoven, as He Played and Taught Them*. Bloomington: Indiana University Press, 1980.

Emery, Walter. *Bach's Ornaments*. London: Novello & Company, Ltd., 1953.

Evans, Edwin. *Handbook to the Pianoforte Works of Johannes Brahms*. New York: Charles Scribner's Sons, 1936. Reprint. New York: Bert Franklin, 1970.

Forman, Denis. *Mozart's Concerto Form: the First Movements of the Piano Concertos*. New York: Praeger Publishers, 1972.

Friskin, James, and Irwin Freundlich. *Music for the Piano: A Handbook of Concert and Teaching Material from 1580 to 1952*. New York: Dover Publications, Inc., 1973. Paper.

Gillespie, John. *Five Centuries of Keyboard Music*. Unabridged republication. New York: Dover Publications, Inc., 1972. Paper.

Hinson, Maurice. *Guide to the Pianist's Repertoire*. 2nd ed. Bloomington: Indiana University Press, 1987.

_____ . *Music for More than One Piano*. Bloomington: Indiana University Press, 1983.

_____ . *Music for Piano and Orchestra*. Bloomington: Indiana University Press, 1981.

_____ . *The Pianist's Reference Guide, a Bibliographical Survey*. Van Nuys: Alfred Publishing Company, Inc. 1988. Paper.

_____ . *The Piano in Chamber Ensemble*. Bloomington: Indiana University Press, 1978.

Iliffe, Frederick. *Analysis of Bach's 48 Preludes & Fugues, Books 1 and 2*. London: Novello (no publication date given). Paper.

Kirby, Frank E. *A Short History of Keyboard Music*. New York: The Free Press, 1966.

Kirkpatrick, Ralph. *Domenico Scarlatti*. Princeton: Princeton University Press, 1955. Paperback reprint. New York: Apollo Editions, 1968.

Krebs, Stanley Dale. *Soviet Composers*. London: George Allen and Unwin, Ltd., 1970.

Lockwood, Albert. *Notes on the Literature of the Piano*. Ann Arbor: University of Michigan Press, 1949. Reprint. New York: Da Capo Press, 1968.

Loesser, Arthur. *Men, Women and Pianos*. New York: Simon and Schuster, 1954.

Newman, William S. *Performance Practices in Beethoven's Piano Sonatas*. New York: W.W. Norton & Company, Inc., 1971.

Powell, Linton E. *A History of Spanish Piano Music*. Bloomington: Indiana University Press, 1980.

Restout, Denise. *Landowska on Music*. New York: Stein and Day, Publishers, 1964.

Schonberg, Harold C. *The Lives of the Great Composers*. New York: W.W. Norton & Company, Inc., 1970.

Suchoff, Benjamin. *Guide to Bartók's Mikrokosmos*. Rev. ed. London: Boosey & Hawkes, 1971.

Swan, Alfred J. *Russian Music*. London: John Baker, 1973.

Wolff, Konrad. *Masters of the Keyboard*. Bloomington: Indiana University Press, 1983.

Pedagogy

Agay, Denes. *Teaching Piano*. 2 vols. New York: Yorktown Music Press, Inc., 1981. Paper.

Ahrens, Cora, and G.D. Atkinson. *For All Piano Teachers*. Oakville, Ontario, Canada: Frederick Harris Music Company, Ltd., 1955.

Banowetz, Joseph. *The Pianist's Guide to Pedaling*. Bloomington: Indiana University Press, 1985.

Bastien, James. *How to Teach Piano Successfully*. 3rd ed., rev. San Diego: Neil A. Kjos Music Company, 1988. Paper.

Bernstein, Seymour. *With Your Own Two Hands*. New York: Schirmer Books/Macmillan, 1981.

Bolton, Hetty. *How to Practice: A Handbook for Pianoforte Students*. London: Elkin & Company, Ltd., 1939.

——————————. *On Teaching the Piano*. London: Novell and Company, Ltd., 1954.

Booth, Victor. *We Piano Teachers*. Rev. by Adele Franklin. London: Hutchinson University Library, 1971.

Broughton, Julia. *Success in Piano Teaching*. New York: Vantage Press, 1956.

Camp, Max W. *Developing Piano Performance*. Chapel Hill: Hinshaw Music, Inc., 1981.

Chronister, Richard, and James Lyke. *The Proceedings of the National Conference on Piano Pedagogy*. Princeton: Published every second year.

D'Abreu, Gerald. *Playing the Piano with Confidence: An Analysis of Technique, Interpretation, Memory, and Performance*. New York: St. Martin's Press, Inc., 1959.

Deutsch, Leonard. *Piano: Guided Sight-Reading*. 2nd ed. Chicago: Nelson-Hall Company, 1959.

Diller, Angela. *The Splendor of Music*. New York: G. Schirmer/Hal Leonard, 1957.

Enoch, Yvonne. *Group Piano-Teaching*. London: Oxford University Press, 1974.

Enoch, Yvonne, and James Lyke. *Creative Piano Teaching*. Champaign: Stipes Publishing Company, 1977. Paper.

Gát, Jósef. *The Technique of Piano Playing*. Translated by Istva Kleszky. (Budapest: Covina Publishing Company), English ed. London: Collet's Holdings, Ltd., 1965.

Kern, R. Fred, and Marguerite Miller. *Projects for Piano Pedagogy, Book 1*. San Diego: Neil A. Kjos Music Company, 1988.

Last, Joan. *The Young Pianist: A New Approach for Teachers and Students*. 2nd ed. London: Oxford University Press, 1972.

——————————. *Interpretation for the Piano Student*. London: Oxford University Press, 1960.

——————————. *Freedom in Piano Technique*. London: Oxford University Press, 1980. Paper.

Maier, Guy. *The Piano Teacher's Companion*. Miami: Belwin/Columbia Pictures Publications, 1963. Paper.

Merrick, Frank. *Practicing the Piano*. New York: Dover Publications, Inc., 1965. Paper.

Neuhaus, Heinrich. *The Art of Piano Playing*. Translated by K.A. Leibovitch. New York: Praeger Publishers, 1973.

Pollei, Paul C. *Pedagogical Tips for Piano Teaching*. Provo: Brigham Young University Press, 1969. Paper.

Reifling, Reimar. *Piano Pedalling*. Translated by Kathleen Dale. London: Oxford University Press, 1962.

Sandor, Gyorgy. *On Piano Playing*. New York: Schirmer Books/Macmillan, 1981.

Seroff, Victor. *Common Sense in Piano Study*. New York: Crescendo Publishing, 1977. Paper.

Slenczynska, Ruth. *Music at Your Fingertips*. 2nd ed, rev. and enlarged, with corrections. New York: Da Capo Press, 1974. Paper.

Whiteside, Abbey. *Indispensables of Piano Playing*. New York: Charles Scribner's Sons, 1955. 2nd ed., 1961.

Wolff, Konrad. *The Teaching of Artur Schnabel: A Guide to Interpretation*. New York: Praeger Publishers, 1971.

Periodicals

American Music Teacher (Music Teachers National Association, 2113 Carew Tower, Cincinnati, OH 45202).

Clavier (200 Northfield Road, Northfield, IL 60093).

Maxwell Music Evaluation Notebook (1245 Kalmia, Boulder, CO 80302).

The Piano Quarterly (P.O. Box 815, Wilmington, VT 05363).

Pianists

Chasins, Abram. *Speaking of Pianists*. 2nd ed. New York: Alfred A. Knopf, Inc., 1961.

Appendices

Dubal, David. *Reflections from the Keyboard*. New York: Summit Books/ Simon & Schuster, Inc., 1984.

Elder, Dean. *Pianists at Play*. Northfield: The Instrumentalist Company, 1982.

Gerig, Reginald R. *Famous Pianists and Their Technique*. Washington: Robert B. Luce, 1974.

Kaiser, Joachim. *Great Pianists of Our Time*. Translated by David Wooldridge and George Unwin. New York: Herder and Herder, 1971.

Mach, Elyse. *Great Pianists Speak for Themselves*. New York: Dodd, Mead & Company, 1980.

Marcus, Adele. *Great Pianists Speak*. Neptune: Paganiniana Publications, Inc., 1979.

Schonberg, Harold C. *Great Pianists From Mozart to the Present*. Rev. and updated. New York: Simon & Schuster, Inc., 1987. Paper.

Wallace, Robert K. *A Century of Music Making* (Josef and Rosina Lhevinne). Bloomington: Indiana University Press, 1976.

SPECIAL SUBJECTS

American Music

Chase, Gilbert. *America's Music*. 2nd ed. New York: McGraw-Hill Book Company, Inc., 1966.

Hitchcock, H. Wiley. *Music in the United States: A Historical Introduction*. Englewood Cliffs: Prentice-Hall, Inc., 1969. Paper.

Howard, John Tasker, and George Kent Bellows. *A Short History of Music in America*. New York: Apollo Edition, 1967. Paper.

Machlis, Joseph. *American Composers of Our Time*. New York: Thomas Y. Crowell Company, 1963.

Mellers, Wilfrid. *Music in a New Found Land*. New York: Alfred A. Knopf, 1964.

Business

Bastien, Jane Smisor. *Music Teacher's Record Book*. San Diego: Neil A. Kjos Music Company, 1976.

Gigante, Beth. *A Business Guide for the Music Teacher*. San Diego: Neil A. Kjos Music Company, 1987.

Shemel, Sidney, and M. William Krasilovsky. *This Business of Music*. 4th ed., rev. and enlarged. New York: Billboard Publishers, Inc., 1979.

Chamber Music

Berger, Melvin. *Guide to Chamber Music*. New York: Dodd, Mead & Company, 1985.

Ferguson, Donald. *Image and Structure in Chamber Music*. Minneapolis: University of Minnesota Press, 1964.

Haroutounian, Joanne. *Chamber Music Sampler, Books 1, 2, 3*. San Diego: Neil A. Kjos Music Company, 1992.

Hinson, Maurice. *The Piano in Chamber Ensemble*. Bloomington: Indiana University Press, 1978.

Ulrich, Homer. *Chamber Music*. 2nd ed. New York: Columbia University Press, 1966.

Concerto

Hinson, Maurice. *Music for Piano and Orchestra*. Bloomington: Indiana University Press, 1981.

Young, Percy M. *Concerto*. Boston: Crescendo Publishers, 1968.

Veinus, Abraham. *The Concerto*. Rev. republication. New York: Dover Publications, Inc., 1964.

Conducting

Green, Elizabeth. *The Modern Conductor*. Englewood Cliffs: Prentice-Hall, Inc., 1961.

Grosbayne, Benjamin. *Techniques of Modern Orchestral Conducting*. Cambridge: Harvard University Press, 1956.

Harpsichord & Clavichord

Harich-Schneider, Eta. *The Harpsichord*. Kassel: Bärenreiter, 1960.

Hoover, Cynthia A. *Harpsichords and Clavichords*. Washington: Smithsonian Institution Press (for sale by the Superintendent of Documents, U.S. Government Printing Office), 1969.

Kenyon, Max. *Harpsichord Music*. London: Cassel & Company, Ltd., 1949.

Neupert, Hanns. *Harpsichord Manual: A Historical and Technical Discussion*. Translated by F. E. Kirby. 2nd ed. Kassel: Bärenreiter, 1968. Paper.

Russell, Raymond. *The Harpsichord and Clavichord*. London: Faber and Faber, 1959.

Troeger, Richard. *Technique and Interpretation on the Harpsichord and Clavichord*. Bloomington: Indiana University Press, 1986.

Zuckerman, Wolfgang Joachim. *The Modern Harpsichord: Twentieth-Century Instruments and Their Makers*. New York: October House, 1969.

Instruments

Kendall, Allan. *The World of Musical Instruments*. London: The Hamlyn Publishing Group, Ltd., 1972.

Appendices

Libin, Laurence. *American Musical Instruments*. The Metropolitan Museum of Art. New York: W.W. Norton & Company, Inc., 1985.

Sachs, Curt. *The History of Musical Instruments*. New York: W.W. Norton & Company, Inc., 1940.

Winternitz, Emanuel. *Musical Instruments of the Western World*. New York: McGraw-Hill Books, 1967.

Letters

Gal, Hans, ed. *Letters of the Great Composers*. London: Thames and Hudson, 1965. Paper.

Musical Ability

Bentley, Arnold. *Musical Ability in Children*. London: George G. Harrap & Company, Ltd., 1966.

Bloom, Benjamin S., ed. *Developing Talent in Young People*. New York: Ballantine Books, 1985. Paper.

Shuter, Rosamund. *The Psychology of Musical Ability*. London: Methuen, 1968.

Music Books for Children

Britten, Benjamin, and Imogen Holst. *The Wonderful World of Music*. Garden City: Doubleday, 1968.

McLin, Lena. *Pulse: A History of Music*. San Diego: Neil A. Kjos Music Company, 1977.

Scholes, Percy. *The Oxford Junior Companion to Music*. 2nd ed. by Michael Hurd. London: Oxford University Press, 1979.

Musicology

Haydon, Glen. *Introduction of Musicology*. Englewood Cliffs: Prentice-Hall, Inc., 1941. Unaltered reprint. Chapel Hill: University of North Carolina Press, 1959.

Pruett, James W., compiler. *Studies in Musicology*. Chapel Hill: University of North Carolina Press, 1969.

Reese, Gustave, and Robert J. Snow, compilers. *Essays in Musicology, in Honor of Dragan Plamenac on His 70th Birthday*. Pittsburgh: University of Pittsburgh Press, 1969.

Watanabe, Ruth Taiko. *Introduction to Music Research*. Englewood Cliffs: Prentice-Hall, Inc., 1967.

Notation

Donato, Anthony. *Preparing Music Manuscript*. Englewood Cliffs: Prentice-Hall, Inc., 1963.

Heussenstramm, George. *The Norton Manual of Music Notation*. New York: W.W. Norton & Company, 1987.

Read, Gardner. *Music Notation*. 2nd ed. New York: Crescendo/Taplinger Publishing Company, 1979.

Ross, Ted. *The Art of Music Engraving and Processing*. Miami: Hansen Books, 1970.

Williams, Charles Francis. *The Story of Notation*. New York: Haskell House Publishers, 1969.

Orchestration

Adler, Samuel. *The Study of Orchestration*. New York: W.W. Norton & Company, Inc., 1982.

Kennan, Kent Wheeler. *The Technique of Orchestration*. 2nd ed. Englewood Cliffs: Prentice-Hall, Inc., 1970.

Piston, Walter. *Orchestration*. New York: W.W. Norton & Company, Inc., 1955.

Organ

Anderson, Paul Gerhard. *Organ Building and Design*. Translated by Joanne Curnutt. New York: Oxford University Press, 1969.

Barnes, William Harrison, and Edward B. Gammons. *Two Centuries of American Organ Building*. Glen Rock: J. Fischer, 1970.

Soderlund, Sandra. *Organ Technique: an Historical Approach*. Chapel Hill: Hinshaw, 1980.

Summer, William Leslie. *The Organ*. 3rd ed. London: Macdonald, 1962.

Parents

Bastien, James. *A Parent's Guide to Piano Lessons*. San Diego: Neil A. Kjos Music Company, 1976.

Johnson, Mary Teel. *Keys to Successful Piano Lessons*. Monterey: Funchess-Jones Publishing, 1987.

Performance

Green, Barry, with Timothy Gallwey. *Inner Game of Music*. Garden City: Anchor Press/Doubleday, 1986.

Reubart, Dale. *Anxiety and Musical Performance*. New York: Da Capo Press, 1985.

Appendices

Self-Instruction

Appleby, Martha, and Larry Morton. *Follow Me: A Self-Guide to Playing Electronic Keyboards, Book 1*. San Diego: Neil A. Kjos Music Company, 1988.

Symphony

Cuyler, Louise. *The Symphony*. New York: Harcourt, Brace, Jovanovich, Inc., 1973.

Peyser, Joan. *The Orchestra: Origins and Transformations*. New York: Charles Scribner's Sons, 1986.

Previn, André. *Orchestra*. London: Macdonald and Jane's Publishers, Ltd., 1979.

THEORY

Acoustics

Backus, John. *The Acoustical Foundations of Music*. New York: W.W. Norton & Company, Inc., 1969.

Bartholomew, Wilmer. *Acoustics of Music*. Englewood Cliffs: Prentice-Hall, Inc., 1942.

Sabine, Wallace C. *Collected Papers on Acoustics*. New York: John Wiley, 1962.

Wood, Alexander. *Acoustics*. New York: Dover Publications, Inc., 1967. Paper.

Counterpoint

Bassett, Leslie. *Manual of 16th Century Counterpoint*. New York: Appleton-Century-Crofts, 1967.

Jeppesen, Knud. *Counterpoint*. Translated by Glen Haydon. Englewood Cilffs: Prentice-Hall, Inc., 1960.

Kennan, Kent Wheeler. *Counterpoint*. 2nd ed. Englewood Cliffs: Prentice-Hall, Inc., 1972.

Piston, Walter. *Counterpoint, 18th and 19th Century Styles*. New York: W.W. Norton & Company, Inc., 1947.

Searle, Humphrey. *Twentieth Century Counterpoint*. London: Ernest Benn, Ltd., 1954.

Form

Fontaine, Paul. *Basic Formal Structures in Music*. New York: Appleton-Century-Crofts, 1967.

Kohs, Ellis B. *Musical Form*. Boston: Houghton Miffin Company, 1976.

Walton, Charles W. *Basic Forms in Music*. Sherman Oaks: Alfred Publishing Company, Inc., 1974. Paper.

Harmony

Baur, John. *Music Theory Through Literature*. Englewood Cliffs: Prentice-Hall, Inc., 1985.

Christ, Delone, Kliewer, Rowell, and Thomson. *Materials and Structures of Music*. Englewood Cliffs: Prentice-Hall, Inc., 1966.

Haroutounian, Joanne. *Explorations in Music, Books 1-7; Explorations in Music Teacher's Guides, Books 1-7*. San Diego: Neil A. Kjos Music Company, 1993, 1995.

Ottman, Robert. *Elementary Harmony*. 3rd ed. Englewood Cliffs: Prentice-Hall, Inc., 1983.

Piston, Walter. *Harmony*. 5th ed., rev. and expanded by Mark Devoto. New York: W.W. Norton & Company, Inc., 1987.

Introductory

Harder, Paul. *Basic Materials in Music Theory*. 6th ed. Boston: Allyn and Bacon, Inc., 1986.

Chronological List of Concert Pianists* B

THE PAST GENERATION

Louis Moreau Gottschalk, American (1829–69)
Anton Rubinstein, Russian (1829–94)
Amy Fay, American (1844–1928)
Vladimir de Pachmann, Russian (1848–1933)
Ignace Jan Paderewski, Polish (1860–1941)
Moritz Rosenthal, Polish (1862–1946)
Ferruccio Benvenuto Busoni, Italian (1866–1924)
Leopold Godowsky, Lithuanian-American (1870–1938)
Sergei Rachmaninoff, Russian (1873–1943)
Josef Lhevinne, Russian-American (1874–1944)
Josef Hofmann, Polish-American (1876–1957)
Alfred Cortot, French (1877–1962)
Ossip Gabrilowitsch, Russian-American (1878–1936)
Wanda Landowska, Polish (1877–1959)
Rosina Lhevinne, Russian-American (1880–1976)
Egon Petri, German-American (1881–1962)
Percy Grainger, Australian-American (1882–1961)
Artur Schnabel, Austrian (1882–1951)
Wilhelm Backhaus, German (1884–1969)
Edwin Fischer, Swiss (1886–1960)
Arthur Rubinstein, Polish (1887–1982)
Myra Hess, English (1890–1965)
Benno Moiseiwitsch, Russian (1890–1963)
Simon Barere, Russian (1891–1951)
Walter Gieseking, German (1895–1956)
Clara Haskil, Rumanian (1895–1960)
José Iturbi, Spanish-American (1895–1980)
Alexander Brailowsky, Russian (1896–1976)
Guiomar Novaes, Brazilian (1896–1979)
Robert Casadesus, French (1899–1972)
Lili Kraus, Hungarian-American (1903–86)

*For a complete historical list of pianists, read Wilson Lyle's book *A Dictionary of Pianists* published by Robert Hale, Ltd., 1985 (distributed in the U. S. by Schirmer Books/Macmillan).

Louis Kentner, Hungarian-English (1905–87)
Oscar Levant, American (1906–72)
Clifford Curzon, English (1907–82)
Alexander Uninsky, Russian-American (1910–72)
Hans Richter-Hasser, German (1912–80)
Gina Bachauer, Greek-English (1913–76)
Witold Malcuzynski, Polish (1914–77)
Emil Gilels, Russian (1916–85)
Dinu Lipatti, Rumanian (1917–50)
Eugene List, American (1918–85)
Géza Anda, Hungarian (1921–76)
William Kapell, American (1922–53)
Julius Katchen, American (1926–69)
Glenn Gould, Canadian (1932–82)

THE OLDER GENERATION

Wilhelm Kempff, German (1891-91)
Solomon Cutner, English (1902–88)
Claudio Arrau, Chilian (1903-91)
Rudoff Serkin, German-American (1903-91)
Vladimir Horowitz, Russian-American (1904–89)
Beveridge Webster, American (1908–)
Rudolf Firkusny, Czech-American (1912–)
Gyorgy Sandor, Hungarian-American (1912–)
Jorge Bolet, Cuban-American (1914–90)
Annie Fischer, Hungarian (1914–)
Sviatoslav Richter, Russian (1914–)
Rosalyn Tureck, American (1914–)
Arturo Benedetti Michelangeli, Italian (1920–)
William Masselos, American (1920–)
Gyorgy Cziffra, Hungarian (1921–)
Grant Johannesen, American (1921–)
Abbey Simon, American (1922–)
Alicia de Larrocha, Spanish (1923–)
Leonard Pennario, American (1924–)
Aldo Ciccolini, Italian (1925–)
Eugene Istomin, American (1925–)
Ruth Slenczynska, American (1925–)
Raymond Lewenthal, American (1926–)
Theodore Lettvin, American (1926–)
Paul Badura-Skoda, Austrian (1927–)
Jorg Demus, Austrian (1928–)
Leon Fleischer, American (1928–)
Gary Graffman, American (1928–)

Byron Janis, American (1928–)
Alexis Weissenberg, Bulgarian-American (1929–)
David Bar-Illan, Israeli (1930–)
Lazar Berman, Russian (1930–)
Friedrich Gulda, Austrian (1930–)
Alfred Brendel, Czech (1931–)
Ivan Davis, American (1932–)
John Browning, American (1933–)
Tamas Vásáry, Hungarian (1933–)
Agustin Aneivas, American (1934–)
Van Cliburn, American (1934–)
Philippe Entremont, French (1934–)
Malcolm Frager, American (1935–)
Peter Frankel, Hungarian-English (1935–)
Daniel Pollack, American (1935–)
Vladimir Ashkenazy, Russian-Swiss (1936–)
John Ogdon, English (1937–89)
Michael Ponti, American (1937–)
Anton Kuerti, Austrian (1938–)
Ralph Votapek, American (1939–)

THE YOUNGER GENERATION

Illana Vered, Israeli (1940–)
Stephen Bishop-Kovacevich, American (1940–)
James Dick, American (1940–)
Martha Argerich, Argentine (1941–)
Daniel Barenboim, Argentine-English (1942–)
Maurizio Pollini, Italian (1942–)
Ruth Laredo, American (1942–)
Alexander Slobodyanik, Russian (1942–)
Nelson Freire, Brazilian (1944–)
Lorin Hollander, American (1944–)
John Lill, English (1944–)
Jean-Bernard Pommier, French (1944–)
Mischa Dichter, American (1945–)
Radu Lupu, Rumanian (1945–)
Minoru Nojima, Japanese (1945–)
Rafael Orozco, Spanish (1946–)
André Watts, American (1946–)
Murray Perahia, American (1947–)
Peter Serkin, American (1947–)
Horacio Gutierrez, Cuban-American (1948–)
Garrick Ohlsson, American (1948–)
Gregory Allen, American (1949–)

Emanuel Ax, American (1949–)
Christina Ortiz, Brazilian (1950–)
Vladimir Viardo, Russian (1950–)
Santiago Rodriguez, Cuban-American (1952–)
Stephen de Groote, South African-American (1953– 89)
Andras Schiff, Hungarian (1953–)
André-Michel Schub, American (1953–)
Krystian Zimerman, Polish (1956–)
Ivo Pogorelich, Yugoslavian (1958–)
Ken Noda, American (1963–)

Chronological List of Keyboard Composers C

BAROQUE PERIOD (1600–1750)

Jean-Baptiste Lully, French (1632–87)
Henry Purcell, English (1658–95)
François Couperin, French (1668–1733)
George Philipp Telemann, German (1681–1767)
Jean-Philippe Rameau, French (1683–1764)
Johann Sebastian Bach, German (1685–1750)
Domenico Scarlatti, Italian (1685–1757)
George Frideric Handel, German (1685–1759)

PRE-CLASSICAL PERIOD (1720–75)

Wilhelm Friedemann Bach, German (1710–84)
Carl Philipp Emanuel Bach, German (1714–88)
Johann Philipp Kirnberger, German (1721–83)
Johann Christian Bach, German (1735–82)

CLASSICAL PERIOD (1775–1825)

Franz Joseph Haydn, Austrian (1732–1809)
Muzio Clementi, Italian (1752–1832)
Wolfgang Amadeus Mozart, Austrian (1756–91)
Daniel Gottlieb Türk, German (1756–1813)
Johann Dussek, Bohemian (1760–1812)
Ludwig van Beethoven, German (1770–1827)
Anton Diabelli, Austrian (1781–1858)
Friedrich Kuhlau, German (1786–1832)

ROMANTIC PERIOD (1800–1900)

Franz Schubert, Austrian (1797–1828)
Friedrich Burgmüller, German (1806–74)

Felix Mendelssohn, German (1809–47)
Frédéric François Chopin, Polish (1810–49)
Robert Schumann, German (1810–56)
Franz Liszt, Hungarian (1811–86)
Stephen Heller, Hungarian (1813–88)
Fritz Spindler, German (1817–1905)
Theodor Kullak, German (1818–82)
Louis Köhler, German (1820–86)
Cornelius Gurlitt, German (1820–1901)
César Auguste Franck, French (1822–90)
Louis Moreau Gottschalk, American (1829–69)
Johannes Brahms, German (1833–97)
Camille Saint-Saëns, French (1835–1921)
Mili Balakirev, Russian (1837–1910)
Modest Mussorgsky, Russian (1839–81)
Peter Ilyich Tchaikovsky, Russian (1840–93)
Edvard Grieg, Norwegian (1844–1908)
Gabriel Fauré, French (1845–1924)
Moritz Moskowski, German (1854-1925)
Isaac Albéniz, Spanish (1860–1909)
Anton Arensky, Russian (1861–1906)
Vladimir Rebikoff, Russian (1866–1920)

CONTEMPORARY PERIOD (1900–)

Edward MacDowell, American (1861–1908)
Claude Debussy, French (1862–1918)
Alexander Gretchaninoff, Russian (1864–1956)
Erik Satie, French (1866–1925)
Alexander Scriabin, Russian (1872–1915)
Max Reger, German (1873–1916)
Sergei Rachmaninoff, Russian (1873–1943)
Arnold Schoenberg, German (1874–1951)
Maurice Ravel, French (1875–1937)
Manuel de Falla, Spanish (1876–1946)
Ernst von Dohnanyi, Hungarian (1877–1960)
Ernest Bloch, Swiss-American (1880–1959)
Béla Bartók, Hungarian (1881–1945)
Joaquin Turina, Spanish (1882–1949)
Igor Stravinsky, Russian (1882–1971)
Anton von Webern, Austrian (1883–1945)
Alfredo Casella, Italian (1883–1947)
Alban Berg, Austrian (1885–1935)
Heitor Villa-Lobos, Brazilian (1887–1959)
Jacques Ibert, French (1890–1962)
Sergei Prokofiev, Russian (1891–1953)

Darius Milhaud, French-American (1892–1974)
Paul Hindemith, German (1895–1963)
George Gershwin, American (1898–1937)
Francis Poulenc, French (1899–1963)
Alexander Tcherepnin, Russian-American (1899–1977)
Aaron Copland, American (1900-1990)
Ernst Krenek, Austrian (1900–)
Aram Khachaturian, Russian (1903–78)
Dmitri Kabalevsky, Russian (1904–87)
Dmitri Shostakovich, Russian (1906–75)
Paul Creston, American (1906–85)
Ross Lee Finney, American (1906–)
Elliott Carter, American (1908–)
Samuel Barber, American (1910–81)
Gian Carlo Menotti, American (1911–)
John Cage, American (1912–)
Norman Dello Joio, American (1913–)
Witold Lutoslawski, Polish (1913–)
David Diamond, American (1915–)
Vincent Persichetti, American (1915–87)
Milton Byron Babbitt, American (1916–)
Hans Werner Henze, German (1916–)
Alberto Ginastera, Argentine (1916–83)
Leonard Bernstein, American (1918–90)
Ned Rorem, American (1923–)
Robert Starer, American (1924–)
Pierre Boulez, French (1925–)
Karlheinz Stockhausen, German (1928–)
George Crumb, American (1929–)
Robert Muczynski, American (1929–)
Stanley Babin, Israeli (1932–)
Krzysztof Penderecki, Polish (1933–)

Basic Theory Outline D

SCALES

A scale is an arbitrary arrangement of tones in a series of ascending or descending pitches. The various scales may be identified by the number of pitches used and their interval sequences. A scale may have the same tones for both ascending and descending, or may have series of tones ascending and another descending. Scales are constructed with half steps (½ step: the smallest interval in Western music), whole steps (two ½ steps), or with larger intervals (1½ steps). In the scales below ⌢ = ½ step, ∧ = 1½ steps.

Commonly Used Scales

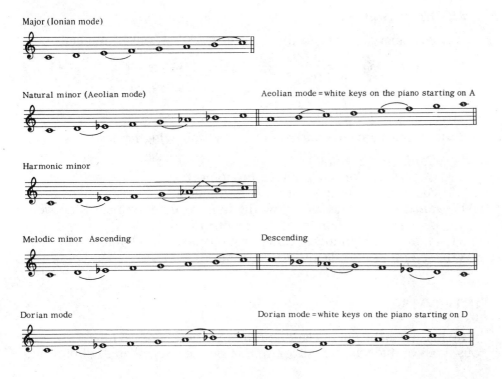

Major (Ionian mode)

Natural minor (Aeolian mode)   Aeolian mode = white keys on the piano starting on A

Harmonic minor

Melodic minor Ascending   Descending

Dorian mode   Dorian mode = white keys on the piano starting on D

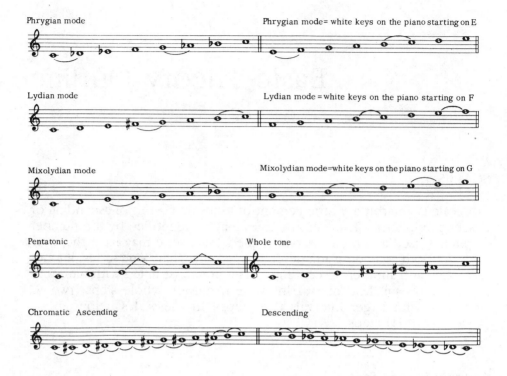

Scale Degree Names

It is customary to refer to the scale degrees by Roman numerals:

Scale degrees are also referred to by the following names:

I. *Tonic* (the key-note)
II. *Supertonic* (one step above the tonic)
III. *Mediant* (midway from tonic to dominant)
IV. *Subdominant* (as far below the tonic as the dominant is above it)
V. *Dominant* (a "dominant" element in the key)
VI. *Submediant* (midway down from tonic to subdominant)
VII. *Leading tone* ("leads" to the tonic)

INTERVALS

An interval is the pitch relation or distance between two tones. The various types of intervals are: Major, minor, perfect, augmented, diminished.

Appendices

Major & Perfect Intervals

unison | M second | M third | P fourth | P fifth | M sixth | M seventh | octave

Chromatically Altered Intervals

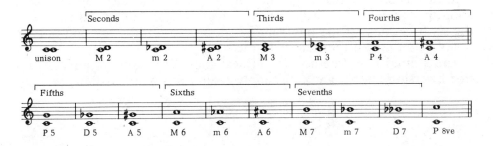

unison | M 2 | m 2 | A 2 | M 3 | m 3 | P 4 | A 4

P 5 | D 5 | A 5 | M 6 | m 6 | A 6 | M 7 | m 7 | D 7 | P 8ve

TYPES OF TRIADS

A triad is a three-note chord comprised of thirds. There are four kinds of triads classified according to the nature of the intervals formed between the root and the other two tones:

1. major triad (Maj.) composed of a major third and perfect fifth
2. minor triad (min.) composed of a minor third and perfect fifth
3. augmented triad (aug.) composed of a major third and augmented fifth
4. diminished triad (dim.) composed of a minor third and diminished fifth

Major | minor | augmented | diminished

Within the Major Scale

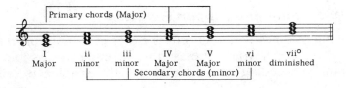

Primary chords (Major)

I | ii | iii | IV | V | vi | vii°
Major | minor | minor | Major | Major | minor | diminished

Secondary chords (minor)

Basic Theory Outline

Within the Harmonic Minor Scale

i	ii°	III+	iv	V	VI	vii°
min.	dim.	aug.	min.	Maj.	Maj.	dim.

First Inversion Triads

An inversion is a rearrangement of the same tones used in the basic chord (root position chord). Triads in first inversion are called chords of the sixth because of the interval of a sixth between the top and bottom notes. The third of the triad is in the bass.

The figured bass (method of musical shorthand) Arabic numerals for first inversion chords are ⁶₃, or simply ⁶, the third being assumed.

I6   ii6   iii6   IV6   V6   vi6   vii°6

Second Inversion Triads

Triads in second inversion are called "six-four chords" because of the interval of a sixth between the top and bottom notes and the fourth between the middle and bottom notes. The fifth of the triad is in the bass.

I⁶₄   ii⁶₄   iii⁶₄   IV⁶₄   V⁶₄   vi⁶₄   vii°⁶₄

FOUR-PART HARMONY

Four-part harmony is based on a vertical construction of four chord tones, and a horizontal movement of four different melodic voices. Voices refers to the standard vocal quartet: soprano, alto, tenor, bass. However, the term "voices" may also refer to the instrumental *parts*. The study of harmony is concerned with the principles that govern the vertical and horizontal movement of these four voices or parts.

Chordal Distribution in Four-part Harmony

The spacing of tones within chords is either in *close* or *open* structure. When the three upper voices are as close together as possible (soprano and tenor not exceeding an octave apart), the spacing is called close position. Any spacing that exceeds a distance greater than an octave between soprano and tenor is called open position. One of the three tones in a triad must be *doubled* to write four-part harmony. The extra tone is obtained by doubling the root in root position chords (as in the example below). Other rules apply for doublings of first and second inversion chords. (Consult a theory text for explanations.)

Close Position   Open Position

CADENCES

Music is analogous to literature because of its essentially linear, horizontal (left to right) motion. The horizontal, melodic movement of music is punctuated by phrases, whereas the vertical (chordal) structure culminates in *cadences* (various points of rest). Below are examples of frequently used cadences.

1. The *authentic cadence* is comparable to a full stop or a period in punctuation, and consists of a V-I harmonic progression.

2. The *half cadence* acts like a comma, indicating a partial stop in an unfinished statement. It ends on a V chord, however approached.

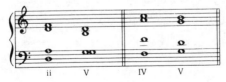

3. The *plagal cadence* is the next most frequently used progression for a full stop or final repose after the authentic cadence. It is also the "amen" sound used in hymns and consists of a IV-I progression.

Basic Theory Outline

IV   I

4. The *deceptive cadence* is a frequent substitute for the authentic cadence. As an alternative to V-I, V-vi (deceptive cadence) is often used.

V   vi

NON-HARMONIC TONES

The texture of music is comprised of melodic tones and rhythms which are interwoven. Some of these tones appear as factors of chords and some do not. *Non-harmonic tones* are tones that become foreign to the prevailing harmony during the course of melodic movement. Below are examples of frequently used non-harmonic tones.

1. A *passing tone* is a dissonant tone interpolated generally between two consonant tones. It usually occurs on a rhythmically weak beat and is approached and left by step without change of direction. The passing tone (or tones) may be either diatonic or chromatic.

I   vi   I   IV   I I_6

2. An *auxiliary tone* (also called a neighboring tone or embellishment) is a dissonant tone of weak rhythmic value that serves to ornament a stationary tone (either from above or below). It is approached and left by step with changes of direction.

3. An *anticipation*, as its name implies, is a non-harmonic tone that occurs just before the harmony to which it belongs. It acts as an upbeat to the tone anticipated. It is a dissonant, rhythmically weak tone, usually approached by step, and becomes consonant without moving as the harmony resolves to it.

4. An *échappée* (French, meaning escape tone) is a dissonant, rhythmically weak tone, approached by step and left by leap.

5. An *appoggiatura* (from the Italian verb *appoggiare*, to lean) is a dissonant tone on a rhythmically strong beat which is usually approached by leap and left by step.

6. A *suspension* (or retardation) is the prolongation of a chordal tone into a chord to which it does not belong. The three elements of the suspension are referred to as the *preparation* (consonant tone), suspension (dissonant tone on a rhythmically strong beat), and resolution (usually by step downward).

Basic Theory Outline

SEVENTH CHORDS

A seventh chord (four-note chord) is formed by imposing an interval of a third upon a triad. A seventh chord may be constructed on any scale degree, with or without chromatic alterations. The dominant seventh chord is the most frequently used of the seventh chords. All other seventh chords (non-dominant) are termed *secondary sevenths*.

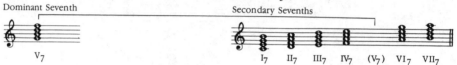

V⁷-I Progression

The resolution of V^7 to I in four-part harmony is one of the most fundamental progressions in music. The tones of the dominant seventh chord have a natural tendency to resolve to the tonic. The root of the chord resolves up a fourth (or down a fifth); the third of the chord (leading tone) usually ascends to the tonic; the fifth of the chord (having no tendency) descends to the tonic; the seventh resolves downward one scale degree to the third of the tonic chord. This results in an incomplete tonic chord resolution (three roots and one third).

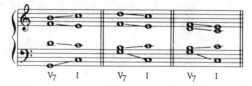

Inversions of the Dominant Seventh

The *first inversion* of the dominant seventh chord (with the third in the bass) is figured V^6_3; the 3 is often omitted, and the chord is most frequently referred to as V^6_5.

Appendices

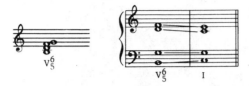

The *second inversion* of the dominant seventh chord (with the fifth in the bass) is figured V^6_3; the 6 is often omitted, and the chord is most frequently referred to as V^4_3.

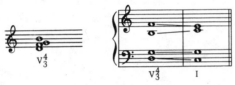

The *third inversion* of the dominant seventh chord (with the seventh in the bass) is figured V^6_2; the 6 is often omitted, and the chord is most frequently referred to as V^4_2 or V^2.

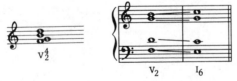

OTHER ASPECTS OF THEORY

Continued theoretical studies would include irregular resolutions of the V^7 chord (and other seventh chords); modulation; diminished seventh chords; ninth, eleventh, thirteenth chords; Neapolitan sixth chords; augmented sixth chords; and other chromatically altered chords. Consult the theory texts listed in Appendix A for specific reference.

Publishers of Keyboard Music E

Alfred Publishing Company, Inc.
16380 Roscoe Boulevard
P. O. Box 10003
Van Nuys, CA 91410-0003

Amsco Music Publishing
See—Music Sales

Ashley Publications, Inc.
113 Industrial Ave.
Hasbrouck Heights, NJ 07604

Associated Music Publishers, Inc.
See—Hal Leonard Publishing Corporation

Mel Bay Publications, Inc.
#4 Industrial Dr.
Pacfic, MO 63069

Belwin-Mills
See—Columbia Pictures Publications

Birch Tree Group Ltd.
P. O. Box 2072
Princeton, NJ 08540

Boosey & Hawkes, Inc.
200 Smith Street
Farmingdale, NY 11735

Boston Music Company
116 Boylston Street
Boston, MA 02116

Bradley Publications
See—Columbia Pictures Publications

Alexander Broude, Inc.
575 W. 8th Avenue
New York, NY 10018

Columbia Pictures Publications
16333 N.W. 54th Avenue
Hialeah, FL 33014

Dover Publications, Inc.
180 Varick Street
New York, NY 10014

Durand
See—Theodore Presser Company

Editions Salabert
See—Hal Leonard Publishing Corporation

European American Music
P. O. Box 850
Valley Forge, PA 19482

Max Eschig
See—Hal Leonard Publishing Corporation

Carl Fischer, Inc.
62 Cooper Square
New York, NY 10003

Galaxy Music Corporation
131 West 86 Street
New York, NY 10024

General Words and Music Company
See—Neil A. Kjos Music Company

Charles Hansen
1870 West Avenue
Miami Beach, FL 33139

G. Henle
P. O. Box 1753
St. Louis, MO 63043

Heritage Music Press
See—Lorenz Publishing Company

Appendices

Hinshaw Music, Inc.
P. O. Box 470
Chapel Hill, NC 27514

Edwin F. Kalmus
See—Columbia Pictures Publications

Neil A. Kjos Music Company
4380 Jutland Drive
P. O. Box 178270
San Diego, CA 92117

Kjos West
See—Neil A. Kjos Music Company

Lee Roberts Music Publications, Inc.
Box 225
Katonah, NY 10536

Hal Leonard Publishing Corporation
8112 West Bluemound Dr.
Milwaukee, WI 53213

Lorenz Industries
501 East Third Street
Dayton, OH 45401

E. B. Marks
See—Hal Leonard Publishing Corporation

MCA
See—Hal Leonard Publishing Corporation

Music Sales Corporation
33 W. 60th St.
New York City, NY 10023

Myklas Press
P. O. Box 929
Boulder, CO 80302

The New School for Music Study Press
P. O. Box 407
Princeton, NJ 08540

Oxford University Press, Inc.
200 Madison Avenue
New York, NY 10016

C. F. Peters Corporation
373 Park Avenue South
New York, NY 10016

Theodore Presser Company
Presser Place
Bryn Mawr, PA 19010

Ricordi
See—Hal Leonard Publishing Corporation

Salabert
See—Hal Leonard Publishing Corporation

Schaum Publications, Inc.
2018 East North Avenue
Milwaukee, WI 53202

G. Schirmer, Inc.
See—Hal Leonard Publishing Corporation

Stipes Publishing Company
10-12 Chester Street
Champaign, IL 61820

Studio P/R Inc.
See—Columbia Pictures Publications

Warner Bros. Music
265 Secaucus Road
Secaucus, NJ 07094

Wiener Urtext Edition (Universal)
See—European American Music

Willis Music Company
7380 Industrial Road
Florence, KY 41042

Yorktown Music Press, Inc.
See—Music Sales

Appendices

Index

Index